I0416001

# The Mediat.

*The Mediation of Power* investigates how those in positions of power use and are influenced by media in their everyday activities. Each chapter examines this theme through an exploration of some of the key topic areas and debates in the field. The topics covered are:

- theories of media and power
- media policy and the economics of information
- news production and journalistic practice
- public relations and media management
- culture and power
- political communication and mediated politics
- new and alternative media
- interest group communication
- media audiences and effects.

In addition, the book presents a series of critical dialogues with the traditional paradigms in the field. These are rethought, supplemented or discarded altogether. The discussions are illustrated with original research material from a range of communication environments and case study examples. These document stock market crashes, e-democracy, the subcultures of the London Stock Exchange and Westminster Parliament, the strategies of corporate and political spin doctors, mass media influences on politicians and the Make Poverty History campaign.

The debates are enlivened by first-hand accounts taken from over 200 high-profile interviews with politicians, journalists, public officials, spin doctors, campaigners and captains of industry. Tim Bell, David Blunkett, Iain Duncan Smith, Simon Heffer, David Hill, Simon Hughes, Trevor Kavanagh, Neil Kinnock, Peter Riddell, Polly Toynbee, Michael White and Ann Widdecombe are some of those cited.

**Aeron Davis** is a Senior Lecturer in Political Communication in the Department of Media and Communications, Goldsmiths College, London. He has published in the areas of political communication, media sociology, promotional culture and financial markets, and is the author of *Public Relations Democracy* (2002).

# Communication and Society
Series Editor: James Curran

# The Mediation of Power

A critical introduction

Aeron Davis

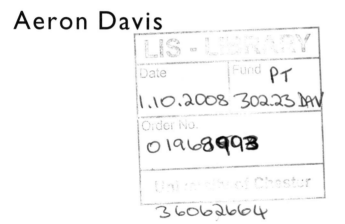

Routledge
Taylor & Francis Group

LONDON AND NEW YORK

First published 2007
by Routledge
2 Park Square, Milton Park, Abingdon, Oxon OX14 4RN

Simultaneously published in the USA and Canada
by Routledge
270 Madison Ave, New York, NY 10016

*Routledge is an imprint of the Taylor & Francis Group, an informa business*

Typeset in Sabon by
Book Now Ltd, London
Printed and bound in Great Britain by
Antony Rowe, Chippenham, Wiltshire

*British Library Cataloguing in Publication Data*
A catalogue record for this book is available from the British Library

*Library of Congress Cataloging in Publication Data*
Davis, Aeron.
The mediation of power: a critical introduction/Aeron Davis.
    p. cm. – (Communication and society)
Includes bibliographical references and index.
[etc.]

1. Mass media–Political aspects. 2. Mass media–Political aspects–Great Britain.
3. Communication in politics. 4. Communication in politics–Great Britain.
5. Communication–Political aspects. 6. Communication–Political aspects–
Great Britain. 7. Press and politics. 8. Press and politics–Great Britain. I. Title.

P95.8.D35 2007
302.23–dc22                                                            2007001862

ISBN10: 0–415–40490–8 (hbk)
ISBN10: 0–415–40491–6 (pbk)
ISBN10: 0–203–94582–4 (ebk)

ISBN13: 978–0–415–40490–7 (hbk)
ISBN13: 978–0–415–40491–4 (pbk)
ISBN13: 978–0–203–94582–7 (ebk)

For Annie

# Contents

# Illustrations

## Tables

## Figures

# Preface and acknowledgements

This book has a dual purpose. First, it is conceived as an advanced textbook that covers many common topic areas that feature in courses on media and power or political communication. Thus the reader is introduced to some of the core literature and debates on: policy and regulation, markets and political economy, media production and journalist practice, critical cultural theory, media–source relations, mediated politics and political communication, new and alternative media, interest groups and civil society, media effects and audiences. Second, the book seeks to engage critically and more fundamentally with the foundational frameworks and assumptions within these research areas. Along the way work from adjacent disciplines is pulled into the debates. Usual topic and theory divides are crossed. Traditional paradigms are confronted, supplemented, reinvented or discarded. In so doing the author sets out an alternative, but complementary, approach for investigating media, communication and power. This 'inverted political economy of communication' perspective focuses on the cultures, practices and mediating processes which evolve at 'sites of power' and influence those actors which inhabit such sites.

In addition, each chapter illuminates its discussion with original case material. The diverse range of cases used include stock market crashes, E-democracy, mediated policy-agendas on crime and Europe, the corruption of international financial information flows, the discursive practices of political journalists, the strategies of corporate and political 'spin doctors', the subcultures of the City and Westminster, and the Make Poverty History campaign. Such case examples draw on the first-hand accounts of some 220 elite interviewees.

This book will appeal, first and foremost, to higher-level undergraduates, postgraduates and scholars in the fields of media and communication, politics and political communication, journalism, and political sociology. It is designed to be 'core' or 'highly recommended' reading for courses on political economy of communication, media and power, politics and media, and political communication. Parts of the book will also be of interest to sociologists and anthropologists, especially those with an interest in power, economic sociology or cultural economy. Lastly it may well appeal to nonacademic observers of, and participants in, financial markets, institutional politics and political campaigns. The views of many high-profile and respected professionals are revealed in the case material sections of each chapter.

I must thank a range of people and institutions. I begin with some of the organisations which provided financial support for the research reproduced in these chapters. These include an earlier Economic and Social Research Council grant (award number R00429824372), pump priming funds from the Sociology Department at City University, and a Nuffield small grant (award number SGS/32887). Thanks go to Sage and the editors of *Media, Culture and Society* for permission to reproduce: 'Media Effects and the Question of the Rational Audience: Lessons from the Financial Markets', vol. 28, no. 4, pp. 603–25 (Chapter 9); and parts of 'Whither Mass Media and Power? Evidence for a Critical Elite Theory Alternative', vol. 25, no. 5, pp. 669–90 (Chapter 4). Thanks to Sage and the editors of *Global Media and Communication*, for permission to reproduce much of 'Information and the Economic Inefficiency of Market Liberalisation: The Case of the London Stock Exchange', forthcoming (Chapter 2). Thanks to Taylor and Francis and the editors of *Political Communication*, for permission to reproduce large parts of 'Investigating Journalist Influences on Political Agendas and Decision-Making at Westminster', forthcoming (Chapter 6). Thanks also to the Bank of England for permission to reproduce figures 2.2 and 2.3 from the Bank's *Quarterly Bulletins*.

I would like to thank the many interviewees who cooperated with this research. Those interviewed since 2004, who were especially helpful or generous with their time, include: David Bailey, David Blunkett, Colin Brown, Rob Clements, Ralph Cox, John Davies, Tony Dye, Neil Gerrard, Tony Golding, Paul Goodman, Andrew Grice, Neil Kinnock, Julie Kirkbride, Martin Linton, Peter Luff, Christine McCafferty, Robert MacLennan, John Maples, Peter Riddell, Michael Rimmer, Angus Robertson, John Rogers, Andrew Smithers, John Thurso, Polly Toynbee, Philip Webster, Michael White, Robert Wilson and Paul Woolley.

For taking on this project and guiding me through it many thanks go to Natalie Foster, Charlie Wood and all those involved at Routledge. The many friends, colleagues and external advisors, who have read and commented on specific chapters, given me useful advice and/or moral support along the way, include: Jay Blumler, Jean Chalaby, Rosemary Crompton, Robert Entman, Natalie Fenton, Bob Franklin, Des Freedman, Julie Froud, Gerassimos Galiatsatos, Peter Golding, Mike Kaye, Adam Leaver, Colin Sparks, Gareth Stanton, Daya Thussu, Howard Tumber, Karel Williams, Tony Woodiwiss and Barbie Zelizer. Above all, I am extremely grateful to Nick Sireau, for working with me on Chapter 8, and James Curran and Frank Webster, who have offered their support and incisive insights on many occasions. Last of all a special mention to my family who, despite the fact that they saw far too little of me in 2006, continued to offer me much-needed love and support: Annie, Hannah, Miriam, Helen and Neville.

# Chapter 1

# Introduction
## Critical engagements with mediated power

## Introduction

This book is part advanced textbook and part critical engagement with the dominant paradigms employed in studies of media and power. In textbook terms its ten chapters cover a broad range of common media and communication topics that might be included in a one term course. These include: policy and regulation; media production; elite media management and media–source relations; culture, ideology/discourse and power; mediated politics and political communication; new and alternative media; interest groups, civil society and mediated mobilisation; media audiences and effects. Each chapter presents some of the key literature, debates and challenges on the topic, followed by new case study material.

However, the book also presents a series of critical dialogues with the prevailing interpretive frameworks of the subject area. Along the way, traditional paradigms may be supplemented, synthesised, resuscitated and reinvented, or discarded altogether. In each chapter media research is combined with literature from outside the discipline to invigorate the discussions and push conceptual boundaries. Work in politics, sociology, economics and anthropology are all drawn upon. At the same time, many of the usual media topic divides are broken down and crossed throughout the book. New and alternative media frequently feature alongside traditional, mass media. Production and consumption are not always investigated as separate processes. Cultural and qualitative perspectives are merged with political economic and quantitative approaches. Presentation of argument moves between micro forms of communication and behaviour, and, macro, mass media forms. Both are linked to larger-scale political and economic patterns.

Each chapter also offers original case material, based on a diverse mix of studies, to illustrate the debates. These come from a range of subjects and communication environments and include the spheres of politics and political parties, journalism and public relations, corporations and financial markets, interest groups and new social movements. Interview material, taken from some 220 first-hand accounts, is used to present the issues and arguments. The recorded views of journalists, cultural and promotional intermediaries, politicians, campaigners, captains of industry, financial managers, public officials and regulators, all enliven the accounts.

## Mass media and power: the elite-mass media-audience paradigm

There is one, central line of reasoning that emerges throughout the chapters of this book: critical enquiry on the links between media, communication and power must look beyond the elite-mass media-audience paradigm. Traditional research has almost invariably been grounded in a framework of elite-mass communication and historical 'media events' transmitted via the mass media. However, social and political developments in recent decades, as well as much contemporary research, suggest that this framework can only explain so much. The utility of media and communication in sustaining unequal power relations in society is rather more complex and varied than this dominant paradigm suggests. For many there is nothing new about these developments. Indeed, they have supplied the justification for switching the research focus away from issues of media and inequality or discussions of power in society altogether. However, it is not the intention of this book to provide further evidence of this trend nor to argue for a complete paradigm shift. Rather it is to set out steps towards an alternative, but in many ways complementary, critical research project.

What evolves through the book might best be described as: *an inverted political economy of communication that focuses on the mediation of sites of power and those actors who inhabit them.* This approach moves away from media-centred investigations of power that seek to document the political, economic and cultural means by which media is shaped to further advantage those in power. Instead, the starting point is to identify political and economic sites of power and those that operate at those sites. Investigation is then led by asking how media and culture are used by, as well as influence, those actors, processes and sites themselves. Further explanation of this approach follows a review of work linking media, communication and power.

Much work in political science, and in the subdisciplines of media politics and political communication, is rooted in an elite-mass media paradigm. Political writing on the establishment of democracy, old and new (see Held, 1989, 1996, for overviews), does not feature media with much frequency. But there is a consistent focus on the legitimate authority of the state and its representatives, and on how that is established and maintained without the regular use of force. Debate, on the ways political leaders are best selected, act according to the public will and are consistently held accountable for their actions, clearly involves public communication. Studies, therefore, hold very securely to an 'ideal type' of democracy that links elite decision-making to the mass of consumer citizenry via mass communication and 'public opinion'.

Consequently, this has directed much research in departments of politics or journalism towards those institutions, individuals and events where legitimate state authority is publicly reinforced or questioned. This usually involves documenting and evaluating the large media events and public personalities associated with 'history'. Thus, there is now a wealth of studies on wars and elections (Blumler and Gurevitch, 1995; Kavanagh, 1995; Crewe *et al.*, 1995, 1998; Hall Jamieson, 1996, 2006; Norris, 1999; Herman and Chomsky, 2002; Hess and Kalb, 2003; Miller, 2004; Tumber and Palmer, 2004). There is also a strong body of work on political party and government communication with leading journalists and citizen-voters (Zaller, 1992; Scammell, 1995; Fallows, 1996; Iyengar and Reeves, 1997; Glasser, 1999; Barnett and Gaber, 2001; Lees-Marshment, 2001; Patterson, 2002; Hess, 2003).

Alongside these studies there has developed a framework of evaluation, grounded in political theory, and applied in studies of media sociology and media history. Drawing on historical treaties and declarations on 'the press', a set of 'ideal' public communication functions in democracies have emerged (see Keane, 1991; Curran, 2002, for discussions). These dictate that the media should provide: a source of 'objective' information widely available to all citizens and interest groups; a check ('watchdog role') on the activities of powerful institutions, organisations and individuals; a platform for rational debate on the issues and policies affecting society and the state; and access for a wide range of citizens and interest groups to put forward their views. Such debates about the media's ability to fulfil its ideal functions have continued in various forms and currently are most commonly discussed in terms of Habermas's account of the 'public sphere' (Habermas, 1989 [1962]). The public sphere concept, documented as the public, deliberative space between the state and private citizens, appears readily adaptable to work on media and politics. It has been applied in the assessment of public communication spaces at the national, transnational and electronic levels (see collections in Calhoun, 1992; Dahlgren and Sparks, 1992, and also Thompson, 1995; Goldsmiths Media Group, 1999; Sparks, 2001; Dahlgren, 2001, 2005).

Indeed, much writing on media and politics, in effect, is based on an evaluation of one of more of these ideals (Hallin, 1994; Schudson, 1995; Norris, 2000; Bennett and Entman, 2001; Meyer, 2002; Corner and Pels, 2003; McNair, 2003; Franklin, 2004; Curran and Gurevitch, 2005; Lewis *et al.*, 2005). Thus, these works variously document and debate: campaign media effects or lack thereof; rising public apathy or alternative forms of political engagement; the growth of political news management or the 'media colonisation' of politics; political marketing as a tool for manipulating or responding to the public; and the tabloidisation or public-responsiveness of news media.

Critical work, in media, sociology and cultural studies, has been directed by other concerns but has similarly adopted the elite-media-mass paradigm. Thinking here was originally driven by a model of society that revolved around economic class inequalities, legitimation crises and conflict. Under such circumstances one central concern drove critical investigation in media and culture: the question of how mass consent was maintained in a patently unequal society. The answer for many was to be located in the dissemination of dominant ideologies and false consciousness. Members of the Frankfurt School (Adorno and Horkheimer, 1979 [1947]) saw modern, mass culture as dulling and distracting public minds. Lukes (1974) argued that the all-important third dimension of power was ideological. Althusser's (1984) 'ideological state apparatus' and 'interpellation' explained the institutional means of mass cultural assimilation. Hall (1973) looked to the encoding of preferred meanings in mass produced texts. The adoption of Gramsci's earlier writing (Forgacs, 1988), particularly his concept of hegemony, added a sense of fluidity and change. Each of these scholars offered a set of intellectual tools with which to observe and explain mass consent.

Arguably, in critical cultural studies, the consent question, along with other research parameters, have continued to determine the way culture and power have been linked. The other parameters are a focus on popular/mass media and culture and an emphasis on investigating culture in the anthropological tradition; that is, as a 'whole way of life'. Each of these research emphases can be traced back to the work of the discipline's founders: Williams (1958, 1961) and Hall and, to a lesser extent, Hoggart (1958) and Thompson (1963). So, 'popular culture' became as significant a subject of study as 'high culture'. Culture, as a 'whole way of life' inseparable from the social fabric of society, was to be observed and documented. Along the way, critical studies enforced the links between each of these elements: popular/mass media and culture, culture as a 'whole way of life' and the mass consent question. These links became firmly established in the work of Hall and later Williams (Hall, 1973, 1980, 1982, 1983; Williams, 1977).

Alongside critical cultural theorists, media political economists have sought to locate the material means by which elites, at the state and corporate levels, influence the production of mass media texts. Usually this has come to mean a focus on news texts (Schiller, 1989, 1992; Garnham, 1990; Eldridge, 1995; Philo, 1995; Stauber and Rampton, 1995, 2002; Ewen, 1996; Herman and McChesney, 1997; Golding and Murdock, 2000; Curran, 2002; Davis, 2002; Herman and Chomsky, 2002 [1988]; Curran and Seaton, 2003; Bagdikian, 2004; McChesney, 2004; Miller, 2004). All offer detailed accounts of the power of state and market forces to shape news media and public information. This top-down influence has been maintained through a mixture of conscious, direct means and unconscious, indirect influences. In terms of overt, conscious influences, ownership, whether by the state or private corporations, has brought with it the power to allocate resources, appoint senior staff and influence editorial agendas. The state has additionally applied pressure through regulation, licensing, censorship and libel laws. Corporate elites have extended their control through overlapping networks of shareholders and directorships, and through advertising – a principal source of media funding. Overt influence has become all the more effective with the steady professionalisation of corporate and state communication operations. These alternate between blocking, 'spinning' and threatening journalists, on the one hand, and guiding, subsidising and offering incentives, on the other. At crisis points, caused by union activity, mass protest, war or economic depression, this full range of overt influences is brought to bear in an attempt to 'manufacture consent'.

Indirect, less conscious influences come down to the economic and organisational conditions that direct media production in a capitalist system. Market pressures, to take advantage of economies of scale and greater advertising revenues, have encouraged production for mass audiences and a steady stream of industry concentration and conglomeration. The results have been cuts in uneconomical public news and information production, and restrictions on entry for alternative and critical news and cultural producers. Several studies have also shown that news organisation and news values encourage journalists to repeatedly seek out and promote certain elite sources over others (Fishman, 1980; Gandy, 1982). For some this results in a self-perpetuating 'primary definer' status (Hall *et al.*, 1978) being bestowed on those who are already politically and economically advantaged. For others, although such a status is fluid and contested, elite groups continue to dominate news coverage (Miller, 1994; Schlesinger and Tumber, 1994; Manning, 1998; Davis, 2002). In some news beats journalists appear to have become such a part of the 'issue communities' they report on they have become all but 'captured' by their sources (Negrine, 1996; Schlesinger *et al.*, 2001; Davis, 2000b).

Over time, investigation of media, culture and inequality has broadened considerably to now include gender, race, ethnicity and sexual identity. In addition, a variety of continental European theorists and concepts have been appropriated by critical cultural theorists. Foucault's (1980) 'discourse' and 'power/knowledge', and Bourdieu's (1979) 'fields', interchangeable forms of 'capital' and 'habitus', have been most widely taken up. More recently Callon (1986, 1998) and Latour's (1987) 'Actor-Network Theory', where 'actants' are 'performed' in 'disentangled material-semiotic networks', have presented an alternative cast-off point. Each set of concepts has reinterpreted the links between individuals, institutions, power and culture. Adoption and interpretation of these theorists and concepts by media and communication scholars has directed the field in several disparate directions; including moves away from discussions of power altogether.

However, when absorbed into the media-power framework, usually the concepts are employed either to emphasise the structural reinforcement of the elite-media-mass paradigm, or forms of resistance to that. Work on active audiences, everyday resistance, oppositional subcultures and 'semiotic guerrillas' (Hebdige, 1979; de Certeau, 1984; Ang, 1986; Fiske, 1989; Silverstone, 1994) has emphasised individual, cultural autonomy but within the same elite-mass framework. Much recent scholarship within media and cultural studies, whatever its stance, has tended to retain a baseline attachment to the paradigm's original research precedents. Typical introductory overviews (e.g., Grossberg *et al.*, 1992; Gray and McGuigan, 1993; Storey, 1998; Turner, 2003) all begin with the Williams and Hall (and Hoggart and Thompson) history and their shaping of the culture and ideology (or discourse) project. Many key works, although quite dispersed and varied, from media production, 'media events' and audience consumption (Dayan and Katz, 1992; Fiske, 1996; Sparks and Tulloch, 2000; Kellner, 2003), to 'political culture' and 'cultural economy' (Kellner, 1995; Street, 1997, 2001; du Gay and Pryke, 2002), have been developed within these conceptual parameters. Wars, conflicts and terrorism, viewed through the critical media lens, continue to be documented as incidents of state management of media and public opinion (Herman and Chomsky, 2002; Thussu and Freedman, 2003; Miller, 2004).

Of course, each of these bodies of work offers an impressive range of research and interpretations and cannot simply be summed up as part of the elite-media-mass power paradigm. However, they do share at their mainstream centres such a set of defining characteristics. Whether mass media and culture are a means of upholding or undermining the legitimacy of democracies, a means of maintaining dominant elite hegemony or ensuring the continued circulation of powerful elites, elite-mass communication is key.

## The elite-mass media-audience paradigm: holes and limitations

The elite-mass media-audience paradigm now appears to contain a number of holes and limitations. By focusing primarily on mass communication and culture, it has tended to take power and its operation as a given. There are few communication-oriented studies of actual sites, actors and processes of power. Of equal significance, many of the material, social and intellectual foundations of the paradigm have been, and continue to be, undermined. Such omissions and continuing trends suggest that the elite-mass framework will, in the longer term, become too restrictive in its explanatory power.

To begin, the ideal principle of direct democracy, to which the mediated public sphere aspires, has never existed outside of small, usually exclusive and exclusionary, collectives. This issue has been highlighted by several of Habermas's critics (see, for example, Behabib, 1992; Fraser, 1992) and is, indeed, acknowledged in his more recent work (1996). Instead, representative democracies, or 'deformed polyarchies' (Dahl and Lindblom, 1953), are much more elaborate and conflictual. Habermas's alternative framework (1996) focuses on a civil society of organisations and interest groups which privately feed public opinion into the increasingly formalised and autonomous institutions of government which then produce law. 'Communicative power' mobilises public opinion, through interest groups, to influence the processes and participants which then enact law largely out of public view. If the public sphere model is outdated so, therefore, are the associated frameworks applied to media and communication (see also Calhoun, 1992; Thompson, 1995, on this). Indeed, for many looking at communication and politics, there exist multiple, linked, public spheres (Behabib, 1992; Curran, 2000) or 'sphericules' (Gitlin, 1998).

Moving a step further, the traditional state-centred model of power is, itself, being undermined. Economic and political resources appear to be seeping away from national governments. The shift in power and resources is towards rather less visible quangos, transnational corporations and financial systems, pressure groups and international bodies (Castells, 1997; Strange, 1998; Hirst and Thompson, 1999; Nash, 2000; Held and McGrew, 2002; Amoore, 2005; Froud et al., 2006). In many post-industrial countries there has been quite a strong decline in support for mainstream political parties and national legislative bodies. Party memberships, electoral support, conventional party ideologies and faith in politicians and the electoral system has gone down as support for social movements and single issue politics has gone up (Blumler and Gurevitch, 1995, 2000; Castells, 1997; Norris, 2000, 2002; Heath et al., 2001; Bromley et al., 2004; Franklin, 2004; Todd and Taylor, 2004; Lewis et al., 2005).

The paradigm has also been regularly undermined by work on media effects and audiences. The majority of studies, be they in political communication (e.g., Curtice and Semetko, 1994; Kavanagh and Gosschalk, 1995; King, 1998; Norris et al., 1999), sociology and social psychology (e.g., Katz and Lazarsfeld, 1955; Blumler and Katz, 1974; Livingstone 1998) or media and cultural studies (Morley, 1980; Ang, 1986; Radway, 1987; Liebes and Katz, 1990; Barker and Petley, 1996; Gauntlett, 1998), conclude that the available evidence can only explain minimal, reinforcement or uses and gratifications-type effects. Effects are difficult to isolate and establish, media texts are complex and contradictory, and audiences are active and influenced by other social and cultural factors (although see challenges in Iyengar and Kinder, 1987; Lewis, 1991, and collections in Bryant and Zillman, 1994; Iyengar and Reeves, 1997).

Connected to this is a significant critique of the 'dominant ideology thesis' (Abercrombie et al., 1984, 1990). This suggests that there is little historical evidence to demonstrate that the ideas of the ruling classes have ever been particularly accepted beyond the ruling classes themselves. Certainly, regular polls of public opinion tend to show strong disparities between what corporate elites believe, in terms of the regulation of industry and the economy, and the views of the public (Abercrombie *et al.*, 1984, 1990, see also MORI, 1974 – 2006; Jowell *et al.*, 1992, 1993). Polls have for some time revealed that business leaders and politicians appear to be regarded by the public as being among the least 'trusted' professions. Indeed, for several observers there are many other reasons why the question of ideological consent is a less pressing concern in fairly stable and wealthy democracies (Held, 1989; Abercrombie *et al.*, 1990; Tilly, 1991). The dull compulsion of economic life, pragmatic acquiescence, low-level everyday resistance, commodity fetishism and other forms of personal investment in society, all offer alternative or additional explanations for mass acceptance of the political system.

Whether effects and the ideological elements of media are significant or not may not be that relevant in the future. The influence of individual, mass media outlets on the public appears to be steadily declining as the number of competing news and entertainment media outlets continue to rise. This is matched by a decline in support for national newspapers and public service broadcasting media in many democracies. Evidence suggests that a growing proportion of the public is less inclined to consume 'political news' – at least from the traditional outlets (see Gitlin, 1994; Tunstall, 1996; Herman and McChesney, 1997; McQuail and Suine, 1998; Thussu, 1998; Hallin, 2000; Leys, 2001; Curran, 2002; Doyle, 2002 for overviews and discussions). News quantity is increasing but its focus on those processes that involve power is on the decline. Investigative, contextualised journalism and coverage of complex debates and policy-making, which result in lower audience ratings, is being eased out. Scandal, 'infotainment', personality news and public relations content, which increase ratings, is rising (see Hallin, 1994, 2000; Ewen, 1996; Franklin, 1997; Hess, 2000; Thompson, 2000; Delli Carpini and Williams, 2001; Underwood, 2001; Davis, 2002; Meyer, 2002; Corner and Pels, 2003). Consumers themselves appear to be more interested in information, sport and entertainment than hard news (see surveys in, for example, Morrison, 1991; Negrine, 1996; Seymour-Ure, 1996; Tunstall, 1996).

In cultural studies research there has been a steady drift away from investigating culture and power. This is not surprising as the original disciplinary parameters, which connected ideologies/discourses to mass/popular culture and the struggle for consent between repressors and repressed, have become unsustainable. The culture of large, complex societies cannot be observed in the same 'whole way of life' sense previously applied in ethnographies of smaller cultures. It becomes increasingly difficult to identify homogenous groups of 'repressors' and 'repressed'. Such groups, which were first class-based, came to be more finely segmented in terms of race, gender, ethnicity, age and other facets of individual identity. They were then further fragmented by the emphasis on consumption, pleasure and polysemy. Work on 'new media', globalisation, transnationalism and identity all suggest increasing cultural fragmentation, hypersegmentation and pluralist diversity

(Hebdige, 1988; Fiske, 1989; Ang, 1991; Nava, 1992; Fowles, 1996; Storey, 1999). None of these research directions have hindered the study of media and culture; but they have hindered exploration of the links between culture and power.

Taken together, these studies suggest that the elite-mass paradigm, that has dominated critical media and cultural studies and political communication, can only explain so much about communication and power. This does not mean that we have reached the 'end of history' (Fukuyama, 1992), that political power is entirely decentred and we have entered into a period of 'cultural chaos' (McNair, 2006), or that inequality, minimal norms of justice and human rights are simply components of modernist 'meta-narratives', now to be discarded (Lyotard, 1984).

Clearly, the case is still strong for continuing to document and evaluate issues of power and inequality. The ongoing concerns associated with capitalist democracies – such as corporate conglomeration and abuses of power; rising economic inequality and poverty; lack of women and ethnic minority representation at the higher levels of politics and business; environmental degradation; over-production and economic crises – still persist. Other trends – such as levels of obesity, personal debt, depression and mental health problems; inequality on the national and global scales; per capita waste and pollution; restrictive union legislation; indirect taxation which hits the poorest hardest; attacks on the welfare state and public spending; long working hours and casualised employment; and civic disengagement – have all steadily emerged and/or increased in the last quarter of a century (see, for example, Bauman, 1997; Castells, 1997, 1998; Panitch and Leys, 1999; Klein, 2000; Monbiot, 2000; Putnam, 2000; Hutton, 2001; Moore, 2001; Schlosser, 2001; Stiglitz, 2002; Sennett, 2006).

That mass media can have a profound influence on peoples and events is also still very much in evidence. Media coverage of, and related public beliefs about, 11 September and subsequent events, is a powerful indication of that. In spite of official US and UN assessments to the contrary, a March 2006 poll found that 60 per cent of Republican voters thought Iraq had weapons of mass destruction prior to the 2003 invasion. Sixty-three per cent of Republican voters also thought Iraq had 'substantially' supported al Qaeda (PIPA). In the UK, although such beliefs are not so common, media coverage and public debate about the invasion were still framed in terms of potential military threats rather than the international legality of a 'pre-emptive' attack or the real divisions within the UN Security Council. Indeed, the terms '9/11' and 'WMD' appear to have developed a symbolic and ideological power all of their own. Similarly, on the issue of climate change, while a majority of citizens now support government action being taken against global warming, doubts still remain about the science (PIPA). As late as 2004 a majority of US Citizens still believed that there was no 'scientific consensus' on the issue. In July 2005 39 per cent still held this opinion (see

Stauber and Rampton, 1995, 2002, 2003; Brookes *et al.*, 2004; Miller, 2004; Monbiot, 2006, for critical accounts).

However, there is a need for supplementary forms of critical enquiry into the links between media, communication and power. At the moment, the current alternatives appear frustratingly limited for critical researchers in media and communication. For many the way forward is simply to keep documenting new wars, instances of corporate abuse, state propaganda, the destructive consequences of globalisation, or organised opposition to such. For others, the links between communication and power are a given and intellectual passions are more engaged by other issues and topics. For others still, it is actually time to celebrate the end of history and ideology, embrace the individual freedoms of the consumer-citizen and/or join the cultural and intellectual liberation brought by postmodernity. This book seeks to supplement the first option, reengage those on the second path, and challenge those who have taken the third line.

## Inverted political economy and mediated power

Research and thinking presented in this book seeks to locate processes, participants and sites of power at the centre of enquiry. It also attempts to come to terms with today's fast-evolving and fragmenting communication environments. Its alternative starting point is perhaps best described as an *inverted political economy*. It is political economy because, at root, it assumes that power originates, and is played out and recorded in material forms. It is inverted because it reverses the line of investigation normally taken in typical political economy studies of communication. Such a research approach traditionally chooses to investigate the political and economic forces which work to shape media content in ways that support the material and ideological bases of power. It also tends to focus on the big, historical media events and public actions of powerful individuals. An inverted political economy, instead, takes those actors and processes operating at the centres of political and economic power and then asks: what is the part played by media and culture in the activities of those actors and the evolution of those processes? The emphasis here is on the micro and less visible forms of communication at these sites, and on the private actions of powerful individuals.

### Elites and sites of power

The sites of power selected are those that have a more significant part in the economic, politico-legal and military spheres (see Mills, 1956; Mann, 1986). Politics and political sociology have long been concerned with political decision-making and relationships between state, corporate and other elites, at local and national levels (Mills, 1956; Dahl, 1961; Domhoff, 1967;

Miliband, 1969; Poulantzas, 1975; Lindblom, 1977; Grant, 1978; Offe, 1984). Such studies are not usually media oriented but, clearly, such decision-making and elite relations involve private and mediated forms of communication. In fact, many of the processes that significantly influence the shape of power involve multiple and intensive forms of private communication. Such processes and communication forms take place outside the public sphere and without reference to the majority of consumer-citizens. They are not, therefore, part of any society-wide hegemonic struggle or mass circuit of cultural production. The same is even more true of sites of power centred on corporate, military and international institutions. Thus, as Lukes states (2005: 1) 'we need to attend to those aspects of power that are least accessible to observation: that, indeed, power is at its most effective when least observable'.

Research enquiry therefore entails looking at specific sites of institutional power, such as a legislative assembly, a civil service centre, a United Nations body, the headquarters of a multinational company, a local council or other local institution. Alternatively, it may involve investigating geographically dispersed elite networks or policy communities (see Castells, 1996; Marsh, 1998). In the case of this book the research territory covers legislative assemblies, political parties, corporate bodies and financial markets, policy networks and social movements.

At each of these sites, localised or networked actions and decision-making have wider social and economic impacts. As such, it is assumed that the experiences, discursive practices, beliefs and ideologies, that inform decisions and actions within those sites, do too. Thus, localised forms of communication come to be implicated in the long-term 'mobilisation of bias' (Schattschneider, 1960) which guides decision-making and practices in certain directions. Legislation, regulation and corporate strategies, from employment to housing, from environmental regulation to taxation systems, from take-overs to international investments, are influenced in such ways. Incrementally, over time, they contribute to larger scale imbalances and inequalities.

'Power' at these sites has many 'dimensions' (see Clegg, 1989; Lukes, 2005, for useful overviews). The first of these is the power of actors to make decisions, and set the agendas for decision-making, that benefit themselves to the possible detriment of others (Dahl, 1961; Bachrach and Baratz, 1962). In the classic literature this is described as the power of A *over* B documented in terms of A's ability to get B to do something against B's own best interests. Such dimensions of power tend to involve conscious actors operating as part of well-defined elite groups or classes.

This turns the focus towards those 'classes' or 'elites' who tend to occupy these sites of economic and political power. A number of neo-Marxist and critical elite studies have been produced which have such a focus (Mills, 1956; Domhoff, 1967; Fidler 1981; Useem, 1984; Lazar, 1990; Scott, 1997; Sklair, 2001). Each of these has sought to identify the social and material bases of elite/class cohesion and reproduction. It is often assumed that they exercise power consciously, work or 'conspire' in unity, and, by virtue of their positions, accumulate economic and political power and status. One or more of these things may, and often do, hold true.

Arguably, however, they frequently do not apply. The object of study should not, therefore, be reduced to the social and cultural reproduction of materially defined classes or the reinforcement of pre-existing habitus. More significantly, traditional class or elite-based perspectives have a narrow interpretation of the way power operates. They tend to neglect other 'dimensions' or conceptions of power that move away from elite/class agency and rational intent. Thus, Lukes's (1974) third dimension of power, that of ideology, may equally guide elites and be fundamental to forms of decision-making at elite sites of power. Other conceptions of power link its operation to practice, discipline, organisational structures, networks or performativity (Foucault, 1975, 1980; Callon, 1986, 1998; Mann, 1986), each of which also guides those who occupy such sites of power. As such, this suggests a need to investigate the cultures, communication, beliefs, discourses and practices that exist within elite sites of power.

### Elite cultures at sites of power

Thus, while the research starting point is political and economic, the means of investigation are very much cultural and social. The methods for exploring micro and less publicly visible forms of communication necessitate more qualitative research tools and concepts. One research tradition that is appropriate is the subcultures one. Not subcultural research in the Birmingham School vein but, rather, in the Chicago and 'post-Birmingham School' traditions. Such work on subcultures looks at culture as 'a whole way of life' but as it operates locally and discretely in 'a world within a world' (Gordon, 1997 [1947]). Developing organically, around any combination of vocational, spatial, lifestyle or cultural commonalities, such subcultures can also be central to discrete systems of social relations, organisation and localised cultures. Within them, certain beliefs, practices and ideologies evolve from a mixture of 'lived social relations', processes and symbolic exchanges.

More recently, such forms of investigation have turned to the work and conceptual tools of Foucault (1975, 1980, 2000), Bourdieu (1979, 1993) or Callon (1998). For Foucault it is discourses and practices which invisibly direct individuals. Thus the institutions and technologies of power, from the prison to the asylum, evolve and shape power throughout society. Similarly, the practices, technologies, tactics and discourses of 'governmentality' in part shape government (Rose, 1999; Foucault, 2000). For Bourdieu, actors are guided by life-long, evolving 'habitus'. They exchange forms of cultural, symbolic and economic capital as they progress through positions of power within defined 'fields'. For Callon, in his work on markets, agents enter into 'actor-networks' which are 'disentangled' from wider, external social and cultural influences. All parts of a market actor-network – individuals, institutions, tools, prices and measures – are so constituted in ongoing practices within the market itself. As such, agents calculate and act within the localised logics of the market network. In each of these approaches actors are guided, or performed, by cultures, cognitions and practices that develop exclusively within the spaces they temporarily inhabit.

Many would argue that research cannot include all of these dimensions or conceptions of power. One cannot have both conscious agency and disciplinary power, ideology and discourse, 'power over' and 'power to', 'habitus' and 'performativity'. Such differences now commonly separate scholarly camps. I disagree. The chapters that follow reveal each of these kinds of power in operation. Each approach offers tools with which to research power at elite-centred sites. The need to place one interpretive framework and set of tools over another all too often acts as a barrier to more productive empirical engagements.

The main point to note is that the research focus should be on exploring the social, cultural, ideological and discursive elements of those elite-centred sites (or 'networks' or 'fields') of power in which such actors operate. Individuals at these sites do not have any greater cognitive capacities – understanding, intelligence, taste or autonomy – from the mass of citizens engaged in everyday work and leisure activities. Indeed, they may be just as guided by dominant norms, values, discourses and practices as those elsewhere. However, it is their activities that are likely to have a more fundamental influence on material power because of their positions within sites which influence wider economic and political power.

### Mediated power

Another concern of this research involves investigating how *mediation* influences individuals, cultures and practices at elite sites of power. Much recent enquiry in media and cultural studies has focused on the 'mediation' of social and political processes (Martin-Barbero, 1993; Thompson, 1995; Livingstone, 1999). Such works ask: how do individuals and institutions use media and communication and, conversely, how do media and communication shape individuals and institutions? How, in other words, do individuals, in their use of media, inadvertently alter their behaviours, relations and discursive practices? In Science and Technology Studies (STS) and work on new media (see MacKenzie and Wajcman, 1999; Lievrouw, 2004; Livingstone, 2005; Lievrouw and Livingstone, 2006) 'recombinant' and 'social shaping' approaches follow a similar line. In each of these, media, individuals and social practices are 'co-determining'.

To date, work on processes of mediation and social shaping, like that on subcultures, has not really been applied to the elite actors and sites of power singled out here. Presented as alternatives to dominant, elite ideologies and media effects, and opposed to economic and technological determinisms, such studies emphasise individual autonomy, diversity, and postmodern flux and shift. The research territory favoured is one of the everyday and every person (de Certeau, 1984; Silverstone, 1994; Livingstone, 1998). When issues of power are engaged with it is in relation to resistance or opposition and on the cultural or mundane level.

However, there is no reason that the mediation concept cannot be employed in the study of elite actors and sites. Indeed, it seems more than appropriate to apply it to elite actors operating in such sites of power. As the following chapters demonstrate, elite understandings of, and relationships to, media and media workers are often quite different from most citizens. In many cases, they work closely with media producers, consciously attempt to influence media production, and consume specific kinds of media texts in vast quantities. These differences are significant.

The research objectives of an inverted political economy thus become directed towards: a) locating sites of economic, political (and military or legal) power, b) investigating the formation of the micro cultures, beliefs, ideologies/discourses and practices at those sites, c) documenting the ways media influences, and is used by, actors in these sites, and d) identifying the non-cultural/ideological mechanisms by which such cultures and mediated practices impact upon wider material relations. In other words, investigating the links between discrete elite cultures, practices, beliefs and ideologies and wider social and material developments, discourses and discursive practices.

At these sites a series of communication-oriented questions are asked. How do those involved perceive the issues, develop cognitive short cuts and interpretive frameworks? What are the dominant norms, values and discursive practices that they share in their everyday activities? How do politicians, corporate managers, international investors and political activists consume and use media in their daily activities? How do they adapt their behaviour and decision-making processes in relation to the evolving media environment that they are faced with? What is their relationship with media producers, individual media workers and cultural intermediaries? What influence do they think they have over the shaping of media texts? What messages do they want to convey and to which particular audiences?

To ask such questions requires observing and talking to those in power first and those in the media and communication industries second. It means initially asking 'where do media, communication and culture relate to sites and processes of power?' rather than 'how do the powerful influence media?' Consequently it necessitates engaging with the language of economic theory and free-market norms, when dealing with fund managers or market regulators, or political theory and democratic ideals when observing politicians, or social movement theory and campaign issues when documenting interest group actors.

Along the way I have found several sources of inspiration; works which have sought to ask questions and observe individuals in positions of power and, do so, by inhabiting those same worlds within worlds. Such works also researched at the micro, qualitative levels but, at the same time, sought to make links to wider consequences and did so with more extended frameworks of power in mind. In starting out, initially, there were several classic studies in media sociology that built up comprehensive accounts, or developed 'grounded theory', of journalists at work or journalist–source relations (e.g., Schlesinger, 1987; Protess *et al.*, 1991). However, inspiration was also to be found in studies set in entertainment industries, stock markets and political assemblies. Gitlin's (1994) work on how network executives decide what television programmes get made, Abolafia's (1996) observations of financial traders and their movements between opportunity and restraint, and Herbst's (1998) investigation of political staffers' understanding of what public opinion is, all stood out during the research period.

## Chapter outlines and arguments

The book's chapters all start with topic overviews before engaging more critically with the literature through an exploration of case material. Chapter 2, on policy and regulation, discusses the 'ideals' of liberal democratic media theory and explores the long-running public service-free market debate in media and communication. This debate revolves around the social and political 'public goods', emphasised by public service advocates, versus the economic 'public goods', championed by free marketeers. However, as the chapter argues, the assumption that free markets naturally bring economic goods is not so clear cut. The case material here centres on media and information systems operating in the London Stock Exchange.

Chapter 3, on media production, looks specifically at elements of news construction. Professional norms and practices, and organisational methods and processes, have all evolved to produce news that documents and reflects the social world accurately. Such elements have enabled journalists to retain their autonomy when faced with a range of external influences such as market forces, corporate or government power. What is argued here, however, is that these same journalistic ideals, norms and practices, are themselves a potential cause of media distortion. Key, long-term and chronic issues, linked to power and inequality, are regularly omitted from coverage and, consequently, become a lower political priority in media-oriented democracies.

Chapter 4 looks at elite group and institutional strategies for media and pubic information management. In particular it documents the rise of the public relations profession and its employment in political and business circles. As argued here, one missing consideration in the work on media management is that mass media also acts as a forum for elite-to-elite communication and conflict. Political and corporate elites use a combination of communication strategies, oriented towards a range of public and elite audiences, in order to sustain their positions. The study examples come from political party and corporate communications departments.

Chapter 5 traces the cultural studies literature linking culture and power, including ideology, discourse, fields, networks and everyday oppositional cultures and subcultures. It is argued that much of this has been hindered by a strong focus on the question of mass consent achieved through the shaping of mass culture. Such an approach has also left a glaring research gap: the study of elite cultures that develop in elite networks/fields and spaces of economic or political power. The significance of such 'elite micro cultures' is explained in case sketches of the City and Parliament.

Chapter 6 looks more specifically at the power of media to influence political agendas and elite decision-making. Two research traditions are identified and set out: the agenda-setting paradigm, adopted in much US political science research, and the 'media colonisation' thesis, suggesting political media management and adaptation strategies direct agendas. The chapter then suggests that there is much to be gained by exploring a mediated approach where the interactions of news texts, politicians and journalists all combine. The case material comes from Westminster.

Chapter 7 reviews a range of perspectives on new media's impact on power and politics. Technological determinist and social shaping approaches, and technophile and technophobic positions are discussed. The chapter then focuses on the issue of E-democracy, politician–citizen interaction, and the possibilities for an Internet-enhanced public sphere. Sample research is offered from the UK Parliamentary public sphere.

Chapter 8 looks in depth at the literature on interest groups and mediated mobilisation. It focuses, in particular, on the communication strategy choices available to new social movements as they try to instigate social change. Is change better effected by placing a group closer to, or further from, centres of power and decision-making (an 'insider' or 'outsider' approach)? Is it better to orient campaigns towards mass media and mass opinion, or to focus communication on active memberships and elite decision-makers? The case study presented is the 2005 Make Poverty History (MPH) campaign.

Chapter 9 reviews the literature on mass media effects and audiences and offers an alternative perspective on the debate. It briefly traces the decline of the strong effects and irrational, mass audience paradigm through uses and gratifications and active audience research. However, as argued here, active audiences may be rational and autonomous but that still does not exclude the possibility of mediated mass-level responses. The case material comes from the professional investor audience at the London Stock Exchange.

Chapter 10 pulls together the findings from the preceding chapters.

# Chapter 2

# Media policy

## Communication and the economic inefficiencies of market liberalisation

## Introduction

This chapter returns to the long-running free market–public service debates that have been at the heart of media policy-making and regulation. In so doing it restates the case for greater financial support for, and regulation of, public service media and communication systems. However, it does so on grounds rather different from the norm. Instead of focusing on the social and political consequences of marketisation, the usual starting point for critiques of neo-liberal economic policy, the emphasis here is on economic consequences. Rather than looking backwards, at a 'golden age' of public service media, this piece looks forwards at a communication system that has been subjected to a period of intense market liberalisation. In place of social crises and democratic deficits it is economic crises which are observed. Instead of nation states and citizens it is markets and market participants which provide the case study material.

## Media policy and the public good

Media work on history and politics or policy and regulation has identified a number of 'ideal' media and communication functions that should operate in healthy democracies (see Keane, 1991; Curran, 2002, for overviews). These ideals dictate that public media should: be a source of 'objective' information that is widely available to all citizens and interest groups; act as a check ('watchdog role') on the activities of powerful institutions, organisations and individuals; present a platform, for the expression of free speech, accessible to a wide range of citizens and interest groups and; support a space for rational debate on the issues and policies affecting society and the state. Debates about the media's ability to fulfil these ideal functions have continued in various forms and currently are most commonly discussed in terms of Habermas's writings on the 'public sphere' (Habermas, 1989 [1962]).[1]

In terms of practical legislation and regulation, policy advocates, for some years, have been divided into two broad camps: those who want publicly supported media systems and those pushing for greater market liberalisation. Such divisions can be traced back to the conflicting ideals inherent in liberal democratic theory itself: that is, between the principles of liberty, equality and fraternity. Such principles cannot all be fulfilled equally and, accordingly, policy advocates prioritise one or two of these ideals over the other(s).

Public service advocates, objecting to the ascendancy of neo-liberal public policy-making, have made their criticisms largely on social and political grounds (see, for example, Postman, 1985; Schiller, 1989; Herman and McChesney, 1997; McChesney *et al.*, 1998; Golding and Murdock, 2000; Sparks, 2000; Herman and Chomsky, 2002; Bagdikian, 2004; Franklin, 2004; Miller, 2004; and CMD). Such policies, they argue, have contributed to social inequality at all levels and a weakening of democratic systems. Powerful corporations have too much influence over media production. Too many sections of society are neither adequately catered for nor given adequate, public opportunities to express themselves. Market pressures have forced media producers to cut production resources, especially in areas of uneconomical public news and information production. Media therefore becomes less diverse, overly dependent on corrupted information subsidies and unable to hold the powerful to account. In effect, the steady marketisation of public media and information systems means that information is being increasingly guided by market needs rather than public ideals. Economic progress is achieved to the detriment of the greater 'public good'. A 'refeudalised' public sphere and a crisis of public confidence and political participation are the consequences (Habermas, 1989; Deacon and Golding, 1994; Blumler and Gurevitch, 1995; Herman and Chomsky, 2002).

Market advocates (see, for example, Sola Pool, 1983; Peacock, 1986; Murdoch, 1989; Veljanovski, 1989; Waters, 1995; Beesley, 1996; Norris, 2000; Lull, 2001; Street, 2001; Lees-Marshment, 2004) have responded with two lines of reasoning. One is to contest the social and political assumptions about what best advances the 'public good'. Politically autonomous communication industries with greater diversity, audience choice and access, are regarded as social and political advances and, therefore, also a 'public good'. Thus, the 'golden age' thesis of an earlier, 'better' public service media, public sphere and social system, is questionable.

Second, they have argued that economic advancement, encouraged by free-market policies, can in itself make a significant contribution to the 'public good'. This emphasis on the market, as the means to harmonise individual self-interests with the greater social and economic good, has an intellectual history dating back to Adam Smith. In its contemporary form, free market advocates argue that liberalisation brings economic advancements, measurable in terms of greater efficiency, productivity, competitiveness, investment and innovation. Such economic developments, in turn, bring positive, measurable, social consequences as a natural by-product. These include greater employment, lower prices and more consumer choice (see, for example, Brittan, 1983; Littlechild, 2000). The same arguments have been applied directly to Britain's communication industries (Peacock, 1986; Veljanovski, 1989; Beesley, 1996) and driven negotiations at successive international trade talks (Freedman, 2005). Whatever the debates, it appears that free market advocates, and economic arguments, appear to be driving the long-term communication policy agenda in Britain, as they are in the USA and most OECD (Organization for Economic Cooperation and Development) countries. Those industries which have not been fully privatised have still been restructured and funded according to market thinking (see Leys, 2001; Curran and Seaton, 2003, for overviews of the UK case). With a few notable exceptions, what is rarely questioned or tested, at least in media studies, is the assumption of economic advancement made by the free market lobby.[2]

This study, centred on the production and dissemination of financial media and information in the equities market (company shares) of the London Stock Exchange (LSE or 'City'), does just this. The LSE, like any financial market, is an information-rich environment. The production and dissemination of accurate market data exercises the thoughts of its participants and authorities more than any other issue. In recent decades the City has been subjected to intensive competition and deregulation. In many ways, these liberalisation policies have had a debilitating impact on the information produced and disseminated within the stock market itself. This, in turn, has had a negative impact on the economic strength of the LSE. Greater marketisation has not necessarily brought greater economic advancement.

The research treated the LSE as a self contained socio-economic system. In terms of employment (over 300,000 people) and assets managed, the City is the third largest stock market in the world and, by some way, the largest in Europe. In many ways it is an autonomous entity with its own legal, cultural and economic rules and systems. The arguments put here are mostly supported by assessing media, information, social and economic developments within this system. However, at the same time, the LSE has a significant effect on, and is also affected by, the UK economy and the global financial system. It is more dominated by large, international 'institutional investors' and banks (as opposed to individual, 'retail' investors) than most international financial exchanges. Thus, any arguments developed about the LSE also have obvious implications for these other systems. Findings are based on approximately 95 semi-structured interviews, at over 80 City locations, during two extended research periods (1998–99, 2004).

## The social information market meets the free information market in the London Stock Exchange

Financial markets, like nation states, are social systems which seek to balance the needs of individuals with those of the general public good. Thus, markets

must balance the needs of individual market participants (citizens) with
those of the market itself (society) and, in the process, establish ideals and
principles that best achieve that balance. The freedom of participants, as
profit-maximising individuals, must be balanced with the needs of a cohesive market, dependent on elements of consensus and cooperation in order
to function. Like all systems, information is a central element of this tension.
On the one hand, it is assumed that markets work most efficiently (are 'fric-
tionless') when prices reflect all available information. For that to happen
all price-sensitive information should be as cheaply, accurately and widely
distributed as possible.[3] Market authorities thus want to achieve a level
playing field in information terms in order that participants might have
sufficient confidence to come and trade. On the other hand, individuals will
also only participate if they believe they can gain information that will give
them a trading advantage over others. Thus, like states, financial market
regulators are faced with a similar free-market/public service dilemma in
regard to the regulation of information. Financial information is a public
resource that must be freely available and widely disseminated, yet participants continue to seek exclusive, private, alternative (or commodified)
sources of information to gain a trading edge.

Legislation and regulation of the City under the Thatcher Government
(1979–89), particularly that put into force in 1985/86 ('Big Bang'), was
strongly determined by the principles of financial market theory. One part
of this involved introducing greater competition into the City to lower
trading costs and attract more investors. In terms of competition, the once
'closed shop' of the City was forcibly opened up. Stock Exchange monopoly
trading conditions were broken, competition increased and transaction costs
decreased. Another part of the legislation demanded better regulation and
greater availability of the 'price-sensitive' information produced by quoted
companies. Better regulation of the release and content of company information reduced the possibilities for insider trading, increased investor confidence, and drew more investors (see Marston, 1996; Kynaston, 2001, vol. 4;
Chapman, 2002, for general accounts).[4]

For many observers these changes brought great economic success. The
combination of deregulation and regulated information supply led to significant growth in the LSE in terms of market infrastructure, trading activity,
capital investment and employment. International financial services grew at
an average of 7 per cent per year. By 2000, the City had an annual surplus in
overseas trade of £31.1 billion (Golding, 2003: 11). The positive knock-on
effects for the British economy and international financial system were also
noted. The intense marketisation of the LSE helped it to successfully maintain its position as Europe's premier financial centre.

However, in the longer term, such intense marketisation has also had a
very detrimental impact on the production and dissemination of financial
information in the LSE itself. This is primarily because information regula-

tion focused exclusively on the information produced and disseminated by companies about themselves. In a national media system, this would be akin to putting the onus on governments and others to honestly disseminate information about themselves through a passive, central media system and then to deregulate all other media entirely. It misses the points that: a) companies (and governments) are only one source of information about themselves, b) such information is unlikely to be neutral, and c) alternative media producers then operate in a completely unregulated environment. Although financial information is regulated in terms of standard accounting requirements, most of the non-company-generated information is not really treated as a competitively produced commodity in itself: that is, in terms of its independence, quality, cost or efficiency of production.

In terms of the equities market of the LSE, the main occupation of most participating organisations, indeed, involves the generation of large quantities of price-sensitive information in order to inform trading decisions. Financial news media/information suppliers, research analysts and fund management companies all generate and exchange large quantities of price-sensitive information (see Figure 2.1 below). A whole set of smaller information service providers also exist, including legal and accounting firms, financial public relations and investor relations companies, and investment consultants. What became apparent through both research periods was that intense competition in all these sectors of the LSE had had an extremely negative impact on the production of these same sources of financial information. Obvious trading costs have been reduced but, in the process,

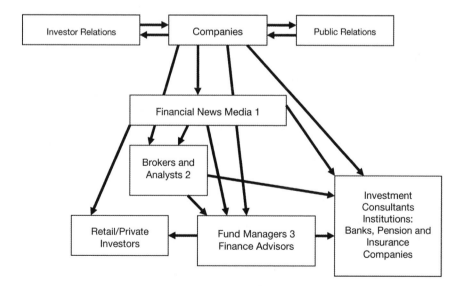

*Figure 2.1* The financial information chain of the London Stock Exchange.

price-sensitive information, the lifeblood of the LSE, has become commodified to an extreme level.

At each stage of the research a similar set of developments and consequences was apparent. Increased financial sector competition had led to
attempts to cut the costs of information production and/or hide those costs
from those further down the investment chain. This caused several problems, one of which was information over-production. More levels of information intermediaries appeared and, at each level, too many of them
generated very similar information. Since much of that information came
from the same original company sources, competition and diversity, among
information intermediaries, was rather more limited than appeared. Many
in the investment chain also attempted to cut or hide their costs by relying
on 'information subsidies' (Gandy, 1982) supplied by those they were
supposed to be independently evaluating. Consequently, much information
was unreliable or corrupt. Investors, at the end of the information chain,
were then left to take their chances with such information or, alternatively,
use investment strategies that excluded the necessity for such information
altogether. In all cases the trading practices and patterns that resulted did
not appear to operate efficiently. In effect, unfettered free-market policies,
applied to the institutions and financial information providers of the
London Stock Exchange, have had a detrimental effect on the market's
operations. Thus, the long-term hidden impact of liberalising the LSE's
financial market structure has been to deregulate financial information
production which, in turn, has made equities trading less rather than more
efficient.

## The market corruption of information in the London Stock Exchange

The research looked at the three main producers and disseminators of financial information about traded companies (excluding the companies themselves) within the equities market of the LSE (see Figure 2.1). According
to interviews with professional investors (see also MORI, 2000) these are: a)
financial media/news wire services, b) brokers' (or 'sell-side') analyst
research, and c) fund manager (or 'buy-side') research.

### Financial journalism

One obvious source of financial information in the LSE is the financial
media, including news wire services. It is the most common information
source for amateur (retail) investors and closely attended to by fund
managers (see Davis, 2005). In financial journalism, expansion, combined
with greater media and financial competition, has forced journalists to
produce more copy with fewer resources. This has increased journalist

dependency on a range of 'information subsidies' from quoted companies, financial public relations and investor relations professionals, and brokers' analysts. Since all these sources are, in the main, using information produced by quoted companies themselves, news content is rather more selective and rather less diverse than appears to traders.

The post-war rise in financial/business journalism (television and newspaper) has been noted in many studies (Parsons, 1989; Tumber, 1993; Tunstall, 1996; Cassidy, 2002). Such journalism now makes up approximately a third of serious news space. However, during the 1980s and 1990s, just as competition reached new levels in the financial sector so it did in the news media industries (Seymour-Ure, 1996; Tunstall, 1996; Franklin, 1997). Financial journalism, like journalism generally, was continually forced to increase output while often making cuts in staffing and other resource levels. This made financial news particularly reliant on the information supplied by corporate advertising and public relations to support its expansion (Curran, 1978; Newman, 1984; Davis, 2002). As interviews revealed, not only are there not enough specialist journalists, the 'beats' they cover are extensive and require complex knowledge of financial accounting and City practices. As two explained: 'Even for the most experienced reporters there do not exist the resources to check the fine details and financial figures produced in company documents' (Nick Chaloner);

> There are a large number of people with interests a mile wide and with knowledge an inch deep. Newspapers just don't have the specialists. Standards per se have not got worse. If a single journalist has to cover banking, aviation, etc., then your level of knowledge gets worse because there is just too much.
>
> (Paul Barber)

The resource gap, since the 1980s, has instead been filled by companies employing financial public relations specialists. For many observers public relations and advertising have indeed had a greater influence on financial media than any other sector of the national news media (Parsons, 1989; Cassidy, 2002; Davis, 2002; Golding, 2003). This was the assessment of two former financial journalists now working in financial PR: (Roland Rudd) 'Undoubtedly there is more PR in financial news than other sections'; (Martin Adeney) 'I would say it [financial news] was 85 or even 90 per cent driven by formal announcements or events . . . The majority of journalists wouldn't even go down to Companies House to look up the annual reports and accounts.'

During the 1990s a third source of information subsidies for financial journalists developed and expanded. The investor relations industry began supplying specialists to promote companies to investors, especially large, international institutions. They do so, in large part, by communicating and supplying information to brokers' analysts and journalists. According to several accounts (Marston, 1996, 1999; Holland, 1997) the investor relations function has been central to a rapid increase in 'controlled information disclosure' between companies and analysts. According to the Investor Relations Society (IRS, 1998: 33), by the end of the 1990s, 77 per cent of analysts had at least weekly contact with their investor relations counterparts. Since journalists regard analysts as the independent 'experts' on companies, and regularly use their comments, this has become yet another form of company-supplied information subsidy for financial journalism. Thus the rise of investor relations has, accordingly, not only impacted on journalists directly, but indirectly through their relations with analysts.

Fund managers, interviewed some years later, were clearly sceptical about the content of financial news and its reliance on company, public relations and investor relations information. It seemed common knowledge that many company intermediaries attempted to 'manage expectations' and share prices by regularly leaking information to journalists:

> But a lot are just fed by the financial PR machine and that's all they do; they regurgitate the financial PR, which ain't much good. There are journalists who are conscientious and experienced, but there aren't many these days.
>
> (anonymous Fund Manager)

> Most of the financial media get their ideas from the analysts they talk to, their mates in the City tell them what's going on and what's likely to go on. They are basically trying to sell things and then the journalists pick up on the trends – by and large.
>
> (Tony Dye)

During both research periods it became apparent that financial news coverage had become overly influenced by the very companies journalists reported on. Quite apart from the overt pressures companies could exert – in terms of advertising clout and controlled access – journalism was extremely dependent on a variety of information subsidies provided by companies and their promotional intermediaries. In cutting news research costs financial journalism had become more dependent on, and encouraged the growth of, several unregulated sources of financial information production. That information was over-produced, unreliable and lacking in diversity.

### Brokers' analyst research

The most central and prolific set of information producers in the LSE are the research analysts working for the broking houses (also known as the 'sell-side' analysts). There are an estimated 14,000 people employed in stock broking and analysis (City Business Series, 2003), each of which produces and disseminates company research on a daily basis. According to the Financial Services Authority (FSA/Deloitte and Touche, April 2004) 52 per cent of all financial research on companies is conducted by such analysts.

Like journalism, increased marketisation in the 1980s caused a number of problems in information production. These included under-funding, hiding research costs, general over-production of information and biased or corrupt research. Prior to the 1986 Financial Services Act a small number of London-based brokers controlled access to the market by managing all trading activity, and at fixed rates of commission. High commission rates effectively paid for analyst research costs and investors therefore selected brokers according to their ability to provide good analysis and trading recommendations. After 1986, fixed commission rates were abandoned and any outside company could act as broker and 'market maker'. This had the obvious benefit of reducing trading costs and encouraging more trading. However, it also meant that brokers, the main producers and suppliers of company information, no longer had their research operations properly funded as commission rates dropped significantly. They also now had to compete in an international, intensely competitive market. As one former broker explained:

> And this is why a lot of the brokers then [post-Big Bang] went into market making because they knew their standalone business on 0.25 per cent wouldn't survive really . . . The research departments got too big and became very expensive, and the day-to-day flow wasn't paying enough money to generate income so they had to cull some of the research department.
>
> (Mike Cunnane)

Fewer resources thus meant a greater reliance on company information subsidies, either directly or indirectly, via investor relations practitioners (see above). Equally significantly, it also left broking houses open to take-over by larger financial companies seeking an influential stake in the LSE. They were almost all bought up by wealthier international investment banks. Investment banks have multiple forms of income, the largest of which involves offering financial services to publicly quoted companies. Since these are the same companies that brokers' analysts are researching and promoting, obvious conflicts of interest have arisen (see Kynaston, 2001; Chapman, 2002; Golding, 2003, for accounts). As Tony Golding explained:

> In the 1970s, pre Big-Bang, the advice of analysts was listened to and there was a natural mechanism and they were paid more for having good judgement. After Big Bang, when investment banks bought up

brokers and the profitability of broking went way down, it became quite clear that you couldn't justify analysts just being analysts. You had to use them to open doors to other kinds of corporate business. So the whole thing became distorted.

The conflicted and unreliable nature of broker research was clear to many on the fund management side:

> Brokers at the various houses will have their own agenda which has been set for the day – because these are information dissemination, selling operations. That is what they are – It's like double glazing salesmen.
>
> (Michael Rimmer)

> It's all a big promotional thing . . . To the corporations they [analysts] are saying 'we know all about your industry and we would be very good to advise you on all your financial business'. To the fund managers they are saying 'we know all about these companies and we can advise you on investments in them'. The great incentive for the investment bank is to push itself all the time.
>
> (Gordon Midgley)

Just how corrupted analyst information has become became apparent in research on analyst recommendations during the 1990s stock market boom period. During this time brokers became increasingly reluctant to make 'sell' recommendations, for fear of offending the companies they analysed. By 2000, according to Golding (2003: 209) only 1.6 per cent of analyst recommendations were to 'sell' a company. According to FSA research (July 2002: 12) 'buy' recommendations in 2000 outnumbered 'sell' by a ratio of nine to one. Even through the period 2000–02, when share prices fell heavily, the ratio remained at five 'buys' to one 'sell'. This positive bias was even worse if a broker's parent investment banking company was found to directly advise the company traded. In 2000, 80 per cent of FTSE 100 company recommendations, by connected brokers, were to buy and 2 per cent were to sell; a ratio of 40:1 (FSA, July 2002: 18, see also Chan *et al.*, 2003, on this).

Following the post-2000 crash in the equities market, the FSA and Treasury have begun devoting greater attention to the problem in a series of discussion papers and policy statements (FSA, July 2002, February 2003, October 2003, March 2004). These papers revealed, in the words of Howard Davies, then Chairman of the FSA (press release, 12 February 2003) 'evidence of systematic bias in analysts' recommendations, and of bad management of conflicts of interest'. The picture built up was one in which analysts have become subsidised, rewarded, pressurised and threatened by companies, in much the same way journalists are by powerful news sources.

Thus, like financial journalism, market competition has had a negative impact on information production in the broking sector. There is a general over-supply of information by too many analysts. That information is increasingly dependent on company and company intermediary supply and is, thus, lacking diversity or objectivity. Analysts are not rewarded for the quality of their information but, instead, through promoting other financial services and/or pleasing clients with conflicting objectives.

### Fund manager research

The third major source of financial information production is the fund management sector. Fund managers make most of the major trading decisions and, at the same time, are producers of research and analysis on companies. Fund management (or 'buy-side') analysts produce an estimated 45 per cent of company research (FSA/Deloitte and Touche, April 2004), much of which consists of analysing and following up broker ('sell-side') research.

Once again, increased market competition has impacted on the information production process at this level. Deregulation of the financial markets led to intense concentration in the industry and the rapid influx of international financial institutions. The London Stock Exchange is now the most concentrated, and has the largest overseas investment presence, of any of the major international exchanges (see Kynaston, 2001; Golding, 2003). On the one hand fund managers seek to digest as much price-sensitive information as they can to make better trading decisions and get better results to attract big investors. On the other, resources of time and money are limited and have to be justified when trying to offer a competitive commission rate to those same investors. According to one senior financial actuary, increased competition has indeed resulted in a reduction in fund manager research:

> All the competition on percentage of funds does the wrong thing as well. It may drive the fees down as a percentage of funds under management, but, what that does, if you then look at the mechanics of your business, is it forces you to cut your research staff and cut your overheads, which is the lifeblood of the information that's valuable to the client. So competition does the wrong thing for the clients . . . They are competing over funds under management charge instead of competing over a more matched fee for research.
>
> (Jeremy Goford)

Consequently, fund managers have, in one way or another, attempted to economise on their information gathering costs and/or hide those costs from their investing clients. The most obvious way that is done is through the use of brokers' analyst information subsidies. Even the most broker-critical fund managers interviewed relied on broker research in some way. For many, brokers simply did the essential 'donkey work' and the 'buy-side' then did the serious evaluation. As two explained:

> No buy-side institution could ever afford to pay for that kind of quality of [broker] analyst . . . typically, sell-side can be much more concentrated because there are more of them than buy-side, who are covering several sectors. They [sell-side] go to industry functions, read all the specialist press, chat to chief executives and finance directors all the time.
>
> (John Davies)

> In the ideal the broker's role is simply to break bulk . . . I think there is a legitimate and defensible role that the fund manager should not read all 150 pages of [an annual results statement] and that it's fair for him to ring up somebody who has and ask the question 'What's the important bit in here?' It would be a great waste of everybody's time if every fund manager had to read all 150 pages.
>
> (anonymous fund manager)

However, recent Treasury/FSA investigations of the LSE (Myners, 2001; FSA, April 2003; FSA/OXERA, April 2003; FSA/Deloitte and Touche, April 2004; FSA, May 2004) have found that the information dependency of fund managers on brokers, generally, is rather more extensive and costly than that. This research estimated that, in 2000, £2.3 billion was paid in commission to brokers, of which approximately 40 per cent went towards research and other information services. 'Bundled brokerage' and 'soft commission' arrangements, as these services were labelled, posed several problems for market efficiency.

First, their costs were not formally accounted for. No documentation was kept and investing institutions therefore had no knowledge of the costs, efficiency or reliability of the information/research production they were paying for. As one FSA report summed up (May 2004: 10–11):

> We concluded from this analysis that there was evidence of a market failure. Control of conflicts of interest was deficient, and the opacity of the arrangements meant that investors had insufficient information to judge whether they were getting good value for money from expenditure on ancillary [information/research] services.

Second, fund managers were encouraged to do business with brokers because of their ability to supply free information subsidies rather than their trading skills. As another FSA report stated (April 2003: 4):

Bundled and soft commission arrangements create powerful incentives that have a strong influence on fund managers' trading decisions and the routing of business to brokers. In some circumstances, buying additional services may be a stronger driver for trading decisions than execution quality.

Third, information over-supply, as well as a false picture of information diversity, was encouraged as every broker competed to supply the same information to their clients. As one top actuary explained:

> I mean the whole soft commission thing . . . arguably encourages over supply of research. It's like having 50 TV channels. Is 50 TV channels better than four or five? Well, yes and no. You're getting more choice, but you're probably getting much lower quality, which is why people flick channels a lot. There's a big debate about that.
>
> (Andrew Kirton)

Alternatively, fund management companies have sought to save on information/research costs, and so offer lower commission rates to investors, by doing away with research altogether. A number of investment approaches simply buy and sell company shares according to price movements in the market itself. 'Index tracker' funds typically buy and keep FTSE 100 shares and are run automatically by computer programmes. According to estimates by Myners (2001) and Golding (2003), 20–30 per cent of shares are managed in tracker funds or in 'closet indexers' (fund managers consciously sticking close to an index). Surveys by Phillips and Drew (1999, 2000: 5) put this figure higher at 41–42 per cent. Alternatively 'momentum' investing looks at the recent history of all shares and buys those which are going up fastest and sells those which are dropping. It also relies on computer analysis. Similarly, hedge funds exploit trading anomalies within the market itself. Each of these approaches, which have increased significantly since the early 1990s, have considerably reduced research costs but have not, according to financial market theory, encouraged efficient trading in the market as a whole.

According to one interviewee, such approaches: disconnect trading prices from real prices; reduce the amount of active buyers in the market, thus giving more power to sellers; and encourage volatile and 'herd-like' trading patterns. As Paul Woolley explained (interview, see also Myners, 2001; Woolley, May 2002, December 2002):

> If you don't think you can outperform because it's an efficient market you index. It pays everybody individually to index but, collectively, the market suffers because there is no efficient pricing. However efficient or

inefficient the market is it's a zero-sum gain. Second thing is momentum. It pays everyone to use momentum but momentum causes bubbles and collapses and is damaging. The third thing is hedge funds. It pays everyone to use them but collectively it's extremely damaging . . . we get a bubble like that in 1999 or 2000 which is highly damaging and people don't realise the damage bubbles do. They just think they go up and come back down again. But they distort investment. We had half a trillion of fruitless investment in telecoms infrastructure as a result of that bubble.

In attempting to reduce the spiralling costs of information and research, fund management companies have taken two routes. The first is to rely on a mix of overt and covert information subsidies supplied by brokers' analysts which are themselves subsidised and overly influenced by companies. The second is to do away with research altogether and manage their investments electronically and purely in relation to the internal market. Both these options are likely to lead to less efficiency in trading in the market overall. They are certainly not likely to encourage better allocation of capital to businesses in the wider economy.

## Consequences for economic efficiency

The ultimate consequence of liberalising the LSE's market structures has been to liberalise most information production also, which, in turn, has made the LSE a less efficient market. In terms of information production and dissemination, the LSE increasingly suffers from: overproduction of financial information and information overload; the false presentation of a competitive and diverse market in information where too little actually exists; a number of hidden costs in information production; and the fundamental corruption of the information production process.

First, a large amount of financial information production and dissemination is extremely unproductive. Much of it consists of the same information being repeated and repackaged and presented by multiple intermediaries. Public/investor relations practitioners, journalists and analysts all pick up, process and pass on the same information being generated by companies. For several fund managers interviewed there were clearly too many suppliers for each piece of information and an ongoing problem of information overload:

> It's an industry with over-capacity. On average for a large company there will be 20–25 analysts per company and that must be an oversupply because basically their information comes from the same source, which is the company.

> (Tony Golding)

20 or 30 years ago in fund management, having the information was a key advantage. But now there is lots of information, you have to decide what's noise, what's irrelevant.

(Edward Bonham-Carter)

There's too much information. So, you could spend your life analysing things to the end and not coming to a decision. Like *100 years of Solitude*, that book by Gabriel Marquez. You get to the end and there's nothing.

(Andy Brough)

Of equal significance, a large proportion of information produced is extremely unreliable. At each stage in the investment chain two corrupting processes take place. Competition means economising on research costs. This results in 'objective' research relying on the information subsidies that are supplied by the very companies and experts that are the subject of evaluation. Consequently, I found a high level of skepticism about the value and objectivity of much financial information in circulation. The output of financial journalists and analysts alike was either dismissed completely or treated with some caution by investors:

The main thing is we don't trust anything we get from the company and we don't trust anything from sell-side analysts. They offer a tainted product. They all get money from the companies they comment on . . . The sell-side are all journalists really. They are no better then journalists using company information.

(Richard Krammer)

I think the whole business has changed . . . The only credible source as far as we are concerned is us. That's the way it should be for anyone who's got any sense in the City. There's incredible sources and there's less credible sources but there's no credible sources at all . . . They are all out there trying to market to the City and some of them do it with a high level of verbosity and hyperbole.

(Tony Dye)

An inefficient and corrupt information production process, in turn, contributes to clear inaccuracies in, or inconsistent valuation approaches to, the way company shares are gauged (see above). This has resulted in pricing for the stock exchange, as a whole, to move away from historical measures and/or become less stable. From the late 1980s, until stock markets crashed in 2000, the LSE became increasingly over-priced.[5] Annual returns for investors were impressive but, according to historical market data, bore little relation to conventional accounting values. According to Bank of England data (see Figure 2.2), the LSE's price-earnings ratio was 50 per cent higher than its long-term average in the 1990s and by 2000 was two and a half times that average.[6] The average dividend yield (dividends paid to shareholders) was also markedly lower than its long-term average and also hit a new low in 2000 (see Figure 2.3). Both these trends[7] meant that valuable short-term profits were made but, in the long term, contributed to the LSE being as over-priced as at any point in the twentieth century. Long-term profits were sacrificed and long-term stability of the market put in doubt. Obviously, the

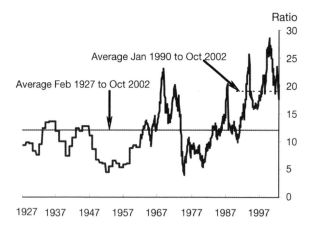

*Figure 2.2* FTSE all-share P/E ratio[a] (1927–2002).

Source: Wetherilt and Weeken (2002).

Note
a Annual data until 1962, monthly data thereafter.

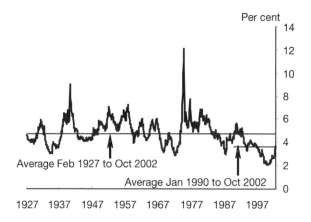

*Figure 2.3* FTSE all-share dividend yield (1927–2002).

Source: Wetherilt and Weeken (2002).

corruption of information production was only one contributing factor to this state of affairs, but it is hard to argue it was not a significant factor.

Ultimately, the costs to the City and those professionally involved in the LSE were high. Following the 2000 crash, the market lost almost 50 per cent of its value over three years. The most severe job losses in any sector of the UK economy were in the City itself. Despite a modest recovery since 2003, at the time of going to press, six years later, it has just regained its 2000 levels but, at the same time, is regarded as over-valued. Monthly surveys of fund managers in the industry (Merrill Lynch) indicate that, since 2003, the LSE equities market has been regarded with suspicion. In that time the 'outlook for corporate profits' has been either the least or second least 'favourable' of the major international equities markets. It has also been consistently labelled the second most 'over-valued' of the markets after the New York Stock Exchange (see also Smithers and Wright, 2004, on this). Many of the largest financial investors, such as pension funds and insurance companies, have since withdrawn a proportion of their funds from the equities market (IMA, 2004) and/or invested in passively managed funds. Since 2000 the LSE's owners and regulators have been regularly criticised in business and political circles. In recent years four other international exchanges have made, or come close to making, take-over bids for the LSE itself. At the time of writing its future is far from assured.

In effect, the LSE has become less efficient according to financial market theory. While direct transaction costs in the City have gone down, indirect costs have gone up. The companies and investors at either end of the investment/information chain, directly or indirectly, have to pay the rising costs of these multiple layers of information intermediaries and their excessive information outputs. As one independent analyst explained:

> At the moment the evidence is . . . there is far more research and effort made in the management of research than is needed to keep the market efficient. The City of London and Wall Street make more money than they should.
>
> (Andrew Smithers)

Information may be more universally available but its quality, and hence trading utility, is questionable. It is less diverse or pluralist in nature and its producers are not rewarded for greater accuracy or attempted objectivity. Arguably, this encourages pricing irregularities and less market stability.

All these concerns were echoed, rather vociferously, by some of the interviewees:

> So maybe the conclusion that you come to is that competition doesn't work . . . It's only because the OFT [Office of Fair Trading] doesn't understand that competition does the wrong thing for customers and

they still don't understand that . . . they just believe that competition will just solve everything. People who don't understand the financial services business.

(anonymous actuary)

I think the whole thing is utterly disreputable. Competitive markets are not efficient markets. The academics have taken us all up the garden path and the practitioners have enjoyed making money from the whole thing.

(anonymous fund manager)

Once you have lost [even] self regulation, which is what we now have in the City, to all intents and purposes, then everything goes by the board. You get the lunatics running the asylum quite frankly . . . The UK is wide, wide open and if anyone is going to bring a tin opener to any part of capitalism it's going to come in the UK. It really is very very worrying. In 35 years of it I've never been so concerned.

(David Bailey, company chairman)

The arguments put here have been in terms of the social sphere of the London Stock Exchange. But, because the LSE is embedded in both the British economy and global financial system, there are also economic (not to mention social and political) consequences at these higher levels. Inefficient allocation of capital in industries in the UK and elsewhere, costly and wasteful take-over activity, industrial and employment decline and displacement, financial instability and unpredictability in national budgets, large-scale corporate frauds, banking crises and pension fund collapses are some of the many repercussions noted by observers.[8] These are not considered to be 'public goods'.

## Conclusion

Initially, the combination of market deregulation and company information regulation appeared to have contributed to the overall health of the London Stock Exchange. Changes were key to the break-up of a privileged and exclusionary market system, to encourage international investment and maintain the LSE's position in the global financial system. In financial market (Efficient Markets Hypothesis) theory terms the City began operating more efficiently. However, the pressures brought about by such extreme liberalisation have also had a longer-term, detrimental impact on the LSE. The argument put here is that most financial information production, essential to trading in the Exchange, has been subjected to extreme marketisation rather than regulation. Information concerns, such as independence and objectivity, quality, cost and efficiency of production, have not been properly addressed. The production and dissemination of price-sensitive information has thus become less economically efficient, not more. There is over-capacity in information production with the same information and analysis being reproduced again and again. Market participants suffer from information overload and have to pay hidden information costs. Much of the information produced, at every stage in the information chain, is unreliable and lacking in diversity, and has few incentives to be accurate or objective.

This state of affairs has contributed to the LSE becoming, in plain economic terms, less efficient and cost effective, not more. The costs of sustaining the market and its many information intermediaries grows. Investment has become increasingly haphazard as decision-making comes to rely on 'promotional' rather than 'objective' information. In the longer term, the survival of the equities market, in its current state, has come into question. Greater volatility, wasted investment, corporate fraud and a market crash have followed. Stock market trust, external investment and employment in the equities market itself has declined. In essence, free market policies, given free reign in the LSE, have worked to corrupt information. Such developments have, to an extent, helped put in jeopardy the long-term survival of the market itself.

Interestingly, the problems associated with liberalising the LSE have also been documented in other accounts of international markets and the global financial system more generally. The issues of information corruption have similarly been noted in the New York Stock Exchange where competition and deregulation were also extended in the same period.[9]

The general conclusion is that media and information are key resources that are essential for the stable functioning of any social sphere – be it on any scale and in any social, political or economic context. If they are subjected to unrestrained market forces, left under-resourced and under-regulated, the stability and longevity of that sphere is jeopardised. These arguments have usually been put in terms of the social and political consequences of economic liberalisation. These, in turn, have been contested by those who emphasise that social gains are a natural by-product of economic stability which, in turn, is aided by free-market policies. However, as argued here, economic stability becomes just as insecure and unsustainable if simply guided by neo-liberal economic thinking. The core assumption that free-markets are purely beneficial on economic grounds can not be taken for granted.

# Chapter 3

# Media production

## Discursive practices, news production and the mobilisation of bias in public discourse

### Introduction

This chapter looks at news production. It discusses the issue of whether power imbalances and inequalities in society are reflected or reinforced in the news production process. It is argued that the same procedures and ideals of journalism, developed as a means of producing professional, objective and socially reflective news, have also become a cause of less visible forms of distortion.

According to many historical and sociological accounts, the journalist profession has, over time, developed a set of practices and cultures which now shape news production according to normative ideals. The market, 'occupational ideology', professional associations, codes of ethics, organisational hierarchies and operating conventions, all encourage journalism to neutrally document and reflect the world as it is. Such elements have similarly enabled journalism, under most circumstances, to fend off the attempts of powerful groups or institutions to control outputs.

However, as argued here, these same market forces, professional cultures and practices have also become a means by which power imbalances are maintained in a less visible way. They lead to crucial reporting omissions or over-emphases on a systematic basis and so contribute to a subtle, long-term 'mobilisation of bias' in media reporting. This excludes certain groups in society. More significantly, it also ensures that chronic, long-term problems, many of which contribute to power imbalances, remain a minor part of public sphere discussions until they reach crisis point. Such tendencies have become all the more exacerbated by rising competition. Thus, the very discursive practices that are supposed to reveal the world as it is also, unwittingly, serve to leave crucial causal elements of inequality and crisis uncovered.

### Directing the production of 'ideal' journalism

It is difficult to find either academic or journalist who would declare that journalism has managed to produce and sustain news outputs that are truly impartial, fact-centred and socially reflective. Reporters constantly have to overcome a number of time, resource and knowledge barriers in order to produce immediate, factual and informed news on a regular basis. Although news publications are no longer the openly partisan tools of political and business patrons they are still subject to attempts at influence by powerful interests. The journalist profession, when surveyed in most circumstances, is skewed on grounds of gender, class, ethnicity, political outlook and geographical location and, thus, does not share the demographic profile of society that it seeks to reflect (Media Information Centre, 1971–2002; Lichter and Rothman, 1988; Protess *et al.*, 1991, NUJ, 1994–2006; NTO/Skillset, 2002; Allan, 2004; CRE, 2005). All of which hinder the production of the kind of news that professional journalists aspire to produce.

Instead, journalism, of the 'Anglo-American' kind at least (Chalaby, 1996), is presented historically as an evolving profession. Over time it has adopted a series of market responses, cultures, tools and processes to make it as reflective, factual and objective as possible (see accounts in Curran, 2002; Schudson, 2003; Zellizer, 2004). One obvious signifier of autonomy and social reflectiveness is, ultimately, the market success or failure of a media organisation. As news producers expanded their operations and sought to attract larger consumer bases and accompanying advertising revenues, so journalism was forced to become a 'profession' that catered to its consumers rather than its patrons. In current times, media that is too state controlled or censored (McNair, 2000; Sparks, 2000), will always decline as market-driven alternatives develop. A commercially produced news product will lose sales and, consequently, advertising if it is not regarded as legitimate and consumer-led in the eyes of its public (Veljanovski, 1989; Beesley, 1996). Thus, the market, if operating under the right balance of competition and regulation, will ensure journalist objectivity and sensitivity to the public.

Producing such forms of news has entailed the establishment of organisational and cultural norms in order to originate regular, objective and public-oriented outputs. So emerged the 'occupational ideology' of professional journalism. This consisted of a set of normative values which included a public service ethos (see Chapter 2), a sense of objectivity and ethics, immediacy and autonomy (see Schudson, 2001; Deuze, 2005). Ethical norms, of accuracy, impartiality and sincerity, are now passed on during journalist training, through membership of professional associations, in codes of conduct and via established editorial hierarchies. They are frequently the subject of discussion in industry journals and conferences. Periodic surveys of journalists, in the United Kingdom and United States (e.g., Media Information Centre, 2002; NTO/Skillset, 2002), reveal that news organisations are increasingly staffed by graduates with professional journalist training. Through such means 'public journalism' (see Glasser, 1999) has developed.

Such an ethos requires the selection of stories according to perceived public interest. Journalists and editors, accordingly, adopt universal 'news values' to guide them in their role as news 'gatekeepers' (Manning White, 1950). There have been several attempts to identify and classify news values (Galtung and Ruge, 1965; Tunstall, 1971; Gans, 1979; Tiffen, 1989). Even though these accounts are written in different time periods and countries there appears considerable overlap. This leads many to conclude that news values transcend the preferences and attitudes of individual journalists and are most obviously in evidence during mass 'media events' (Dayan and Katz, 1992). Such events generate simultaneous, multi-outlet coverage.

Objectivity similarly becomes ingrained in reporters at work. For Tuchman (1972) journalists adopt a number of strategic practices in order to produce balanced, 'factual' news with limited resources and expertise. These include presenting opposing views, generating expert/authoritative source quotations and supplying speculative evidence to support news story claims. Such practices helped to firmly establish journalism's professional credentials and its 'fourth estate' reputation during the Vietnam War and Watergate (Lang and Lang, 1983; Hallin, 1994). As long as opposition parties are reported alongside governments, unions and pressure groups are covered as well as corporations, so journalists retain an independent, arbiter-like status.

For many, news organisation is another vital means of maintaining professionalism in journalism (Gans, 1979; Fishman, 1980; Tiffen, 1989; Tunstall, 1996). Organisation ensures that unpredictable, immediate and unprocessed news material is regularly made to fill set spaces and times, to deadlines, and in recognisable house styles. There are several means for managing such unpredictable and risky elements, including top-down editorial hierarchies, news sections and assembly lines. Journalists internalise such professional norms and operating procedures by being subject to a succession of incentives. These include 'big' story allocation, story acceptance and priority placing, more autonomy and promotion. The other key organising principle of news production revolves around news sections, 'beats' and news sources (Sigal, 1973; Fishman, 1980; Ericson et al., 1989; Schlesinger and Tumber, 1994; Manning, 2000). Most journalists are given beats to cover, within a news section, which include physical locations, personal contacts, information sources and procedures. Beats and sources are selected according to their 'public interest' status and their ability to supply newsworthy comment and information. As long as journalists maintain their professionalism and autonomy a healthy 'tug of war' between reporters and their sources is established (Gans, 1979).

Many of these same studies of news production reveal that these processes, tools and cultures can occasionally lead to unreflective or erratic news coverage. There may be an over-dependence on 'diary events', news features and press release-instigated stories. News events may become too compressed and shaped to fit news slots. Journalists may be too oriented towards established beats. However, all these latter-day faults and suscepti-bilities do not, in themselves, represent an overall failure or pattern of bias. Ultimately, news production can never entirely fulfil its professional, 'ideal' remit. Its adoption of techniques, codes, norms and practices, simply work to ensure mistakes and instances of bias are minimised or evened out. For some (Lichtenberg, 2000; McNair, 2003; Schudson, 2003), any long-term comparison of news outputs over time would conclude that journalism has been significantly strengthened. The way forward is to keep acknowledging professional short-comings, re-evaluate practices during 'critical incidents' (Zellizer, 1992) and continue to adapt to changing circumstances.

## Ideal journalism and invisible power

A proportion of media scholars take their criticism of news production a step further. The inefficiencies, inaccuracies and omissions of journalism do not follow some random path. Instead, they result from powerful, external influences in society and produce partial outputs which favour certain groups, norms and values over others. It is corporate, political and military groups (or classes) and institutions which benefit. There are a range of studies seeking to demonstrate such bias in reporting. These may be loosely grouped into overt and conscious, on the one hand, and invisible and systematic, on the other.

The overt and conscious forms of media management and influence have been widely documented (see, for example, Eldridge, 1995; Philo, 1995; Stauber and Rampton, 1995; Herman and Chomsky, 2002 [1988]; Bagdikian, 2004; Miller, 2004) and are discussed further in Chapter 4. In summary, these detail a number of control mechanisms through which domi-nant elites attempt to exert control over journalists and the news production process. This 'propaganda model' (Herman and Chomsky, 2002) has a powerful case to make, especially in times of war or international crisis. However, the critique seems rather less consistent when applied to many other areas of national and daily news reporting. Much of the time, coverage of events and people is less dramatic and elite control mechanisms are used more sparingly.

An alternative approach to documenting 'mobilisations of bias' in news production focuses on less visible and more systematic processes. It can be traced back to the very practices, cultures and discourses that are meant to have shaped and propelled journalism towards its contemporary 'ideal' incarnation. Like the evolution of other professional discourses the shifts are more micro-level and incremental but with equally significant impacts on the macro-scale. The communicative consequences for news journalism, in terms of societal power, are expressed by what, systematically, is not included, recorded or engaged with in daily news content.

First, the market mechanism is not simply about making news media autonomous from government and responsive to public interest. Advertisers choose to advertise in media outlets and particular sections where there are either large audiences, with moderate spending power, or smaller or specialist audiences with higher spending power (see Curran, 1978; Garnham, 1990; Curran and Seaton, 2003). This explains why many radical, working class papers have, in spite of large circulations, failed in the past. It also explains why minority groups are not adequately catered for, and, why business/financial news sections are far larger than their audience figures can justify (Newman, 1984; Davis, 2002). Intensified market forces often result in a competition for audiences and advertising revenues which, in turn, can result in news commodification, news recycling, the adoption of populist, entertainment-oriented news values and non-news outputs (Postman, 1985; McManus, 1994; Bennett, 1997; Franklin, 1997, 2005; Delli Carpini and Williams, 2001; Underwood, 2001; Altheide, 2004; Entman, 2005).

Several elements of the professional, 'occupational ideology' are problematic in that, in practice, they are achieved more symbolically than substantively. For Hall *et al.* (1978), journalists, in attempting to fulfil these public interest aims and present authoritative accounts, purposively seek out those who already appear knowledgeable, authoritative or representative. As such, they reinforce, as well as reflect, power imbalances by awarding such 'primary definers' greater visibility and legitimacy. Other studies (Protess *et al.*, 1991; Herbst, 1998; Entman and Herbst, 2001; Lewis, 2001; Davis, 2003b; Brookes *et al.*, 2004) have revealed that journalists often determine public interest concerns and public opinion through exchanges with other journalists and these same elite sources. Consequently, on a day-to-day basis, public interest is narrowly defined, not by the wider public, but by those already in positions of power.

The fourth estate, autonomy and objectivity directives of reporters are similarly achieved more on a symbolic level. As Hallin (1994) demonstrates, objectivity which is signified by reporting a balance of elite sources, still constrains debate within these elite-defined spheres of legitimate conflict and consensus. For others (Blumler and Gurevitch, 1995; Tiffen, 1999; Thompson, 2000; Barnett and Gaber, 2001) fourth estate values, which critically hold the powerful to account, have come to be represented by personal conflicts and scandals rather than real evaluations of policy and competency. Balancing views, as an objective practice, can instead become quite distorting if coverage masks the fact that one set of views is either a minority one or artificially created and presented (see examples in Stauber and Rampton, 1995, 2003; Bennett and Manheim, 2001, and many contributions in Allan *et al.*, 2000).

News organisation, while aiding the dissemination of professional values and practices, is also a means of restricting journalists. Reporters, in trying to produce news to deadline and to set spaces, come to produce items that are ahistorical and in soundbite form (Schlesinger, 1987; Hallin, 1994). Production needs discourage context and complexity. As editorial hierarchies become tighter so journalists reduce risk-taking and adopt methods of self-censorship to maximise chances of story publication (Sigelman, 1973; Schlesinger, 1987). At some point, beats, organisations and sources, come to encroach on the organisation of news itself. Journalists increasingly include organisations and sources on the basis of their ability to regularly supply newsworthy information subsidies (Sigal, 1973; Fishman, 1980; Gandy, 1982) and, conversely, organisations and sources proactively orient themselves towards journalists.

In effect, many of the market mechanisms, tools, cultures and practices that have evolved to support independent, reflective journalism, in time, have also come to have a strong shaping character of their own. This is problematic because many of these elements are, in practice, no more than short-cuts or proxy substitutes for what is required. They are as symbolic as they are substantial. They have developed to make up for the fact that journalists do not have the necessary resources of time, money and knowledge required to fulfil professional expectations. Put under strain by a further tightening of resources simply makes the gap between expectations and practice larger. Consequently, these elements are themselves a potential cause of distorted reporting.

What is significant here is not whether journalism is more subject to top-down control and overt influence, or whether it is more autonomous, diverse, anarchic and responsive to consumer-public demand. The key concern is that professional practices mean that certain topics, individuals and forms of debate are continually highlighted while others become systematically omitted from public discourse altogether.

Thus, issues which matter to those who do not consume news become excluded. Reporting on those public interest issues that are costly, require investigative resources or lack headline appeal, declines. This has been the fate of foreign news, parliamentary coverage, investigative reporting and current affairs programming (Seymour-Ure, 1996; Tunstall, 1996; Van Ginneken, 1998; McLachlan and Golding, 2000). Issues that are complex, long-term and/or not presentable in human interest form are either avoided altogether or drastically reshaped to fit the needs of news producers. Thus, reporting on social and welfare issues, industrial relations, inner-city deprivation, racial tensions, white collar crime, financial and market instabilities, and environmental topics, continually fail to register until a crisis arises (Parsons, 1989; Cottle, 1993; Hansen, 1993; Schlesinger and Tumber, 1994; Franklin, 1997; Gavin, 1998; Manning, 1998; Franklin and Parton, 1999; Allan *et al.*, 2000; Cassidy, 2002; Davis, 2002). Perhaps most significantly, journalism remains oriented to, and dependent on, those beats and sources which best deliver rather than those that most need investigation and coverage. Power may be moving towards large corporations, the world's financial centres, the EU, IMF and other supranational bodies. But, as they are too expensive to cover, inaccessible to journalists, poor suppliers of information subsidies and not perceived as newsworthy, they will not be adequately reported or held to account.

## Political and business print journalism in the United Kingdom

The following findings pull together a loose collection of observations and data gathered over a ten-year period. They draw on over 50 interviews – mostly with national journalists reporting on business and finance or politics and parliament. Unlike the case material presented in other chapters, the interviews are linked to different studies and dispersed across a lengthy time span. The findings come out of a review of interview transcripts and an identification of those experiences and practices which were revealed across the disparate studies.

## Market pressures and the demands for greater 'productivity'

Looking at news journalism in the United Kingdom over the last quarter of a century, there are two contrasting trends. On the one hand, there are more news outlets, organisational outputs and journalists (see NTO/Skillset, 2002). The news industry appears to be growing. On the other, there is greater competition and fragmentation, and fewer consumers, and often fewer journalists, per individual outlet (Tunstall, 1996; Williams, 1996; Franklin, 1997, 2005; Barnett and Gaber, 2001; Davis, 2002; Curran and Seaton, 2003; McNair, 2006). New technologies and news formats, 24 hour news, market deregulation, price wars and global market pressures, have all contributed to these trends. Consequently, most national newspaper and terrestrial broadcasters have presided over a long-term decline in audience figures since the 1970s. A steady decrease in advertising revenues for most single, commercial news outlets has followed.

A snapshot of developments in the mid-1990s revealed a continuing annual decline in national newspaper sales. In an effort to remain profitable, papers raised prices above inflation, increased output and sections, and cut back on staff. The page numbers of many papers doubled over the previous 10-year period while journalist numbers per publication were cut or, in the best cases, increased slightly. Broadcasting companies fared little differently as the BBC and ITN introduced 24 hour news channels without employing the staff numbers to match. In the same 10-year period the BBC shed 7,000 jobs (Franklin, 1994) and announced a further 25 per cent cut in 1997. ITN removed its own flagship news programme *News at Ten*. For the majority of remaining staff, working conditions were clearly getting more difficult as union recognition declined, journalist rights were eroded and output per journalist rose. Tunstall estimated that (1971, 1996: 136), between the 1960s and 1990s individual output had at least doubled. By 1998, approximately 40 per cent of journalists worked on a freelance basis or were employed on part-time or short-term contracts (NUJ, 1998). In a 1996 survey, 62 per cent of journalists claimed to work 59 or more hours in the office each week (*Press Gazette*, 12.7.96). In Jon Snow's assessment (*Press Gazette*, 20.9.96: 5):

> We are under siege, there is no question . . . Ratings will be the determinant because the money comes from advertisers . . . Within a couple of years there could be no serious analytical news programmes on American TV and that is the way we are heading.

Ten years later a quick glance reveals the industry picture to be similarly bleak for many journalists. In December 2004, the new Director General of the BBC, Mark Thompson, announced cuts of 5,300 staff over three years and, by early 2005, 400 specific cuts were identified in the Corporation's news operations. At the end of 2005 ITN's 24 hour news channel was closed down. In 2006, the NUJ documented thousands of job cuts in local, regional and national news operations (NUJ, March 2006). Currently (NUJ, 2006) 31 per cent of journalists are part-time or work 'flexible hours' and 41 per cent are 'freelance' (there is some overlap between these groups). The average salary has gone up but a greater proportion (11.6 per cent) than in 1994 (9.6 per cent) earn less than £10,000 per year. According to Tim Lezard, the NUJ President (NUJ, March 2006):

> No longer are reporters given time to go and get stories, to cultivate contacts, and meet the people that make news . . . accountants have decided a reporter out of the office cannot be writing stories . . . so reporters are chained to their desks, ordered to rewrite press releases by large corporations, or to localise a story sent over the wires by the national press agencies.

Similar findings and concerns have been reported by journalists in the United States.[1]

Virtually every journalist interviewed over the years, regardless of paper or news section, offered personal accounts which supported these snapshot views. All spoke of daily pressures rising as a consequence of competition. Several described the following experiences: declining employment security and job cuts; the hiring of cheaper, junior staff replacements; decreasing editorial resources; an increase in output and paper supplements; efficiency drives; the growing power of accountants within firms; and a greater dependency on externally supplied 'information subsidies' (see Chapter 2 on this). The story was relayed by experienced journalists in finance, business and politics:

> There is the drive to ever greater efficiency. A whole cross current of things that one has to try and take into account. It's become wider and broader . . . There is a lot more information and a lot more companies pumping out their information. There is a lot of pressure to cover and manage it all.
>
> (Roland Gribben)

> They [demands] have increased. There is a lot more financial pressure to deliver . . . There is a greater pressure on financial budgets and, at the same time, the amount of supplements, and therefore page numbers, have kept going up. As these pressures have increased, people have to work longer hours to keep up. It's now a very busy and stressful occupation.
>
> (Raymond Snoddy)

> But they [newspapers] will also fight tooth and claw for circulation, and they shouldn't be kept going, there should be fewer of them. The irony is that the market really doesn't work for newspapers . . . Competition is very bad in the media, where it's very good for selling widgets . . . the lethal competition means that people have less time and you have to shout louder.
>
> (Polly Toynbee)

Several journalists acknowledged the benefits of new communication technologies. The information sources on the Internet and the multiple means of news transmission over distance had clearly brought occupational gains. However, many also complained that new technologies had contributed to their daily pressures. This was partly down to the speeding up of the news cycle and partly a consequence of organisations using ICT introduction to cut staff:

> Technology is the biggest change . . . Output has increased at the same time numbers have gone down. That's across writers and subs. The output of the subs has increased phenomenally with new technologies.
>
> (anonymous financial journalist)

> All of this marketisation of society and technical transformation of communications are both pointed in the same direction: enormously more speed and the need to get your message across rapidly because if you don't somebody else will.
>
> (Michael White)

It has become more competitive and it's quicker. We are now in a 24 hours a day seven days a week news cycle. More instant analysis. The criticism is that it has become broader but shallower . . . more speculative . . . Partly because of the speed we have to read things – far less time to follow up and assess the information.

(George Jones)

## Editorial pressures, risk reduction and the restriction of journalist practices

Organisational pressures on journalists to become more productive has had the effect of restricting their daily practices. Story selection is influenced by calculations based on what editors will accept and what is more likely to produce a 'newsworthy' story. Thus, market-oriented considerations are internalised through an attempt to accede to editor expectations. As many explained, editors are a key consideration when reporting:

Journalists are all human beings and have all sorts of things in mind when writing. First of all, what you write has to get past your editor so it has to be acceptable to him.

(Michael White)

Journalists want to see their by-lines in newspapers so they work out what will get in the papers. They don't get an order from above. They know instinctively after a few months being on the newspaper what works for them.

(Colin Brown)

Physical movement of reporters also becomes more constrained. Initially, there is a greater tendency to stay at a terminal and to be seen to be writing: 'Now it is all more tightly staffed. Their ability to get out of the office and handle lots of stories just on the doorstep is gone' (anonymous former financial journalist);

With less reporters the papers think twice about sending people out to get stories. It's much more bums on seats now and people don't get out much. So people are increasingly reliant on the wire services and Internet and other information coming to you . . . journalists sit in the office much more because that's what management want them to do. It's like a comfort blanket. They like to look around and see lots of bodies at their desks.

(Barrie Clement)

Activities, such as time-consuming investigations which cannot guarantee a news story, are less likely to be embarked upon: 'These days, if you get something that isn't going to contribute to today's news you don't do it' (anonymous financial journalist);

> Because of the pressures on journalists there is less and less investigative journalism . . . If you are doing an investigative piece you can spend a week or two finding out information and not come out with a real story.
>
> (Michael Walters)

> The Members' Lobby is where lobby correspondents traditionally could go . . . they could stay there and chat to MPs, and that used to be one of the principal areas of where they would meet one another and get stories . . . They still do it a bit but it's not the same . . . Because if you meet people like that, and you're just chatting, you don't get a story.
>
> (Julie Kirkbride)

Another means of improving the odds of news story acceptance is through close monitoring of other news organisations and journalists. If others are covering an issue then it is more likely to be taken up. Journalists following similar beats have regular opportunities to watch each other and exchange information. Arguably, as editorial pressures grow so journalists are more likely to become reflexive as a means of personal risk reduction. This begins at the level of the news organisation: 'There is also an enormous me-too-ism in the sections. If one paper introduces something they all try and do it' (Richard Northedge);

> I had calls from *Sky News*, *BBC News 24*, *Radio 5 Live*, *BBC Breakfast Show*. I agreed to do them the next day, and the first one I did was *Radio 5 Live* in the morning and they got a car around to my house, the radio car. Before I got into the radio car I'd had *BBC Radio Breakfast*, *BBC Radio Wales* and *BBC Radio Scotland* all onto me . . . through computers, they can see the running order of various programmes and they hack into them and steal guests basically . . . one talking head can be all around the country for 24 hours simply because all these programmes need to fill up. And that can really distort the way that news is delivered, and it can distort the truth massively.
>
> (Colin Brown)

Journalists on financial and political beats, while competing for exclusives, are also very aware of the movements and outputs of others. No journalist would say they simply followed others but all agreed that there are many opportunities to exchange opinions and monitor the outputs of others:

> When they leave after Question Time, they're all congregating outside the seating area for the press gallery, and they will take a view then. I mean the sort of doyens, the George Joneses, the Phil Websters and the Mike Whites. They would say 'what do you think? Oh well yes . . .' and they'd have little confabs. It's like a rabbit warren up there so they're all on top of one another really.
>
> (Julie Kirkbride)

> I mean there's absolutely no doubt that when a story is not exclusive we would often as a group discuss a speech. For example, 'What do you think of Brown's speech tonight? What do you think the best line is?' Sometimes there's consensus . . . And, by the way, so does every other branch of journalism. I know the home affairs correspondents discuss the stories. I know the defence correspondents all do it because a sensible way of doing a story is to knock ideas around amongst yourselves.
>
> (Philip Webster)

Many also explained that such practices and exchanges take place as a means of anticipating possible editorial demands to follow up on a popular story: 'There are many times, like this, when I didn't care and I just made calls so I could cover my arse, so I could say that I tried' (Michael Walters);

> I rang him on something different, I said 'it's a very tight night' – in other words not much space in the paper – 'are you making much of so and so?' And he said 'I'm doing three hundred words' and I said 'that's fine that's all I needed to know' . . . it's what they call defensive filing . . . if you're looking at something which you gave a hundred words to which is the lead in rival newspapers and the lead item on the *Today Programme* and then somebody says 'Why did we fuck up?'
>
> (Michael White)

> I think you have one very big adverse effect – less true of the senior correspondents and their deputies – is it makes everyone risk averse . . . the news desk go 'why haven't we got this story?' So people are acting in a risk averse way, so ensuring that they will cover something because someone else might have it . . . we cover ourselves if we cover the story and someone else has got it, you know, if the *Telegraph* has got it we ought to have it otherwise someone will be asking 'why?'
>
> (Peter Riddell)

Financial and organisational demands for increased productivity have subtly constrained the working practices of journalists. Thus reporters restrict their own movements, are less likely to spend time conducting investigations and, increasingly, look to others to gauge what is newsworthy. Consequently, journalists, in attempting to reduce the risks of unproductive reporting, move in smaller circles, are less speculative and are more inclined to 'follow the pack'. Indeed, most political journalists interviewed were very critical of the all-too-apparent herding tendencies within their profession.

## Proxy fourth estate journalism in political journalism

The 'occupational ideology' of journalism directs journalists towards holding politicians to account and adopting an adversarial stance in their engagements. At the same time journalists understand that news values encourage a personal focus on issues rather than abstract details. This means less space for ideological differences, public policy debate and reporting of legislative details. Taking the perspective of politicians, party leaders are as keen to cover up party splits and contentious policy debates as they are to gain positive publicity. These two parallel tendencies have resulted in a hybrid form of proxy fourth estate journalism. In this journalists can be seen to be holding politicians to account but, in practice, this is at a very personal and symbolic, rather than substantive, level.

For political parties the lesser of two evils appears to be to cover up public policy debates and disagreements as far as possible:

> Now we are in a cleft stick as regards the question of public debate. Those of the public who are interested in politics hold two incompatible views. One, they want independent, objective, unconstrained politicians who can debate freely. Two, they want non-divided, non-split, smoothly functioning parties. Parties look at this second perspective and therefore work hard to cut down on divisions and conflicts . . . So all parties say they value debate but they are also desperate to stop too much public debate.
>
> (Tim Collins)

> If presentation becomes more important than formation of policy there is an obvious argument not to have rows in public. If appearance rather than outcome becomes key then one either has to repress dissent or get it away from public view.
>
> (Andy McSmith)

This suits reporters and news organisations. As experienced journalists all admitted, public discussions of legislation and the details of policy are unlikely to gain publication space or increase readership:

> Circulation actually goes down if there is a lot of political coverage . . . At one point I had three memos leaked from Blair's office. I got the scoop of the year. But sales actually went down.
>
> (Trevor Kavanagh)

> I think one of the reasons that ministers have such contempt for the press, quite rightly really, is that what they're doing day after day is hard policy work on things that are interesting and important, that never ever get anywhere near the light of day. So there the press is . . . not remotely interested in the very important stuff that's out there, and people are longing to tell them about, because it's boring policy . . . We report nothing of what really happens, what the stuff of Government really is, and what they're really doing and thinking about all the time.
>
> (Polly Toynbee)

Instead, the focus of even broadsheet papers moves to personalities and personal party conflicts:

> The media have probably contributed by giving more attention to those kind of personality-driven stories than highlighting the policy stories, focusing on the good work, maybe the politicians do at Westminster and in their constituencies.
>
> (Philip Webster)

> The media are constantly looking for divisions and splits. Journalists find that fascinating . . . When Clark or Duncan-Smith attack the Labour government they get very little coverage for it. But when they attack each other a lot of it gets coverage.
>
> (Andrew Grice)

The media watchdog remit is also more easily fulfilled by revealing sleaze and scandal:

> If we could have found something on Prescott that he had been doing corruptly and, you know, we're still looking as you can tell from the newspaper, then we could have got rid of him.
>
> (Simon Heffer)

Journalists found out that stories with sleaze automatically get into newspapers, because news desks knee jerk over the word sleaze . . . If you've got a long-term investigation into, say, the Trident weapon programme, or you've got a Minister getting his leg over with his secretary, you'll make a lot of money out of the second and you'll hardly get anybody to publish the first.

(Colin Brown)

From the point of view of several politicians journalists now automatically take an adversarial stance regardless of the political affiliations of the papers. This has come to represent objective, fourth estate journalism without the need for complex political evaluations of policy:

I think that something entirely new has developed recently, which is a kind of gotcha both ways culture where anything the Government does is wrong . . . the BBC has increasingly interpreted that duty to be impartial as a duty to criticise both sides equally. Now I'm not denying that they should . . . but there's a big difference between being impartial, by making sure your criticism is equal, and being impartial, by criticising everybody all the time almost regardless of what they do.

(Martin Linton)

It was a clinical decision by the press in general. They tottered into the view that it was essential to attack politics, and the conduct and process of politics as well as politicians, in order to show their gift of insight and cleverness. Now, I have to say that I prefer that, with all its slings and arrows, to any form of deferential press . . . But the problem is that, unless they are prepared to represent political engagement – activity and representation more as an honourable and worthwhile activity – they are feeding all the devils of disillusionment and disengagement.

(Neil Kinnock)

Ultimately, such proxy forms of fourth estate journalism give a misleading impression that political activity is being scrutinised and politicians being held to account. However, such practices mean that public scrutiny of actual policies and decisions, which may have significant consequences for large parts of the public, is minimally done.

## Journalist practices and mobilisations of bias in public discourse

Members of Parliament (see Chapter 6) and political journalists were usually asked which kinds of issue drew too much media coverage and scrutiny/pressure and which too little. Something commonly mentioned was the greater focus on the perceived concerns of middle class readers in central and South Eastern England: 'It's always directed at a middle England middle class world' (Kevin Maguire);

> By omission there are a whole host of developments in Scotland, Wales, Northern Ireland, I would suggest probably in the North of England as well, which are completely overlooked by the metropolitan press.
>
> (Angus Robertson)

> I keep meaning to write about skills, which is desperately important. Skills never gets into the papers, never, and everybody knows it's really important. Every education correspondent knows that writing about skills policy and what the hell they're going do in adult education and FE is far more important than rubbish about whether A-levels are slightly dumbed down or not. But because it's mostly middle class people who read newspapers, or their newspapers, they're never going to go near the skills agenda.
>
> (Polly Toynbee)

For both politicians and journalists the policies most likely to be covered were those with a 'strong headline impact', that were 'emotive', 'sensitive' and had a 'human interest' angle: 'the more emotive the issue the more [it is covered] . . . drinking hours, fox hunting . . . casinos, yes, the gambling one was a huge' (Philip Webster). In fact, during interviewing in 2006, by far the most commonly cited example of a piece of legislation gaining news coverage was the debate over the introduction of new super casinos:

> When the Gambling Bill was going through there was a joint committee of both houses . . . virtually nothing happened until really late in the day . . . and then the press got interested and then there was a tremendous row about would we have ten casinos or five or whatever.
>
> (Peter Riddell)

> Casinos is interesting because we had gambling in the Culture Committee and we did an enquiry . . . And there wasn't an ounce of controversy about it, about the whole issue, about the introduction of new casinos, about a loosening of the gambling laws. And then, suddenly, a year and half later after . . . it was picked up by the press, particularly the *Daily Mail*, and became a major issue.
>
> (Frank Doran)

After casinos, the most frequently mentioned topics were those involving crime, law and order, and immigration: 'The *Sun* would undoubtedly have an impact on the way issues like criminal justice legislation and immigration matters are treated' (Philip Webster); 'Oh yes, of course yes, they're influenced to go after populist issues . . . Crime is an easy one' (Michael White);

> Street crime, street robbery would be a good example where . . . the media picked it up. Once they'd picked it up it took off like a snowball rolling down a hill . . . it was a self-fulfilling hot air balloon.
>
> (David Blunkett)

> Asylum was huge during our time . . . I don't think the media actually dictated policy but it did create an atmosphere in which it was felt something had to be addressed. Something had to be done about it.
>
> (Ann Widdecombe)

Similarly, journalists and politicians could give several examples where certain issues were under-reported. Either parties were afraid to raise the issue, because of the fear of negative coverage, or journalists would not report it, because of a perceived lack of editorial or popular interest. Topics regarded as 'technical', 'complex' or 'boring' were frequently mentioned. Constitutional affairs, pensions, and energy policy were all mentioned as issues that were rarely covered unless a crisis or dramatic shift in government policy occurred:

> Process things, administration, anything which is regarded as technical, 'boring' will get ignored . . . on the whole if you mention constitutional issues to a news desk, or parliamentary procedure, or reform of parliament, there's a problem.
>
> (Peter Riddell)

> Some select committees will be dealing with rather technical issues, complicated issues, ones which don't so much obviously impact on people's daily lives and the media, therefore, are less interested. It's not to say they're less important than they are, but if you look at the reports of committees like Work and Pensions or Constitutional Affairs, they don't get a lot of media attention.
>
> (John Whittingdale)

> The getting attention for the underlying cause of the problem to face is the difficulty you always have – and this means that important issues can go unnoticed for a very long time . . . The debate about energy policy, when it becomes a debate on energy policy, where gas prices go through the roof and my [Trade and Industry] Select Committee, six months ago, produced a report which basically predicted what's happened, you know, and that got some but not much attention. And

now people are screaming that something must be done. We pointed out the limits to what could be done six months ago.

(Peter Luff)

The lack of reporting on foreign affairs, especially in Europe, was also frequently mentioned (see also Chapter 5 on this):

And if the media aren't interested it's dead effectively. They're not much interested in issues of international development, environmental issues, debt, world poverty. But if it doesn't get in the newspapers it doesn't strike chords outside.

(Austin Mitchell)

But even when you look at foreign pages in all the broadsheets now they are gee whiz stories . . . much more than they are serious policy stories, and particularly not Europe, unless it's a Euro row.

(Polly Toynbee)

Interestingly, several politicians and journalists, from across the political spectrum, spoke of the lack of public debate about the long-term funding and organisation of the Welfare State. All sides felt that the topic, especially in relation to the National Health Service, was too politically sensitive and too complex to discuss:

We've never had the proper debate because they're scared of it . . . They fight for the NHS but they're up against the *Daily Mail*'s third world NHS campaign which is quite destructive of public attitudes.

(Michael White)

This government will not tackle the large bogeys of British politics . . . long-term important things like the Welfare State or spending on the health service.

(Trevor Kavanagh)

I think that there is a very strong intellectual case for introducing incentives too, with healthcare, for people to pay for themselves when they can . . . [but] it is absolutely impossible for the Conservatives to launch a discussion about that because you're instantly going towards 'oh well the Tories want to privatise the Health Service'.

(John Maples)

I think there's a debate that we're sort of not having about the role of the welfare state, social welfare and the NHS. The New Labour agenda is essentially based on news management, and so hospital bad news stories equals bad news, therefore do something about it . . . What they're not looking at is an underlying agenda which is essentially an undermining of the principle of the welfare state . . . and that is a huge change which has gone fairly unnoticed.

(Jeremy Corbyn)

## Conclusion

News producers have continued to promote a professional image of journalism in which reporting manages, to a reasonable degree at least, to reflect the world as it is. Its imperfections and failures, which are frequently acknowledged, are not systematic and, in the larger picture, cancel each other out. As argued here, the errors do follow certain patterns and do contribute to 'mobilisations of bias' in public discourse. Many critical accounts tie such trends to the conscious attempts of powerful elites and institutions to influence news outputs. In the discussion presented here, however, bias is linked to the very tools, cultures and practices that journalists themselves adopt as a means of producing objective and reflective accounts of society.

The real issue here, perhaps, is that the news profession has always attempted to hide the fact that many of its methods and practices involve using short-cuts or proxy means of attaining 'ideal' outputs. They have been developed because journalists do not have the resources – time, money, expertise – necessary to produce news to the standards they aspire to. Organisational hierarchies, professional values, reporting methods, beats, presentational styles, are all practical solutions for bridging the gap between reporting limitations and expectations. They all offer routine, internalised practices that make reporting possible. Journalists rarely have time to question them. When financial pressures are applied these short-cuts and proxy methods become constraining ends rather than means. Beats and reporter activities come to be directed towards what is most likely to produce news. The powerful are held to account for their personal weaknesses rather than their professional aptitudes, policies or decisions. Conflicting opinions take the place of balance. News values are very much market oriented and influenced by what other journalists are following rather then being driven by what is perceived to be in the public interest.

As a consequence the biases in journalism are influenced by economic pressures without necessarily being shaped by elites. Long-term issues of power and inequality are not adequately addressed in public discourse because of consistent omission rather than conscious influence or conspiracy. The same is true in a number of reporting areas that include business and financial affairs, environmental reporting, international political and economic negotiations, energy and water supply issues, and global health and farming patterns.

# Chapter 4

# Media management and public relations
## Public media, inter-elite conflict and power

## Introduction

This chapter discusses the attempts of elite groups to manage the media as a means of achieving and sustaining positions of power in society. In particular, it looks at the rise of the professional public relations sector and the employment of communication professionals to manage news media and information in the public sphere.

Many established, critical accounts have focused on documenting the range of strategies developed by corporate, political and military elites, to manipulate the media and public opinion. However, this 'propaganda model', or 'dominance paradigm', contains some blind spots and cannot be consistently applied to all forms of news and in all time periods. Of equal significance, the model fails to engage with the issue of inter-elite conflict and with how elites gain or lose power over time.

This chapter attempts to fill these gaps by offering an alternative, but complementary, perspective on power, conflict and media management. This observes that inter-elite conflicts and negotiations are as important for sustaining elite power bases as elite attempts at influencing mass media and opinion. Both forms of engagement draw in news media and journalists and, accordingly, are a part of media management strategies. However, inter-elite contestation does not, as political pluralists suggest, merely result in polyarchy and dispersed power. It also leads to public exclusion as the parameters for debate and negotiation become narrower. Under these circumstances, journalists and elites come to form part of the same 'elite discourse networks' or 'iron triangles'. As the chapter therefore concludes, both elite-mass media management and mediated, inter-elite competition are contributors to power imbalances and inequalities in society.

## Media management: critical accounts

There is now a long-established political economy literature that seeks to explain the means by which political, corporate and military organisations manage media and public information. This diverse work (Schiller, 1989, 1992; Garnham, 1990; Eldridge, 1995; Philo, 1995; Mosco, 1996; Herman and McChesney, 1997; Golding and Murdock, 2000; Curran, 2002; Herman and Chomsky, 2002; Bagdikian, 2004), explains the multiple 'filters' or 'top-down' influences which shape media and public opinion in ways that benefit those in power.

The most obvious means by which state and corporate elites have attempted to manage media is through the ownership and management (direct and indirect) of news organisations themselves. Ownership power is wielded in the allocation of resources, the appointment of senior editorial and management staff, and the directing of editorial agendas. This 'allocative' form of control filters directly through to editors and journalists down the chain and thus results in daily 'operational control' (Murdock, 1982). Most recent media legislation in the United States, United Kingdom and continental Europe has encouraged privatisation, deregulation and corporate conglomeration in the sector (McChesney, 1997; Goodwin, 1998; Doyle, 2002; Bagdikian, 2004). Only a handful of conglomerates now control the majority of all media and communication infrastructure and content in the United States and United Kingdom/European Union. Non-media corporate elites may also exert influence through their shareholdings, board directorships, and through advertising – a principal source of media funding. Thus, relatively small, corporate networks can potentially influence large quantities of news and public information content.

Democratic governments directly own and manage a declining proportion of news media outlets. However, they continue to use other forms of influence. These include enacting new media laws, operating regulatory regimes, controlling licensing, and instigating and applying legislation that affects reporting freedoms. Such legislation, on matters of libel, privacy, copyright, data protection, insider trading and, of course, censorship, may all be used to restrict journalists. As many accounts have documented (Schlesinger et al., 1983; Glasgow University Media Group, 1985; Hollingsworth, 1986; Tunstall and Palmer, 1991; Neil, 1996; Herman and Chomsky, 2002), both states and corporate owners have frequently abused their control and sought to influence journalist employees and political administrations. The ultimate tool of government or military media management is, of course, the physical threat that hangs over the life of a journalist in conflict zones and under some political regimes. In late 2006, according to the Committee to Protect Journalists (CPJ), 85 journalists have died in Iraq since the war began in March 2003 and some 226 have been killed world-wide since 2000.

Power is also exercised, on a more routine basis, in elite source–journalist relationships. It has been readily advanced by the adoption of promotional techniques and personnel. Historically, the promotional professions usually expand during periods of political or corporate crisis. So they come to be increasingly utilised by the corporate sector (Dreier, 1988; Nelson, 1989; Stauber and Rampton, 1995; Ewen, 1996; Marchand, 1998; Tye, 1998; Cutlip *et al.*, 2004; Monbiot, 2006), during industrial shifts, corporate expansions and large-scale union activity. Governments, political parties and military institutions turn to them during periods of economic instability, elections and wars (Miller, 1994, 2004; Hall Jamieson, 1996, 2006; Kurtz, 1998; Herman and Chomsky, 2002; Knightley, 2003; Stauber and Rampton, 2003; Philo and Berry, 2004). Thus the needs of governments and corporations – to control information flows within the public sphere in the name of the consumer citizen – necessitate the creation and expansion of a professional communication and media management sector.

The budgets and numbers of communication staff, working in corporate, military and government settings, far outnumber those working for NGOs, trade unions and other opposition groups (see examples in Miller, 1994; Davis, 2002; Herman and Chomsky, 2002). Elite sources, and their communication employees, also benefit from a number of cultural and organisational advantages which enable them to have routine access to journalists. As 'primary definers' (Hall *et al.*, 1978, but see also Eldridge, 1995; Philo, 1995; Parenti, 1993), they then get to set news agendas and reporting frameworks. Being in demand such sources are also able to control journalist access, both to themselves and also to newsworthy information and restricted areas. Thus, media access to prominent politicians and legislative spaces (Jones, 1995; Barnett and Gaber, 2001), to heads of business and economic spheres (Parsons, 1989; Davis, 2002, 2003b), and to military leaders and zones (Thussu and Freedman, 2003; Tumber and Palmer, 2004), can all be granted or withdrawn accordingly.

Apart from exercising power over journalist access, powerful sources and their communication staff have the resources to 'spin' journalists, subject them to public attacks ('flak'), and engineer mass propaganda campaigns. Of increasing concern is the rise of 'astro-turf' and other 'third-party' campaigns. In these cases propaganda is organised through seemingly independent, public and scientific bodies but, actually, is directed and funded by the same powerful corporate and political groups (see Stauber and Rampton, 1995, 2002; Ewen, 1996; Monbiot, 2006, see also CMD and Spinwatch).

For advocates of the 'propaganda model' there is ample evidence of overt control being exerted over news content on behalf of powerful groups and institutions in society. Such means of media management have been a fundamental tool during the steady shift towards neo-liberal (or 'neo-con') political, economic and military agendas since the Reagan–Thatcher years. Taxation systems, union legislation, welfare state management and employment law, have all been altered in ways that benefit large corporations and the wealthy. International conflicts and the post-2001 'war on terror' have been accompanied by an expansion of military and government communication operations to levels not seen since World War Two.

## Critical media management accounts: gaps and limitations

However, such top-down attempts at information and news management have rarely been entirely successful for more than short periods. The 'countervailing', bottom-up forces that elite media managers have to contend with have always made the process of information control fairly erratic and complex. For some critics, contemporary social, political and technological developments mean that this 'dominance paradigm' (McNair, 2006) is increasingly implausible. Of equal significance to the discussion here, the model does not account for inter-elite conflicts or explain how certain elite groups come to replace others over time.

Beginning with the first of these lines of argument top-down communicative power is rarely as uniform or efficient as the propaganda model suggests. Most news coverage in established democracies is not simply about wars, terror and other instances of national crisis. Outside of these periods, such forms of media management are rather less assured. For many, such centralised forms of state and corporate power are becoming harder, rather than easier, to sustain. In all post-industrial countries economic and political power is seeping away from national governments. Party membership, electoral support and faith in politicians and the electoral system has gone down as support for protest movements and single issue pressure groups has gone up (Castells, 1997; Blumler and Kavanagh, 1999; Norris *et al.*, 1999; Blumler and Gurevitch, 2000; Heath *et al.*, 2001; Bromley *et al.*, 2004; Todd and Taylor, 2004). The shift in power and resources is towards rather less visible quangos, transnational corporations and financial systems, pressure groups and international bodies (Castells, 1997; Strange, 1998; Held *et al.*, 1999; Hirst and Thompson, 1999; Nash, 2000; Amoore, 2005; Froud *et al.*, 2006).

The same is true in the corporate sector. Latter-day media moguls, such as Berlusconi and Murdoch, are a shrinking anomaly in an age of transnational, manager-led conglomerates. Globalisation and new information and communication technologies (NICTs) are making centralised communicative power difficult as cultural fragmentation takes place (Tomlinson, 1999). New media players, such as Google, Yahoo and AOL, are taking over from established market leaders as the traditional barriers to entry break down.

Smaller, oppositional groups have become better at accessing news media and challenging primary definers (Anderson, 1997; Davis, 2002; Deacon, 2003). Alternative voices, at the community and NGO levels, are increasingly able to take advantage of the multiplicity of new channels, internet platforms and cheap video technologies (Downing, 2001; Couldry and Curran, 2003; Atton, 2004) to challenge elite messages. Journalists are not always relegated to the role of 'secondary definers' (Schlesinger, 1990). Journalism itself has not simply become 'dumbed down' and politically sterile. It is now also more subversive, critical and sceptical of authority, and responsive to wider audiences (Connell, 1992; Lull and Hinerman, 1997; Bird, 2000; Langer 2003; McNair, 2003). Strong media effects and dominant ideologies are not simply disseminated through media and absorbed by the public (Morley, 1980; Abercrombie *et al.*, 1984; Liebes and Katz, 1990; Gauntlett, 1998; Norris *et al.*, 1999).

Thus, for opponents of the critical media management perspective, the approach appears increasingly redundant (Scammell, 1995, 2004; Norris, 2000, 2002; McNair, 2003, 2006). For McNair such developments mean that the global communication environment has become much too anarchic and chaotic to be managed by dominant groups and institutions. 'Cultural chaos' is the result. Thus, for McNair, Norris and Scammell, continued 'pessimism' is unwarranted as pluralist, democratic communication continues to flourish.

What critical accounts of communication also fail to engage with is the rise and fall of elite groups themselves. Much of the content of Marx and Engels's original works is concerned with the rise and fall of different dominant classes as the predominant mode of production changes. Post-Marxist writers, from Lenin (1970 [1902]) and Gramsci (Forgacs, 1988) to Miliband (1969) and Poulantzas (1975) have been similarly concerned with conflicts and/or negotiations and balances of power between elite groups. Modern, liberal pluralist theory, from Truman (1951) and Dahl (1961) onwards, also argues that the exercise of political power is 'fragmented', shared and competed over by powerful groups in society. Corporations and business associations are frequently in conflict with each other and often fail to work together when making demands of government (Richardson, 1993; Grant, 1995, 2000; Boswell and Peters, 1997). 'Deformed polyarchies' are the result (Dahl and Lindblom, 1953; Dahl, 1989). Such elite conflicts and divisions come to be reflected in the media and wider public sphere (Deacon and Golding, 1994; Hallin, 1994; Schlesinger and Tumber, 1994; Miller *et al.*, 1998).

Both lines of reasoning, taken together, suggest that the traditional 'dominance paradigm' is, on its own, no longer adequate for explaining the utility of communication in the sustenance of unequal power relations in society. Neither line, however, means that power itself is now dispersed and chaotic, or that issues of power, inequality and environmental crisis are no longer pressing. Nor do they conclusively demonstrate that media and communication are not integral to the attainment and maintenance of power. Instead, it is argued that the critical media management literature is in need of some kind of adaptation and/or supplementation.

## Public media, inter-elite communication and power

An alternative, but supplementary, critical interpretation is offered here. The first component in its construction is to be found in the study of media–source relations. Work here consistently reveals that elite sources dominate news production. In studies of the reporting of politics (Gans, 1980; Tiffen, 1989; Bennett, 1990; Hess, 2000; Herman and Chomsky, 2002), crime (Hall *et al.*, 1978; Ericson *et al.*, 1989; Schlesinger and Tumber, 1994), environmental issues (Anderson, 1997; Allan *et al.*, 2000), tax, welfare and financial matters (Deacon and Golding, 1994; Davis, 2002), and war (Glasgow University Media Group, 1985, 1993; Bennett and Paletz, 1994; Hallin, 1994; Brookes *et al.*, 2004) institutional/governmental (political and military) and, to a lesser extent, corporate elite sources are the most cited and the greatest suppliers of news 'information subsidies'. This fits in with the propaganda model.

However, what is not included in the model is the fact that there is quite a bit of dispersed research which indicates that elites are themselves susceptible to a range of media and ideological influences (Abercrombie *et al.*, 1984, 1990; MacKuen, 1984; Miller and Krosnick, 1997; Herbst, 1998; Meyer, 2002, see also Chapter 6). Certainly there are several documented cases of elites being influenced in their decision-making by media campaigns (Nelson, 1989; Manheim, 1994; Stauber and Rampton, 1995; Davis, 2002). This leads naturally on to a third point, one that is documented with the following case examples of professional communication staff working for corporate and political elites. This reveals that much elite promotional activity is aimed, not at the mass of consumer-citizens but, rather, at other, rival elites. Corporate and political elites, while needing to communicate with larger publics, also spend a significant amount of time targeting rival elites at all levels: within organisations, with rival organisations and with organisations in relevant, influential sectors.

Together, these points suggest a scenario in which elites are simultaneously the main sources, main targets and some of the most influenced recipients of news. If this is so, it could be concluded that a major function of the news media is not merely to reflect political differences but to act as a communication channel for the regular conflicts, negotiations and decision-making that take place between different elite groups. This is also to the exclusion of the mass of consumer-citizens. Decisions, which involve such things as the development of institutional policies, corporate strategies, legislation, budgets, investment decisions, regulatory regimes and power structures, take place in communication networks in which the mass of consumer-citizens can be no more than ill-informed spectators.

The following research findings come out of several sets of semi-structured interviews, mainly with some 85 corporate and political public relations professionals and journalists. These interviews, in addition to revealing the regular targeting of other elites, also indicate a number of other trends which offer further evidence of this alternative paradigm. These are: a) the blocking of larger audiences and media coverage, b) the development of small elite communication networks, which include top journalists, and c) the 'capture' of reporters by the 'policy communities' they report on.

## The corporate sector

The rapid expansion of corporate public relations in recent decades has been well documented (Ewen, 1996; Miller and Dinan, 2000; Davis, 2002; Cutlip *et al.*, 2004). In the United Kingdom, by the mid-1980s (PRCA, 1986) it became the norm rather than the exception for top companies to use PR with 69 per cent of the United Kingdom's top 500 companies using PR consultancies. According to Miller and Dinan (2000) the sector rose as a whole by a factor of 31 (or elevenfold in real terms) between 1979 and 1998. The 2005 estimated total turnover of the industry, consultancy and in-house, was £6.6 billion (Key Note, 2006). Approximately 47,800 people were employed in the profession and 2,500 consultancies existed. These figures exclude the 125,000 people working in the associated advertising and marketing industries, those working in PR support industries (e.g., press cutting, media evaluation, news distribution services) and the many professionals who have had media training.

Several studies of corporate public relations have noted that a significant proportion of communication resources are spent in avoiding mainstream coverage (see also Dreier, 1988; Berkman and Kitch, 1989; Ericson *et al.*, 1989, and Tumber, 1993; Davis, 2000b, 2003b; Cutlip *et al.*, 2004). This is because most mainstream news about corporations is likely to involve negative stories such as scandal, environmental problems, financial losses and fraud. Certainly there are frequent objections from business leaders about the tone of coverage they do receive (CBI, 1981; Hoge, 1988; Smith, 1988; Rees-Mogg, 1992).

When conducting interviews it became apparent that a substantial proportion of corporate communication time is indeed taken up with blocking journalists and stifling negative coverage. For virtually all the corporate news sources interviewed, evading wider public scrutiny was an established part of the job. Nick Chaloner, of Abbey National, explained 'There are negative stories that we try to keep out of the press on a daily basis . . . There are so many rumours and so much bar room talk and . . . thousands of journalists trying to write a story.' Richard Oldworth similarly stated that a lot of client work involves attempts to 'kill' stories:

> In terms of the media, a lot of our job is to minimise bad news coverage. We get quite a lot of that. We often get calls on a Friday night from a

Sunday journalist asking about a negative report and we try and get the article scrapped. But that depends on your relationship with the press.

This story was echoed by financial journalists. Indeed, their main complaint about the growing corporate public relations industry was its ability to close down access:

From a company stand point, public relations acts as a block and that works to frustrate journalists who are trying to get to the people who matter.

(Roland Gribben)

Sometimes they act as a block to keep you away from companies in trouble. I try to go to principals as much as possible. But they have some control in terms of who you get to speak to. It's a certain power over access.

(Raymond Snoddy)

At the same time, it was also apparent that, in certain sectors of corporate public relations, more resources were targeted at elite decision-makers than the public. In fact, a breakdown of the major occupations of public relations practitioners working for PRCA consultancies (see Davis, 2000b), in rank order, during the period 1989 – 96 were: Financial, Consumer, Corporate, Trade and Industry, Government Relations, Employee Relations, High Tech and Other. Financial, Corporate and Trade and Industry, three of the four major categories listed, are in fact aimed at the corporate sector itself. Other surveys (see, for example, Newman, 1984; White and Mazur, 1995) have also suggested that corporate sources consider shareholders, analysts and government officials to be rather more important audiences than the mainstream media and general public. The disinterest in the public became very clear when conducting interviews with financial public relations practitioners:

The private investor, most of the time, is regarded as an irrelevance. Ninety per cent of shares are now held by institutions, so they [the public] are generally ignored.

(Tim Jackaman)

Unfortunately, most papers apart from the *FT* think they speak for the private investor but the way the City operates it doesn't give a toss about the private investor.

(Nick Miles)

All interviewees concurred with this. While they were all concerned with the company's 'brand image', as relayed to mass, public audiences (employee and consumer), they also tended to be strongly focused on private, elite targets. This form of elite communication was in fact regarded as a priority for senior communication staff and corporate sources. As Jan Shawe of the Prudential explained:

> The two key functions are the government affairs/policy development section and the investor relations/press office section. These two sections are made up of parts working closely together. Community affairs spend is higher and there are more people on it but, in terms of importance, it comes behind the other two.

These private decision-makers were targeted directly, through lobbying and by way of media-oriented public relations. Starting with government and institutions, PR practitioners focused on ministers, government civil servants and industry regulators. For example, Chris Hopson of the Granada Media Group, described his role as follows:

> The primary focus of the job for me is identifying how the company works, how the profitability of the company can be improved and how PR may be used to gain that profitability. That is my principal task. For example, if the regulations were being re-negotiated, how best would that re-negotiation work for us? A while ago we wanted to change the ownership rules to enable us to takeover LWT and Yorkshire Tyne Tees. Were it not for our and other PR departments' activities, changes would not have happened and we would not have been able to take those companies over. Those changes and takeovers have helped to increase our profits ten times since 1991 ... We have saved the company around £40 million in recent regulatory questions and probably saved the ITV companies £100 million in total.

For publicly quoted companies, resources were periodically devoted to government policy-making and institutional regulation. However, their most consistent area of concern was the financial community. It was deemed vital for publicly quoted companies to keep communicating with and influencing their main shareholders. A strong share price raised the company's value, kept major shareholders supportive, encouraged investment, and diminished the chances of the company suffering a hostile takeover. As Nick Miles professed:

> The primary target is the fund manager. He or she might have to look at 300 companies in the sector and unless he is truly remarkable he won't remember everything. So a lot of what we do is try and hit a button with those people, conform to their view of the world so that they buy the shares.

An integral part of the persuasion of shareholders involved attempts to influence specific opinion formers and the financial community more generally. This translated into communication with business journalists, investment analysts and business leaders:

> Where PR influences opinions, financial PR influences decisions . . . In financial services there is so much room for analyses and so many factors. Therefore one needs to influence people who analyse and make decisions.
>
> (Jonny Elwes)

> One of the two key ingredients of financial PR is preparing the City for [earnings] surprises. If a company takes a decision it must make sure the City is not surprised and you can do that by dropping hints and analysts' forecasts in the Sundays.
>
> (Roland Rudd)

Every corporate communicator and financial consultant interviewed was aware of who were the top analysts and journalists in their field, how to target them, and who might be influenced by them. Within the City, the message repeated by all interviewees was that the potential audience was an extremely small one – usually numbering no more than a hundred people:

> In John Menzies, for example, there are a dozen big shareholders, the business press with maybe 20 key editors and journalists, and 10 analysts, 50 maximum.
>
> (Bob Gregory)

> You have three significant audiences – the press, the sell-side brokers and the buy-side institutions. Any company has three sets of groups interested . . . Out of these there are roughly two dozen journalists who are really influential. On the relevant sell-side you have the top-rated analysts and the most mentioned analysts – out of which about 20 are really key. On top of that you have about 20 top fund managers with about 20 to 50 people. So you could say that the perceptions of a company are dependant on 50–100 individuals.
>
> (Angus Maitland)

What ultimately has evolved in the corporate sector generally, and the City more specifically, is the development of closed, 'elite discourse networks'. These involve heads of industry, their communication staff, large institutional shareholders, analysts and financial journalists. Consequently, business and financial journalists, those who are admitted into these networks, are overly focused on the interests and concerns of those they report on.

Indeed, six out of the eight business journalists interviewed, in one way or another, tended to confirm this picture. On the one hand, many seemed far more aware of their City audience than the wider shareholding public. On the other, their sources were almost exclusively analysts, financial PRs and corporate heads, all operating within the City. According to two financial news editors:

> We have the highest percentage of businessmen and managers – the highest proportion after the *FT*. So it's businessmen, managers of big and small businesses and professional investors [we write for] . . . My diary is still full of lunches with chairmen and chief executives – that hasn't changed . . . But in the end it's a village. They need you as much as you need them. Usually they need you more, so there's always a negotiation to be done.
>
> (anonymous)

> Traditionally we wrote for *Guardian* readers rather than City ones. Now the view is that we are a much more mainstream paper, which means we spend more time on traditional City and business coverage . . . we are working all the time with chief executives and chairmen. I see CEOs four times a week. I also see Treasury officials, Bank of England officials and others on a regular basis.
>
> (Alex Brummer)

What has thus developed in this area of reporting is a situation in which the principal significance of business news coverage lies in its utility as a means of communication and influence for a small select elite. As one director of a financial PR consultancy, explained:

> The national financial press are written for the City by the City. So we know that when we are getting coverage we are getting through. What you use the press for is to provoke a thought or confirm a thought. So if an investor is interested and if it's in the press then it gets discussed.
>
> (anonymous)

Fund managers interviewed were also aware of the roles of journalists and financial news texts in this regard. Accordingly, they tried to pick up clues, read news accounts with suspicion and, also, tried to feed stories or play off them (see Davis, 2005 and Chapter 9):

> [During] the demise of the M and S Chairman there was an enormous amount of stuff in the press. But . . . Where was that stuff coming from because financial journalists, in my experience, don't think of these things themselves. It must come from somewhere. It may have been

planted by rivals, investment banks, analysts, I don't know. Institutional shareholders who are not happy. It's a bit like politics. I'm sure an awful lot of stories are planted but it's difficult to know by whom and for what.

(John Davies)

From the other side, journalists were similarly aware of the tightening restrictions of their job and that their access was in some ways tied to their perceived utility:

The CEOs who are happy not to go through the filter of the PRs are becoming less and less. There are very few now and there is a sense of losing something there . . . there is less direct contact, less a feel for what's really going on.

(Alex Brummer)

It's a very uncomfortable thing for the financial journalist. The financial journalists are very slowly being marginalised. I don't know if they all know it . . . you have to be very stubborn-minded to pursue an investigative story on your own. The companies don't like it, the PRs don't like it, the brokers are against it, and the City doesn't want a knocking story . . . The real scoop, as opposed to financial PR plants, is increasingly rare.

(Michael Walters)

In a sense, journalists operating in business and financial elite circles, have, to a degree, become 'captured' by those they report on. Few experienced reporters would say that 'spin doctors' had much direct influence over them in terms of being able to affect outputs. However, their main sources and main audiences are the same financial elites working within the City. Journalists are highly reliant on these contacts and information flows within the financial district. Consequently, they become a fundamental part of the closed communication networks in which elite decision-makers attempt to influence each other and others are excluded (see also Parsons, 1989; Hutton, 1996). This is evident when looking at financial news coverage 'written by the City for the City'. In a study of the most reported corporate take-over of the 1990s (Davis, 2000b), of the 425 articles analysed, only 2.8 per cent quoted a source that came from outside the City. Only 7.1 per cent of articles referred to employees, 4.2 per cent mentioned customers and 3.5 per cent mentioned the large-scale job losses that would result from the take-over.

## Political parties and government

Similar trends are also in evidence when one looks at the communication practices and media relations of politicians and government officials at Westminster. The rapid growth in PR personnel and communication expenditure, documented in the Thatcher years (Jones, 1995; Kavanagh, 1995; Scammell, 1995), has continued apace during New Labour's period of office (Rawnsley, 2001; Jones, 2002; Franklin, 2004; Price, 2005; Wring, 2005). Table 4.1, showing changes in the number of information officers employed in government departments, illustrates this rise.

Trends observed in these and other accounts include the growing central-isation of party/government communication, the blocking of potentially negative coverage and increasing restrictions being put on journalist access. Most PR advisors who had worked for political parties and/or government stated that they spent the majority of their time blocking and reacting to negative coverage: 'I had ten years in Whitehall, and 70 per cent of press relations there was keeping stuff out of the papers' (Tim Blythe); 'We spend two-thirds to three-quarters of the time reacting to events, unfortunately' (Tim Collins, Conservative);

*Table 4.1* Changes in numbers of information officers employed in government departments 1979–2006

|  | MoD | FCO | Home Office | DTI | Cabinet Office | PM's Office | Treasury |
|---|---|---|---|---|---|---|---|
| 1979 | 58 | 19 | 27 | 38 | – | 6 | 12 |
| 1983 | 34 | 17 | 25 | 77 | – | 6 | 12 |
| 1987 | 34 | 13 | 33 | 67 | 11 | 6 | 13 |
| 1991 | 36 | 20 | 37 | 62 | 10 | 6 | 9 |
| 1995 | 36 | 22 | 43 | 69 | 13 | 10 | 13 |
| 1997 | 47 | 30 | 50 | 67 | 14 | 12 | 16 |
| 2001 | 87 | 51 | 80 | 77 | 28 | 17 | 30 |
| 2006 | 230 | 41 | 145 | 84 | 35 | 24 | 31 |
| 1979–2006 (%) ± | +297 | +116 | +437 | +121 | +218* | +300 | +158 |

Source: figures compiled from COI directories 1979–2006.

Note
All figures accumulated from 'The IPO Directory – Information and Press Officers in Gov-ernment Departments and Public Corporations' (formerly called 'Chief Public Relations, Information and Press Officers in Government Departments, Public Corporations, etc.').
* Increase from 1985 to 2006.

Political party communications is generally more concerned with blocking hostile media coverage and crisis management than it is with proactive campaigning. The proportions are roughly 60:40. Although, when I was with Neil Kinnock . . . at times it felt like the balance was more 90 per cent defence and 10 per cent attack.

(John Underwood, Labour)

This account of public relations barriers and restricted access to government ministers was repeated with some frequency by journalists:

Ministers have to clear announcements with Number 10. Number 10 has a strong grip on the information coming out of departments. From their point of view it's very sensible but, from another point of view, they go to great lengths to limit debate and discussion and to stop journalists from finding out what's going on . . . They are doing their job but they are not serving the democratic process by refusing point blank to open up to public scrutiny.

(Andrew Grice)

Alistair Campbell, because he'd been a lobby journalist, told Ministers not to go through the Members' Lobby. And you find that unless somebody is in trouble and wants to be approached by journalists, Ministers tend to avoid the Members' Lobby . . . the Civil Service will block all calls to Ministers. Now, there's another barrier, which is that the Civil Servants are now blocking calls to Special Advisers.

(Colin Brown)

At the same time there also appears evidence to suggest that the media and journalists are used by politicians and PR advisors to influence political decision-making. Several examples in the United Kingdom are to be found within studies of government reporting (Cockerell *et al.*, 1984; Negrine, 1996; Tunstall, 1996), political (auto)biographies (e.g., Ingham, 1991; Routledge, 1997; Gould, 1998; Lamont, 1999; Major, 1999; Price, 2005; Blunkett, 2006) and in journalist accounts of New Labour (McSmith, 1996; Jones, 1999; Rawnsley, 2001). All the interviewees supported this picture in some shape or form. Clearly, individuals attempt to use the media to influence leadership battles and ministerial appointments:

With the decline of Mrs Thatcher . . . it has become clear to people that if an incumbent PM can be toppled it is therefore much more possible for other leaders to topple. Therefore . . . a number of people are pursuing their agendas and certainly within the parliamentary party they will use the media to influence that.

(Conservative communications)

Well, I think, I mean it's said that the Press knew that Charlie Kennedy was a drunk but it's not true. I've never seen Charlie drunk . . . So there is a feeling around that maybe Charlie was pushed, and the media was used to undermine Charlie and get the leadership contest. That view exists. And we are used for those purposes. We're used as a battering ram as we're being used in other situations.

(Michael White, 2006)

Such mediated conflict also appears to have become a fundamental part of day-to-day policy-making and decision-taking within governments and parties. The studies of government reporting and the political biographies (see above) all offer extensive descriptions of briefing, leaking and kite-flying in the news media in order to affect policy decisions. This description of events was given wide-ranging support by interviewees. David Hill, Head of Communications for Labour, stated: 'The party since 1994 used the media to float ideas, get discussions going, prepare the ground and so on. And that has happened more as the party has consolidated its position in government.' As Charles Lewington, a former Director of Communications at the Conservative Party, recounted: 'In my case we spent huge amounts of time trying to influence colleagues through the media. They were excep-tional circumstances . . . The party was split down the middle.' Similar accounts were relayed by the political journalists:

It [kite-flying] is also used to dominate one's enemies. Ministers get briefed against by other ministers all the time . . . It's part of the Mandelsonisation of the party . . . What Mandelson brought was spin-ning ahead of the meeting in an effort to bounce people into decisions in advance.

(Paul Routledge)

There is a constant jockeying for position in any party and the media is a part of that. It's part of the game of politics . . . If there is a big cabinet discussion coming up, a big disagreement between ministers, lots of briefing goes on. They will often try and bounce the Prime Minister into something or rubbish their opponent's case.

(Andrew Grice)

By such means was old Labour transformed into New Labour (e.g., McSmith, 1996; Routledge, 1997; Gould, 1998; Rawnsley, 2001) as the new Blair–Brown axis established itself between 1994 and 1997. The communication campaigns and the 'spinning' that surrounded the abandon-ment of Clause Four (1994) and the pledge not to raise income tax levels (1997), was aimed at Labour Party members themselves. Such tactics were explained in some detail by two Labour Directors of Communication:

It was necessary for Tony Blair to be seen to be in control of the party and to develop initiatives which showed that he was in control. Bringing the party on board was essential to the project . . . This required confronting the party with a major change. Reforming Clause Four was that change.

(David Hill)

Certain people with press relations skills have used the press to change the party . . . Take the tax and spend announcement on Monday [20.1.97] . . . no change in direct taxation and the public spending freeze . . . all those stories came out of the media. The announcement on taxation was delivered on the *Today Programme*. It was a deliberate policy strategy that hadn't been agreed beyond Blair and Brown. And now there's nothing to be done about it this side of the General Election. And certainly this is what happened repeatedly over the last two years in Labour.

(Joy Johnson)

When interviewing MPs (see Chapter 6), half said they spoke to the media for the explicit purpose of influencing Parliamentary agendas and government decision-making in some way. Many of the government's own backbench MPs had tried to raise issues and promote policy ideas through their contacts with journalists. Some described long-term campaigns which only became successful when they gained a media profile:

The Pension Reform Group, which I am associated with, we're seeing the Prime Minister on Monday with our proposals . . . Last Sunday I gave to the *Sunday Telegraph*, the letter I'd written to the Chancellor, following up a meeting I'd had with him a few days before. And I think the *Guardian* will do something this Friday and then, hopefully, if all the facts are through, we'll get stuff in the media this coming Monday. So I use it to build up the campaign . . . But, also, the sad fact is if the Prime Minister reads it in the press he thinks it's real.

(Frank Field)

I ran a campaign over about three years to get the VAT reduced on sanitary products . . . And the year that he [Gordon Brown] actually did it in the budget, we sat and talked about what else we could do . . . I did a really good interview with them [*Woman's Hour*] and they allowed me the time for the interview. And a couple of newspapers did say that the Chancellor was under pressure . . . And I know that even if he hadn't been going to do it, in the end, he had to do it because the serious newspapers were saying he was expected to do it. And when newspapers say those things ministers become – even Gordon – become quite cornered.

(Christine McCafferty)

Within this inter-elite political conflict journalists get slowly pulled into the closed networks of communication that develop around Westminster and Whitehall. These networks are made up of politicians, civil servants, prominent members of think tanks and powerful pressure groups, and lobby journalists. From the professional communication advisor point of view journalists are targeted and pulled in or excluded accordingly. For David Hill: 'What Alastair Campbell did brilliantly was, for the first time in modern politics, to oblige conservative papers to report what Tony Blair and Gordon Brown were saying. Getting all the key Labour politicians into these papers was an essential element'. In Charles Lewington's account:

> There's an expression in America called the 'Big Feet' . . . the main political correspondents – the White House correspondents in American terms. These are the people that, once they have decided what way to spin a story, most others will follow . . . In Bernard Ingham's day there was a group of newspaper political editors from the *Sun*, the *Daily Mail*, *Telegraph* and *Times* who were the 'Big Feet' of their day. He referred to them as the 'White Commonwealth' and he would make sure that they were always kept in the loop. In the 1990s power switched to the television political editors. These are now undoubtedly the most important opinion formers.

This mixture of threats and rewards was relayed frequently by journalists:

> Things are rarely done straightforwardly any more . . . It's all become a bit Pavlovian – a bit of reward and sanction. Report the way they want and you get more briefings. Report it another way and you get excluded.
> (George Jones)

> They use all sorts of rules to control journalists' access to ministers and relations with journalists. They will feed out story lines regularly – but only to those considered important at the time, the *Mail* one day, *Guardian* the next.
> (Trevor Kavanagh)

The majority also admitted that, when writing, they had ongoing concerns about how these same political sources would respond to their work. Although they saw journalism as being written for the general reader it was difficult to avoid thinking about those within the Parliamentary sphere:

> I try and think of a typical *Independent* reader – but I constantly have to remind myself of that because it's easy to slip into a position where you are thinking more about the people you are mixing with, thinking about those in the Westminster village. You are always aware of how articles

might be perceived by your sources, be they backbenchers, ministers or spin doctors.

(Andrew Grice)

I think it's something that I'd have thought all political columnists worry about in that you don't want to be out of the loop. To be in the loop you have to be quite friendly with people . . . But once you have that relationship of trust, you are then bound to them, to some degree, personally . . . So I think it's a constant dilemma and it causes me a lot of anxiety.

(Polly Toynbee)

It seemed clear that many lobby journalists had become sucked into a process whereby both their principal sources and principal audiences were drawn from these same small networks. Tim Bell and Kevin Maguire's accounts offer further insight:

Politics is a very tiny place . . . Bits of gossip get everywhere, rumours spread around, even if they never appear in the newspapers . . . Nowadays that grapevine is almost entirely the Lobby. Political journalists, lobby journalists, sketch writers, op ed writers, academics. There's a clear network.

(Tim Bell)

I realised a lot of bollocks was written and written from the point of view of people in power. You get sucked into it because these are the people you mingle with and write for. Now I'm out of it I'm very aware of what goes on. It's the same if you look at reporting of the environment, companies, education – in any specialism. As a journalist you want to be in with the audience that you are writing about and, unwittingly, you get pulled in . . . I was always marked out as a Brown man because of my previous work with Charlie Wheelan when he was with the AEEU. I know other journalists who are seen as linked with others – Andrew Grice is seen as a Mandelson man. Others talk to Byers, some to Milburn, some to Prescott. Colin Brown, Prescott's biographer, spoke to him every weekend.

(Kevin Maguire)

Just as business journalists have become captured by the corporate, elite networks they move in, so have political journalists. It is not a matter of conspiracy or journalists writing under direct pressure from their sources. Instead, journalists: are highly reliant on regular source contacts within Westminster; get most of their feedback on what they write from such sources; and are regularly subject to source threats (loss of access) and rewards (generous information/interview supply). Consequently, like their business counterparts, they become a fundamental part of the closed communication networks in which elite decision-makers attempt to influence each other (see also Protess *et al.*, 1991; Hallin, 1994; Hess, 2000, for similar accounts of the Whitehouse press corps in the United States).

## Conclusion

What is clear in these examples is that elite groups are as concerned to use the news media in order to manage communication with other rival elites as they are keen to manage public opinion through the mass media. On the one hand, corporate and political party/government elites need to maintain their communication with large groups of consumer-citizens. They need to develop and promote a long-term 'brand' image of the company or party to ensure continuing sales and electoral support. At times of crisis, significant resources and personnel are employed in attempts to manage the media and public opinion. On the other hand, elites also have an ongoing need to make use of communication to influence complex and less visible elite negotiations, decision-making processes and conflicts. Arguably, mediated, inter-elite conflicts are also likely to contribute to power imbalances and inequalities because they exclude non-elites from either participation or consideration. Both types of elite communication are vital for sustaining the power of an individual, company, government or institution. But while elite-mass communication continues to be explored in media and communication studies, elite-elite communication and its socio-political consequences has been largely ignored.

Accordingly, this moves discussions of power away from both of the typical accounts of media and politics on offer: the (neo) Marxist, class conflict and liberal, pluralist models. Instead, we are left with a description of democracy that, in practice, resembles earlier descriptions of 'competitive elitism' (Schumpeter, 1952). All of which leads one to the conclusion that critical approaches in media studies should be further exploring some form of critical, elite-centred, communication theory. This does not mean taking on some of the less-palatable normative positions of classic elite theory (Mosca, Pareto and Michels). Nor should it entail attempts to mark out clearly identifiable, self-perpetuating groups of elites (Mills, 1956; Domhoff, 1967; Scott, 1991). Instead, it means identifying sites of political, economic and military power and then exploring the communication environments and discourses of those sites. Such an approach, as well as similar findings, are identifiable in some recent studies of media, politics and public opinion (Herbst, 1998; Meyer, 2002; Lewis *et al.*, 2005). These also describe the formation of elite, self-referencing networks, made up of journalists/editors, political elites, professional communication staff and other interest group representatives. Like the study presented here, the public in these cases is either simply imagined or excluded from consideration altogether.

# Chapter 5

# Culture, discourse and power

## The rediscovery of elite culture and power in media studies?

## Introduction

This chapter looks at the topic of culture and power while also extending the arguments and thinking developed in Chapter 4. As such it sets out an alternative approach for conceptualising and researching the links between culture and power in media studies. It begins by re-examining the traditional conceptual parameters that have guided most research linking the two within the discipline. The argument is that such parameters have led to two unintended consequences. First, the cultures and belief systems of powerful elite groups have been largely neglected. Second, the usual conceptual mechanisms used for linking culture and power, such as ideology or discourse, have become increasingly redundant.

An alternative approach, one that builds on Chapter 4, begins with a return to investigating cultures at specific 'elite-centred sites of power'. Not elite cultures in the high 'culture and civilisation' or radical 'power elite' traditions but, rather, in the anthropological, 'whole way of life' sense. Elite cultures and experiences are as central to the evolution of elite identities, beliefs and discursive practices as they are to any identifiable group in society. From this perspective, localised communication, norms and experiences both integrate elites and direct elite decision-making and discursive practices. Such micro-level decisions and practices can, in aggregate, have significant long-term and macro-level impacts on society. In effect, it is argued that elite beliefs and experiences, within a restricted cultural sphere, can have a material impact on wider society without necessarily influencing the belief systems of that society. Thus, in this alternative paradigm, the links between culture, practices, beliefs and power may be investigated in a quite different way.

The theoretical discussion will be illustrated with case study material focusing on the elite micro cultures and practices generated within London's financial and political centres. The research, which investigated communication and decision-making at both these sites, revealed common sets of experiences, practices and beliefs among groups of participants. The material consequences of such localised beliefs and practices have been, and continue to be, widely felt in British society.

## Culture, ideology and power in the media/cultural studies tradition

Arguably, three conceptual parameters have tended to determine the way culture and power have been theoretically linked and researched in mainstream media and cultural studies. These are: a) a focus on popular/mass media and culture, b) an emphasis on culture as a 'whole way of life', and c) the question of ideology and mass consent, be it manufactured, negotiated or opposed. All three can be traced back to the work of the discipline's founders: Williams (1958, 1961) and Hall and, to a lesser extent, Hoggart (1958) and Thompson (1963). First, their work moved the study of 'culture' away from the elite-centred 'culture and civilisation' tradition. Instead, popular culture, which had been neglected, now became the central focus. Second, it was argued that the study of culture, generally, could not be separated from society. Culture was a 'whole way of life, material, intellectual and spiritual', and ought to be observed within the anthropological tradition. Third, it was perceived, especially in the work of Hall (1973, 1980, 1982, 1983) and Williams (1977), that the links between mass culture and ideology were central to unequal power relations.[1] 'The consent question' – how the majority consented to and/or resisted the inequalities imposed by the dominant class – was to be a key object of enquiry.

Under such circumstances, both American, mainstream sociological, and classical Marxist conceptualisations of ideology were rejected. The former, in its pluralist manifestations and emphasis on social consensus, was of little use to this critical project. The latter emphasised the material and class-based nature of control over the cultural. The culture, consciousness and agency of 'the repressed' were excluded and there thus seemed few possibilities for real social/political change to occur. Instead, Hall turned to post-Marxist work in Western (continental) Europe and, above all, to Gramsci and the concept of hegemony. Ideology, for decades a central feature of much research on popular culture, emerged as a fluctuating thing, achieved through struggle and continuing negotiation between ruling groups and the majority.

Most scholarship within the discipline, whatever its political stance, has tended to retain a baseline attachment to these research precedents. Typical introductory overviews (e.g., Grossberg et al., 1992; Gray and McGuigan, 1993; Storey, 1998; Turner, 2003) all begin with the Williams and Hall (and Hoggart and Thompson) history and their shaping of the culture/ideology project. Many key works, although quite dispersed and varied, from media production, 'media events' and audience consumption (Dayan and Katz, 1992; Fiske, 1996; Sparks and Tulloch, 2000), to 'political culture' and 'cultural economy' (Street, 1997; du Gay and Pryke, 2002), have been developed within these conceptual parameters. Over the period, a variety of continental European theorists and concepts have been appropriated by cultural theorists engaged in critical work (Foucault, 1975, 1980; Bourdieu, 1979, 1993; Callon, 1986, 1998) with varying outcomes.

Over time, however, this research remit has resulted in two unintended consequences for media and cultural studies. First, there has developed an ongoing research gap within the discipline: that of the study of elite cultures, ideologies and discursive practices. For media sociologists and political economists, it was the apparatus of communication and their sociology/culture, not the ruling classes per se, which became the object of study. For critical post-Marxists, culture and ideology were to be explored through ideological state apparatus (Althusser), or civil society (Gramsci), or the discourses of professions and institutions (Foucault), or fields of cultural production (Bourdieu); in other words, rarely through the state itself or other sites of power. And for the cultural studies tradition this has generally entailed a continuing interest in either the 'repressed' or those involved with the production of popular culture. In effect, the culture, experiences, practices and 'ruling ideas' of 'the repressors' tend to be assumed or extrapolated from media texts. But, rarely are they actually investigated empirically.

Second, the links between culture and power have been steadily eroded. The original disciplinary parameters determined that ideology (or, latterly, discourse) was to be simultaneously linked with mass/popular culture, culture as a 'whole way of life', and a struggle for consent between repressors and repressed. However, contemporary developments and research foci appear to make these enforced links difficult to sustain. The culture of large, complex societies cannot be observed in the same 'whole way of life' sense previously applied to smaller cultures in anthropological research. It becomes increasingly difficult to identify homogenous groups of 'repressors' and 'repressed'. Such groups, which were first class based, came to be more finely segmented in terms of race, gender, ethnicity, age and so on. They were then further fragmented by the emphasis on identity, mediation and individual consumption. Culture is itself far from being a simple tool of repression or resistance. It is also autonomous, pleasurable, polysemic and productive. Work on 'new media', globalisation, transnationalism and identity all suggest increasing cultural fragmentation, hypersegmentation and pluralist diversity.

None of these research trends and conclusions have hindered the study of media and culture; but they have hindered the study of dominant beliefs and ideologies or discourses and their linking of culture and power. Thus, despite the supposed centrality of ideology in media and cultural studies, in practice, few now publicly declare their allegiance to the concept. At the same time as Turner (2003: 166–67) refers to ideology as 'the single most important conceptual category in cultural studies' he also describes it as 'a slightly clumsy instrument' that has become 'a little out of fashion . . . since the mid-1990s'. For many scholars in the field the weakness of the concept was established a decade or more before that. In many cases, interest in exploring alternatives, or cultural power at all, has waned entirely.

An alternative framework for investigating the links between communication, culture and power is set out as follows. First, the 'whole way of life' approach to investigating culture is returned to the local. One useful body of work to draw on here is that of subcultures. Not subcultural research in the Birmingham School vein but, rather, in the Chicago and 'post-Birmingham School' traditions and, more latterly, in Bourdieu's conception of 'fields' (Bourdieu, 1979, 1993), or Callon's (1986, 1998) (and Latour's) work on 'actor networks'. Such work looks at culture as 'a whole way of life' but as it operates locally and discretely in 'a world within a world' (Gordon, 1997 [1947]). Such cultures are not organised around resistance/opposition to 'mainstream' or dominant cultures (see Thornton, 1995; Gelder and Thornton, 1997: 148) but are 'dependent upon and co-operative with commerce and convention'. Developing organically, around any combination of vocational, spatial, lifestyle or cultural commonalities, such subcultures (or fields or networks) can also be central to discrete systems of social relations, organisation and localised cultures. Within them, certain beliefs, conventions and ideologies/discourses evolve from a mixture of 'lived social relations', in discursive practices, processes and symbolic interchanges. Actors are guided, or 'performed', by cultures, cognitions, relations and practices that develop exclusively within the spaces they temporarily inhabit.

Second, whichever of these research frameworks and sets of conceptual tools is adopted the main point is that the cultures investigated should be those that develop at 'elite sites of power'.[2] 'Sites of power' should include multiple sites and levels, from the local to the global, as well as geographically dispersed elite networks or policy communities (see Castells, 1996; Callon, 1998; Marsh, 1998) where localised elite actions have macro-level consequences. Similarly, at such sites, the object of study should not be reduced to the reproduction of materially defined classes, the reinforcement of pre-existing habitus, or inflexible forms of 'performativity'. Rather, it should be on exploring the evolving 'elite micro cultures', relations and practices of those elite-centred sites of power.[3] Here, elite decision-making and activity has extended material impacts on society. Therefore, the experiences, practices, beliefs and ideologies that inform elite decisions and actions within those sites, do too. Thus, elite cultures are linked to power relations via their influence on private, ongoing cognitions, decision-making and practices that, in aggregate, have significant macro-level, material impacts on wider society.

In this alternative research project, linking culture and power, investigation is not concerned with the construction (or negotiation) of ideological mass consent through culture. Many issues are neither raised in public nor are they discussed with the public in mind. They are negotiated and operationalised in private and are not, therefore, part of any society-wide hegemonic struggle or mass circuit of cultural production. Instead, what is suggested here is that the importance of 'elite micro cultures' lies in their influence on elite decision-making, institutional formation and governance, rules of debate and regulation, and elite negotiation and conflict. Such elements, in turn, have material consequences for society.

The research objectives thus become directed towards: a) locating elite-centred sites of power, b) investigating the formation of elite micro cultures, beliefs and practices at those sites, and c) identifying the non-cultural/ideological mechanisms by which such cultures impact on wider material relations. In other words, investigating the links between discrete elite cultures and wider social and material developments, discourses and discursive practices.

The following snapshot case studies, used to illustrate this alternative paradigm, focus on elements of the culture, practices, beliefs and ideologies/ discourses of Parliament and the London Stock Exchange. They draw on approximately 200 interviews with participants. Most of these took place in or around Westminster and the City. Research also draws on observational notes and collections of secondary and industry survey materials. Each study sketches out specific elements of the intense cultural and communication networks and professional practices that evolve in these sites. Each also offers examples where these contribute to the negotiation, adoption and dissemination of certain prominent beliefs, ideas and discourses. Under certain circumstances such cultures can become disembedded from society and can have a significant material influence on social relations.

## Case study 1: the London Stock Exchange

### Culture and communication in the City

The culture of the London Stock Exchange (LSE) is as intense, cohesive and exclusive as any subculture. Any detailed history of its development (see, e.g., Kynaston, 1994, 1995, 1999; Hutton, 1996; Chapman, 2002, Ch. 2) shows it to have consistently operated as 'a closed shop' with entry severely restricted and controlled by those inside. Social studies of the LSE (Ingham, 1984; Lazar, 1990; Hutton, 1996) and City-linked corporate elites (Fidler, 1981; Useem, 1984; Hill, 1990; Scott, 1997) each observed that the financial sector continues to be bound together by extended financial and personal networks. Despite various attempts to open up the market, some geographical displacement of the City, and an influx of overseas financial institutions, it remains an exclusive and exclusionary culture.

My own experience of researching communication in the City presented a very similar picture. That is, of an intense, focused and exclusive cultural and communication network within which certain consensual beliefs flourished. Specialist language, dress, customs and codes of practice are in evidence everywhere. It is also a very male-dominated environment with very few women attaining the most senior posts. These exclusive cultural networks are readily supported by communication, both public and private. Although, in the post-war period, there has been a steady rise in publicly available financial information and news coverage (Newman, 1984; Parsons, 1989; Tumber, 1993; Tunstall, 1996; Holland, 1997; Cassidy, 2002), that information is very much skewed towards City insiders. In the City no one can be seen reading the *Guardian* or *Independent*. Lobby areas always have the *FT*, followed by the *Telegraph* and *Times*, and a range of business and international publications. The content of financial communication is highly specialised and full of technical jargon, acronyms and coded terms. To engage with others in the market one must be aware of: the difference between financial products (e.g., gilts, equities, futures); a long list of acronyms (e.g., IPO, SETS, AIM); a range of valuation measures (e.g., P/E ratio, EPS, dividend yield); investment styles (e.g., value, growth, momentum); and typical trading concerns (e.g., liquidity, indices, gearing).

This is evident on the public scale in financial news coverage. Here, such reporting has become very much part of the financial elite communication networks that form in the City (see, Parsons, 1989; Davis, 2002; Chapter 4). Consequently, according to many of those interviewed, many financial news items contain information that is only significant for a small, specialist audience. An article appearing in *The Financial Times*, or a public company document, may be distributed to hundreds of thousands of people, but may only make sense to the 50 to 100 people who can decode the information:

> It's all in code and put out by the companies to prepare the market. Everyone in the City knows what it all means. It's prepared by City people for City people . . . It's all in neat columns and everyone knows where to look for them. In some cases the message is only aimed at about 25 people.
>
> (Tim Jackaman)

> Some companies are more prepared to manage their share price than others and some are more adept . . . You look at the *FT* and you will see many quotes using 'sources close to the company', 'it is understood'. It's all PR people who have been semi-licensed by the company to leak this information.
>
> (Tony Golding)

However, it is also clear (see Davis, 2000b, 2002) that it is other, more private forms of communication that have become significant for joining up financial networks and disseminating language, norms and values. There are over 90 specialist financial print publications circulated in the City. Thousands of stockbroking ('sell-side') and fund management ('buy-side') analysts produce and circulate regular research reports. There are also many specialist financial information suppliers. Most of these are available at high subscription rates and are only taken up by large institutional investors based in the LSE.

Private meetings, conversations and phone calls are more intense and focused still. Analysts, brokers, public and investor relations specialists, journalists, fund managers and others are all involved in multiple exchanges every day. Many consist of formal meetings, for example, between company CEOs and fund managers (see also Marston, 1996, 1999; Holland, 1997). When interviewing fund managers it was not uncommon to find them involved in several hundred meetings a year with senior company directors:

> In terms of company meetings, which tend to be in our building, they come to us, we have at least 500 [per year], quite possibly more. I'm at 500.
>
> (anonymous fund manager, 2004)

> We operate as a team rather than individuals and . . . it's something like, for the UK equity side of the business, 700 meetings, maybe more, per year.
>
> (William Claxton-Smith)

However, significantly more exchanges took place in a plethora of daily informal conversations about financial matters:

> There was enormous communication with the brokers . . . They get feedback from the institutions and . . . the press are also talking to the analysts. The press is going to the market and asking what do they think about all this?
>
> (Alistair Defriez)

> Brokers, institutions and the press all wanted and needed more current information. A constant dialogue was created, a daily exchange of views. Some analysts used to speak to me daily, or at least two or three times a week.
>
> (Graham Williams)

> Our current chairman and chief executive are spending more time in the City than the previous ones and those spent more time than their predecessors . . . interaction with the City has steadily increased.
>
> (Martin Adeney)

There also exists a long-hours work ethos and many social and practical facilities which enable participants to further extend the time they spend in the City. I sometimes met interviewees in the evenings, in or near their offices in the Square Mile or Canary Wharf, and would observe a thriving hybrid culture that mixed social and business exchanges. Many participants thus spend far more of their waking hours within the LSE elite micro culture than they do outside it. One interviewee gave an insight into the work–social life crossover:

> There was a long tradition at the *Sunday Telegraph* of putting on a Christmas party. It was the establishment paper read by City-type people. And at that party would come, and still come, very eminent industrialists, businessmen and PRs. They would all stop by, even if it was just for half an hour. And there you had the likes of Lord King and Hanson all in this tacky wine bar – people who would never normally been seen dead there. Everyone would come and be met by John Jay. I remember in the middle of the BA–Virgin clash that I went in and saw Branson and King there having a wild time together in a dingy corner.
>
> (Tim Jackaman)

In essence, the City is made up of a number of overlapping elite communication networks. Communication takes place on multiple, intense levels and for long hours. Participants may be part of wider, popular and more personal cultures, but for most of their waking life they are submerged in the intense, reflexive and exclusionary communication networks of the City. In effect, the culture, institutionalised practices, language and communication of these networks are as extensive as any other observed subculture or field. Clearly, those in this LSE-centred elite micro culture need to accumulate, and maintain, their levels of cultural capital in order to operate and progress successfully. Such levels both distinguish City insiders and exclude outsiders.

### Beliefs, ideologies and discursive practices in the City

Earlier social studies of the City have sought to identify a dominant pro-market ideology among those who work there (Fidler, 1981; Poole *et al.*, 1981; Ingham, 1984; Hill, 1990; Lazar, 1990; Hutton, 1996; Boswell and Peters, 1997). Variously this has been labelled 'entrepreneurialism', 'Thatcherism', 'liberationism' and 'neo-liberalism'. At the heart of each of these accounts is the establishment of a set of core beliefs that link the efficient operation of markets with the public good. This pro-market ideology may be broken down into a number of common beliefs. Anything which hinders markets, such as collectivism, strong unions and greater state intervention, through taxation, regulation or redistribution, are deemed a hindrance. In contrast, privatisation, competition, deregulation and lower taxes are deemed positive for the market. Consequently, City support for free-market parties, such as the Conservatives or Republicans, is particularly high. A collection of opinion and voting surveys shows that the levels of such support is in marked contrast to that of the general public (see Table 5.1).

Interviews, similarly revealed a number of common beliefs and practices which, collectively, contributed to, and were influenced by, a variation on this market ideology. This 'financial-market micro ideology' is linked to the Efficient Markets Hypothesis (EMH) that has dominated finance theory and practice in the post-war period (see Fama, 1970; and Chapter 2 for a description). Most interviewees, when asked about the EMH, expressed a certain level of scepticism. This was not surprising as the theory denies the utility of professional communicators and fund managers themselves. However, it was difficult for participants to conceive of market actions outside this discourse. In fact, with a handful of exceptions, participants seemed to rely on many basic EMH premises to justify their thinking, communication or trading strategies:

> No fund equities manager is going to say the market isn't the best way of allocating capital . . . it would undercut the whole basis of what they do.
>
> (Tony Golding)

> That theory is something that has stood the test of time. It's a very powerful theory, a very elegant theory – the efficient market hypo-

*Table 5.1* Comparisons of City elite and public support for political parties

| Survey | City elite support (%) | Public support (%) |
|---|---|---|
| Vote Conservative 1983 | 84[a] | 44[d] |
| Vote Conservative 1987 | 91[b] | 42[d] |
| Vote Labour 1987 | 1[b] | 31[d] |
| Pro-Conservative Outlook 1990 | 86[a] | 43[d] |
| Pro-Labour Outlook 1990 | 3[a] | 34[d] |
| Vote Conservative 1992 | 94[b] | 42[d] |
| Vote Labour 1992 | 2[b] | 35[d] |
| Vote Conservative 1997 | 69[b] | 35[d] |
| Vote Labour 1997 | 7[b] | 44[d] |
| Prefer Bush 2004 | 41[c] | 16[e] |
| Prefer Kerry 2004 | 9[c] | 47[e] |

Sources: a, from Lazar, 1990, study of 'City' views; b, from MORI *Captains of Industry* surveys (1987, 1992, 1997); c, from Merrill Lynch 'Global Fund-Manager Survey', UK fund managers category (2004); d, from MORI *British Public Opinion* surveys (1983, 1987, 1990, 1992, 1997); e, from Globescan survey of public opinion (2004).

thesis . . . At the end of the day if it's down to [other factors] you can't really do much with that.

(Mark Tapley)

This 'EMH thinking' could be identified in several widespread beliefs that related directly to the experiences and opinions shared across the discourse networks of the City. So, most participants interviewed believed in the long-term accuracy and superior returns of the equities market over other markets. They also assumed that the equities market operated in the same way that industrial markets and the economy did generally, and, similarly, that the health of the former equated to the health of the latter.

Starting with this first belief, there is a general expectation that the market, if not always correct in the short term, will be so in the long term. In many interviews (as well as in daily financial news coverage) the movements of 'the market' or 'the City' were referred to in terms similar to an all-powerful entity that was simply always 'right': 'Prices will change with announcements. But in the end the market is always right because things will settle back down – just like water' (David Blackwell); 'Wherever a market is, whether it's priced at 15 times or 25 times earnings, it's there for a reason. There will be a justification' (Andrew Kirton); 'It's amazing how often the City is right. They are looking ahead a couple of years, looking at trade patterns, the price of sterling, etc, and predicting accordingly. Nine times out of ten the City seems to be right' (Richard Oldworth).

Another belief, linked to EMH thinking and internal communication, is a strong perception that equities markets are the most profitable market sector to invest in. For some decades, industry reports and investor guides (e.g., Siegal, 1998; Glassman and Hassett, 1999) have argued that wise investors should always put most of their capital into equities markets rather than other markets (e.g., bonds, property, currency). According to Shiller's research (2001: 45), in 1999, 96 per cent of wealthy investors agreed that the stock market was the most rewarding and safest place to invest their money. Some years after the 2000 crash, interviewees continued to affirm this pro-equities investment philosophy: 'I am a believer that [equities] markets do tend to go up . . . Everybody says that but there is some logic underlying that' (anonymous fund manager); 'Equities are the cheapest asset class if you compare it to anything on a yield basis, including commercial property. The yields on UK equities are higher than on any other asset class' (Hugh Sergeant).

Another important component of this 'micro financial-market ideology', directly related to City experiences and practices, is the tendency of participants to equate stock markets with the external world. Lazar (1990) observed that City participants assumed that financial markets operated the same way as product or 'flex-price' markets. Similarly, Hutton (1996) noted that those in the City equated the strength or weakness of the LSE, at any one time, with that of the economy more generally. Such thinking was often relayed in remarks made by interviewees:

> I genuinely think that hostile take-overs are a necessary means of keeping British business strong and keeping management on their toes . . . I think in the long run it's good for the business and for the staff and, finally, the customer. Ultimately that all feeds through and is good for the economy as a whole.
>
> (Chris Hopson)

> The stock market, by and large, is efficient at allocating capital, that's what 'stock market' means – market for stock coming from capital. So it allocates capital, takes it away from companies that aren't getting the right returns and allocates it to areas where, risk adjusted, they are making higher returns. So it is efficient every time.
>
> (Edward Bonham-Carter)

The potential for the micro culture, beliefs and activities of the City to become disembedded from wider society was very strongly realised in the 1990s. During this period international markets grew at a rapid rate (see Chapter 2). Many of the key beliefs about the efficiency and profitability of the market, outlined above, became reinforced during the lengthy 'bull market' of the 1990s (see Smithers and Wright, 2000; Shiller, 2001; Cassidy, 2002). A spate of wildly over-optimistic claims about the future growth of stock markets followed. The equation of the LSE with the wider economy became further confused as ideas about the 'new economy' became prominent and influential at the time. All of these beliefs, many generated and exacerbated in the elite micro cultures of the LSE and international financial networks, provided a logic for new investment in equities. Hundreds of billions of pounds were quickly shifted into the LSE.

Figure 5.1 demonstrates the growing gap between City beliefs and those of the outside world in the boom and bust period. The chart, constructed from two different survey series, compares the views of fund managers and the general public on the strength of the economy from January 1999 to December 2000. For much of 1999, the equities market rose quite dramatically as the hi-tech bubble grew. For much of 2000 share prices fell. Arguably this had a strong influence on the general levels of optimism, and then pessimism, of fund managers about the future strength of the wider UK economy. The general public, in contrast, were relatively neutral, or even pessimistic in 1999, and a little pessimistic in 2000. For most of the two-year period there is a significant divergence of opinion between the two. For eight months out of 24 the difference is more than 80 per cent. As the charts in Chapter 2 show, City beliefs had also become disconnected from basic economic 'realities'. Clearly, financial elite perceptions and beliefs can, at

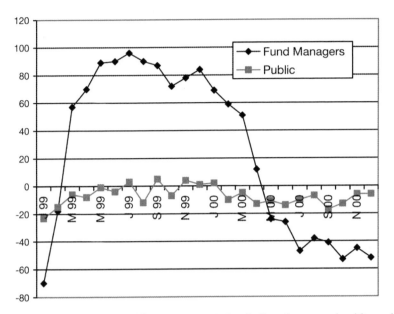

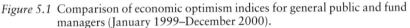

*Figure 5.1* Comparison of economic optimism indices for general public and fund
managers (January 1999–December 2000).

Sources: MORI and Merrill Lynch/Gallup.

times, become very consensual. That consensus can shift quite dramatically.
During such periods, financial elite cultures can become quite disembedded
from wider society.

### Material consequences

The decision-making, practices and activities of this elite-centred 'site of
power' have strong consequences for wider British society. This is because
its participants manage much of Britain's surplus capital and industry. In
2003, UK-based fund managers controlled approximately £2.2 trillion
worth of funds (IMA, 2003). This included a large proportion of the £1.35
trillion in company shares traded in the equities market and £430 billion in
government bonds (government debt) traded on the gilts market. The largest
UK investment institution, Barclays, alone managed £530 billion. To get
this in proportion, the government's annual income and expenditure in
2004 was £430 billion. Therefore, the financial-market micro ideology,
which guides fund manager thinking and practice, is likely to have wider
material impacts on society.

One obvious set of material impacts can be directly traced to the 1990s
market boom and crash of 2000. Both internal, City-based elites and City-
linked, external elites were persuaded to pour surplus capital into equities.

Treasury officials, corporate heads, pension fund trustees, the boards of insurance companies and high street banks, all became convinced that the London equities market was the best place to invest their excess capital. They also made calculations of future wealth and returns based on assumptions about the health of the Market. The 2000 crash resulted in approximately £500 billion of lost investment. Higher insurance premiums, huge pension fund deficits, endowment mortgage shortfalls, and the highest ever levels of personal debt, are some of the consequences for ordinary people of that financial loss.

In addition there are many longer-term trends that have negatively impacted on the shape of UK industry and employment conditions. Fund managers set and agree the goals, rewards and corporate strategies of company managers. However, few fund managers (or analysts) interviewed knew much about the actual industries they evaluated and traded in; nor was that deemed important for the job. Only two of the 22 fund managers interviewed had had any actual industry experience and none visited company industrial sites – although two had in the past (see also Mitchell *et al.*, 1987; Baker, 1997, on this issue). Thus, financial market-oriented goals are imposed on business directors. Short-term investment and price-volatile market experiences inform long-term investment and static-price experiences in industry. Merger and acquisition activity is evaluated on internal financial market, rather than industry, criteria. Similarly, all decision-making excludes social, environmental and macro-economic repercussions. A 1998 poll of 'Captains of Industry' (MORI, 1998) asked 'What, in general, are the most important factors you take into account when making your judgment about companies?'. 'Social responsibility' was noted by only 6 per cent, 'treatment of customers' by 7 per cent and 'treatment of employees' by 6 per cent. A 2001 poll (MORI, summer 2002) came up with similar results. For 'City Investors', 'environmental responsibility' and 'social responsibility' were only mentioned by 2 per cent and 4 per cent respectively.

The consequences for UK industry, in comparison with other OECD countries, have been: a persistent lack of research investment; a bias against smaller public company investment; a rapidly declining manufacturing sector; and an intense take-over culture where most take-overs have left both companies worse off. More significantly, for the workforce, is that such stock market-led developments frequently lead to job cuts, longer working hours, displacement, short-term and flexible contracts, and loss of benefits and pension rights. There is also clearly little support for the imposition of greater environmental taxation or regulation (See Ingham, 1984; Lazar, 1990; Sudarsanam, 1995; Hutton, 1996; Treasury, 1999; Myners, 2001; Golding, 2003; Monbiot, 2006).

## Case study 2: Westminster

### Culture and communication in Westminster

Any historical account of Parliament at Westminster shows that, for most of its long existence, it has also been an exclusionary and exclusive place. Much of this changed during the twentieth century and, just over the last decade, the institution has gone through an extensive period of modernisation (Field, 2002; Hansard, 2004, 2005; HoC, June 2004, December 2005; Brazier *et al.*, 2005). Part of this has involved an acknowledgement that the public feels too distant from Parliament and, accordingly, attempts have been made to remedy that. The general references to 'strangers', meaning all outside members of the public, are being removed. The new Portcullis House building, where many MPs now have offices, is a very open and socially oriented building, as opposed to the dark, maze-like spaces of the traditional parts of Westminster. Outreach programmes and public-oriented communication have expanded (see Chapter 7). Working hours and practices have been made more family-friendly.

Despite these changes there still remain many exclusive and exclusionary cultural elements of Parliamentary life. Although not as extreme as the City, Westminster is also a very white, male-dominated environment with women and ethnic minorities being significantly under-represented. Like the City, specialist language, dress, customs and codes of practice are in evidence everywhere. The language used is full of acronyms and technical or coded terms. To understand the political process, and discuss it with participants, one has to be aware of: the different procedural committees ('general', formerly 'standing order', 'public bill', 'select', 'joint'); the titles and terms of address ('Honourable' or 'The Right Honourable', 'Lord' or 'Baron', 'Minister' or 'Secretary of State'); and terms for physical actions ('crossing the floor', 'making a point of order').

The rules, customs and practices are a mixture of the written and unwritten, centuries old, recent or agreed for a temporary parliamentary period. Despite formal inductions, guides (Flynn, 1997) and regularly updated 'rule books', such as *Erskine May* (MacKay *et al.*, 2004), many experienced MPs and Parliamentary professionals struggle to keep up. New MPs, when asked about learning such rules and procedures, all admitted it was extremely difficult:

> It's the most brutal, medieval and, frankly, managerially dysfunctional place you could possibly imagine. It's so full of unwritten rules and protocols, rituals and ceremonial norms and standards, that you just learn by basically making mistakes.
>
> (Nick Clegg)

It's difficult. I mean, people will tell you about select committees. You know about the structures, you know how legislation is made, you know about first, second, third readings, committee stage . . . But it's little things, like how to try and influence a bill in a constructive manner, how to ask for meetings with ministers and get a meeting with a minister, how to represent your constituents' views properly in this place. It takes time and a lot of it you learn on the job by watching other people and by making your mistakes. And you hope that nobody's watching you when you make them.

(Sadiq Khan)

The communication, be it via news, in formal meetings or via personal exchanges, is extensive. National news, while being publicly available, is consumed in quite different ways (see Chapter 6). The main papers read by the public are the *Sun*, the *Daily Mail* and the *Daily Mirror*. Most Labour (67 per cent) and Liberal Democrat (77 per cent) MPs read the *Guardian*. Most Conservative MPs read the *Daily Telegraph* (82 per cent). The *Times* is the second most read paper by MPs in all three parties. Politicians are also acquainted with the journalists who produce the news, and have first-hand knowledge of the individuals and procedures being covered. Therefore, coverage of events, individuals and statements is full of bits of information that may have a different significance for those in or close to Parliament itself:

The paper which our people would think is most close to party views would be the *Independent*, but . . . if you're talking about members of the party, voters of the Liberal Democrats, then many of those also read the *Daily Mail*.

(Simon Hughes)

This place is a goldfish bowl which we move around in, and the press and the press lobby move around in. You can listen to *Radio 4* in the morning and think that that's everything. But when I go home at weekends and talk [people] haven't got a clue what the *Today Programme* is, never even listen to it . . . we read the papers avidly every day, but most people don't read . . . if you say to people 'What's in the *Guardian*?', most of them haven't read the *Guardian* in their life . . . it's a very unique and strange environment, which means you are concentrating on the issues of the day. The average person doesn't do that, do they? They don't wake up in the morning and think 'Oh, what am I going to think about the Education Bill today', do they?

(Kevan Jones)

Once again, a far greater level of communication and cultural exchange takes place in meetings. Outside the very public debates in the Chamber there are numerous official and unofficial meetings and exchanges. For example, in 2004–05, there were 421 standing committee meetings held to discuss the 44 government bills. There were also 1,286 select committee meetings which produced 190 reports. 54,000 written questions and 14,500 oral questions were put to the government by MPs. An average of 16 EDMs (Early Day Motions) were tabled each day and drew over 100,000 signatures in total from MPs (all figures HoC, July 2005). These figures do not include the many more 'all-Party' and individual party committees that are organised around specific issues, countries and party matters. Most MPs are members of several of these committees and some are members of a dozen or more.

Much of the information in circulation is also only accessible to those politicians and support staff (clerks or civil servants) working within Parliament. All politicians interviewed, when asked about the sources of information used to inform themselves on policy matters and decision-making, listed a number of private sources. The most frequently mentioned information source was 'interest groups'. Party information, the House of Commons Library and party colleagues were all mentioned very frequently. For former Government ministers the primary source was civil servants. So, although MPs also looked to the media and their constituents for information, the reliance on private and internal information sources was, in most cases, higher than public information sources. This seemed especially so in the case of Government ministers.

Beyond the committees there are many tea rooms, bars, restaurants and organised sporting and social activities where MPs and others mix and exchange information. Like the social spaces of the City these are a hybrid mix of social and political exchanges. As many MPs explained, it is through these multiple, formal and informal, exchanges that much Parliamentary business evolves. Opinions are gathered, moods observed and party feeling tested:

> You talk to your colleagues a lot. There are plenty of opportunities, whether it be sitting for a cup of tea in the tea room or a bite to eat in the evening . . . and you pick things up.
>
> (Danny Alexander)

> One shouldn't under-estimate in politics good, old fashioned gossip. It's the bit that makes it interesting, it's the sort of chat up at the tea room table in the tea room . . . people pick up all kinds of things.
>
> (Michael Jack)

> In the main you talk to people. There are people whose opinion you're fairly familiar with, and we've all been involved in enough activities, Parliamentary PLP [Parliamentary Labour Party] elections, whatever, to have a fair idea of the way that our colleagues think . . . when I was at

the PLP meeting last Monday night, I was just looking round the room and watching people's body language, and looking at where they were when Blair was speaking, when people were making their points to Blair. You just gather information that way.

(Frank Doran)

Thus, for many who have closely witnessed Parliament in different capacities, Westminster is a small, insular 'network', 'club' or 'village'. Indeed, many, insiders and outsiders, refer to it as the 'Westminster village' with all that that implies socially and culturally:

The House of Commons has never been very outward looking . . . it's not as though the public are physically excluded, it's just that, when they do come in, they certainly don't get the feeling that the building is for them, everything is designed for the convenience of Parliamentarians and the public are treated almost as intruders.

(Martin Linton)

What the Puttnam Commission found, which looked at this issue, was that people in Parliament spoke to each other, and spoke to the media in a language that each other understood, that the Westminster village understood, but it wasn't accessible for people in the outside world. And it's not to do with language in Parliament. It's to do with the general culture.

(Clare Ettinghausen)

### Beliefs, ideologies and discursive practices in Westminster

There is a sizable body of literature which suggests that party politics has become steadily devoid of ideology. The 'old' divisions that once clearly separated parties have narrowed as each has moved closer to the centre ground. Instead, parties are judged on competency and communication ability (see Evans and Norris, 1999; Heath *et al.*, 2001; Lees-Marshment, 2001). Such views are frequently voiced by interviewees of all descriptions. From the viewpoint of party communicators:

The relationship with the readers is more financial than editorial. People read papers for bingo, free holidays and exclusive offers, not to read about politics and serious issues.

(Tim Bell)

If you look around today the voters of tomorrow are not driven by ideology. Ideological ideas no longer drive voters – especially the young. They support those who are seen to be competent and deliver.

(David Hill)

This position is reflected in many journalist accounts: 'Ideology doesn't matter at all. Competency is what matters. No one talks about ideology any more. They talk about values' (Paul Routledge);

> I look at a lot of people in the Labour Party now who are clearly following a course that they don't believe . . . And that's also something that strikes me very much about the present leader of the Conservative Party . . . it's been said that we live in a post-ideological society and I think that's true.
>
> (Simon Heffer)

It is also an issue mentioned by politicians of all parties:

> In 1983, with Foot versus Thatcher, there were clear differences between the parties, on nationalisation, the EU, CND, tax, etc. . . . By 2001 the differences between what Tories and New Labour would do now are slight in comparison.
>
> (Chris Rennard)

> This isn't an ideological electorate. It wouldn't recognise an ideology if it drove over them in a tank. And they don't like to be frightened . . . Now we're [Labour] part of the middle ground. And once you're there, you're impregnable.
>
> (Austin Mitchell)

> The big issues, which used to get people tremendously excited about partisan politics in the 50s, 60s and 70s, have been settled and there's now a sort of common ground. We're all centrists and politics has become about image and competence and not about principle and ideology.
>
> (John Maples)

Despite this consensus about consensus it is not hard to find examples of issues in which aggregated individual opinions, within parties, are both internally consensual and diverge considerably from others. In some instances such views are in marked contrast to the those of the general public. Some of these issues fit a clear 'left–right' division and some do not. So, for example, views on companies and commerce diverge considerably when comparing Conservatives and Labour MPs. In 1997 (MORI, 1997) 100 per cent of Conservative MPs agreed that 'The main responsibility of companies is to perform competitively, even if this means reducing the number of people they employ'. Only 40 per cent of Labour MPs agreed. In 2001 (MORI, 2001/02), 81 per cent of Labour MPs agreed that 'Industry and commerce do not pay enough attention to their social responsibilities'. Twenty per cent of Conservative MPs agreed. On moral issues that are not easily classifiable on the left–right political spectrum, there were also some clear differences. In 1996 (MORI, December 1996) 98 per cent of Labour electoral candidates supported a ban on fox hunting with hounds. Seventy-three per cent of Conservatives opposed such a ban. In 2004 the differences were between Parliamentarians and the public. Seventy-nine per cent of all MPs (CommunicateResearch, September 2004), including both Conservatives and Labour, opposed new legislation to legalise voluntary euthanasia. Among the public 80 per cent supported the introduction of such a bill and 10 per cent opposed it (YouGov, 06.12.04).

Regardless of whether strong party 'ideologies' still exist or not it is evident that certain beliefs can develop and be widely disseminated within political micro cultures. That process can take place across Westminster or within networks within Westminster, that is, within party networks, or the more exclusive networks inside Government and Whitehall. When discussing the dissemination of ideas, issues agendas and policy evolution, many interviewees used terms like 'fashion', 'mood', 'tipping point' and 'herd':

> It's the mood of the week . . . it's what MPs are talking about in the tea room, and there is no rationale to it. One week, one issue may be deeply fashionable, the next week, it may be completely out.
>
> (Chris Grayling)

> And to a point I suppose there's a, I hesitate to call it a, herd mentality in the House of Commons. But there is a point where, when there are a few Members starting to take an interest in something, certainly jump up and raise points of order, or ask why there aren't debates being allowed on something, you can tell that something's becoming an issue.
>
> (Graham Brady)

Clearly, there are intense and insular cultural and communication networks in Parliament. These provide the basis for the rapid negotiation, adoption and dissemination of consensual beliefs, policy ideas and legislative lines. These, in turn, contribute to ideologies/discourses and practices within Westminster which, at times, can translate into sudden political 'mood swings'. Arguably, under certain conditions and on certain political issues, this may all contribute to a disembedding of political parties, or Parliament generally, from wider public opinion. This may be the case when it comes to engaging with political processes operating within the 'Westminster village'. It may also be on certain issues where the information available and circulating within Parliament may be quite different to that on offer in the wider public sphere. Thus, constitutional affairs, complex economic or scientific issues, or international and military developments, are possible areas of divergence.

Two areas frequently mentioned by MPs and journalists as not being adequately covered in political reporting (see Chapter 3) are constitutional affairs and Europe/Foreign Affairs in general. On the topic of constitutional reform there are strong differences between Labour and Conservative MPs. In 1997, the British Representatives Study (Norris, 1999) found that 95 per cent of Labour MPs wanted to 'replace the Lords with an elected chamber'. Only 2 per cent of Conservatives wanted to. Eighty-five per cent of Labour MPs also wanted a 'written constitution' in contrast to 9 per cent of Conservatives. In 2004 (CommunicateResearch, February 2004), 90 per cent of Labour MPs opposed 'a formal ban on Scottish, Welsh and Northern Irish MPs voting on England-only legislation'. Ninety-two per cent of Conservative MPs supported such a ban. As MORI polls regularly show, the public do not think the issue important at all. Going back to 1974, no more than 2 per cent of the public have ever listed constitutional affairs as being one of the 'most important issues facing Britain'.

The single issue most interviewees listed as being excluded from media coverage and public debate, was European affairs and the activities of EU legislators and administrators. It was a concern of several MPs:

> The media view of the situation is that institutional reform in the European Union is a dull issue now because they don't see it as being part of the agenda, and it's very difficult to get past that blockage.
>
> (Robert MacLennan)

> Very few journalists understand European affairs, and that pool of journalists is ever reducing . . . If it is the job of the media to reflect and report on what is important why, when 60 per cent to 70 per cent of legislation emanates from Brussels, do we read next to nothing about anything beyond straight bananas, Peter Mandelson and an annual bust up in the EU fisheries negotiations?
>
> (Angus Robertson)

In one survey (Baker *et al.*, 1999) the one issue that MPs did agree upon was that there was a 'paucity of debate' on Europe, both in the media (80 per cent Labour, 76 per cent Conservative, 84 per cent Liberal Democrat) and amongst the electorate (88 per cent Labour, 88 per cent Conservative, 100 per cent Liberal Democrat). In 2004 a majority of the public acknowledged that it was an area they knew little about (YouGov, 25.05.04). Asked 'How much do you think you know about the powers and responsibilities of the European Parliament?', 71 per cent answered 'not much' or 'nothing at all'. For journalists, European affairs were regarded as too politically sensitive a topic for politicians to publicly discuss, and too uninteresting a topic for news editors to allocate news space to: 'I suspect that as long as the *Sun* is against the Euro there will never be a referendum on the issue' (Trevor Kavanagh);

I think the Eurosceptics would claim that the press gives far too little attention to European directives that pass quietly through this place in distant committees. They are open to the press. But the press never attend because they're very boring meetings which, nine times out of ten, wouldn't produce a story. It's on that tenth occasion when something is going through that we haven't noticed.

(Philip Webster)

Despite this widespread perception of a lack of public debate it is clear that there are strong, contrasting views on European issues. Among Parliamentarians, Labour and Liberal Democrat MPs, as well as civil servants, are generally in favour of greater integration with Europe. Conservative MPs and the public are generally against. In 1991 (Sanders and Edwards, 1992), before Britain's failed attempt to enter the ERM (Exchange Rate Mechanism), 100 per cent of the 190 'foreign policy elite' interviewees agreed that 'The "EC Connection" is crucial or very important to Britain's international role and interests'. In 1998 (Baker et al., 1999), 87 per cent of Liberal Democrats and 65 per cent of Labour MPs, agreed that 'European membership is crucial to Britain's prosperity'. Only 13 per cent of Conservatives thought the same. In 2004 (CommunicateResearch, February 2004) 95 per cent of Conservative MPs supported the initiation of a referendum on the new EU Constitution. Seventy-seven per cent of Labour MPs opposed this. In 2005 (Smith, 2006) 80.3 per cent of civil servants, and 87.7 per cent of Labour MPs, agreed that 'For Britain the benefits of European integration outweigh the costs'; 74.2 per cent of Conservative MPs disagreed. Public opinion throughout this period has remained fairly sceptical. From 1990 up to the present, support for the Single Currency has wavered between 22 and 33 per cent; opposition has moved between 50 and 60 per cent (MORI, *Long Term Trends*, 1990–98, 1998–2005). In 2000, 46 per cent said, if given the opportunity, they would vote to leave the European Union; 43 per cent would vote to stay. In another survey (YouGov, June 2005) 80 per cent said they wanted less political integration with the European Union and 10 per cent more.

In some ways constitutional and European Union affairs are some of the most important parts of the political process. They have a bearing on the practices, technologies, tactics and discourses of government itself. Yet, while they engage many Parliamentarians on a day-to-day level, and contribute to widespread beliefs about Europe within party and civil service networks, they remain rather vague issues for the general public.

## Conclusion

In both the theoretical and case study parts of this chapter I have proposed an alternative line of critical research for linking culture, ideology/discourse and power in media studies. This begins by taking a different approach to the study of culture, ideology and power to that set out in the classical (post-) Marxist and Western Marxist/cultural studies traditions that have guided work within the discipline.

Instead, this complementary critical research project begins with a renewed interest in researching cultures, beliefs and practices in localised, 'elite sites of power'. These sites should be treated, for research purposes, as any other subculture or field. Such 'disentangled', 'elite micro cultures' impact on the behaviour of elites, their day-to-day practices, decision-making and the shaping of institutions. All of this has wider, but less visible, consequences for society. In many cases, although the inhabitants of some elite sites are engaged in very public dialogues (politicians, most obviously), they spend a significant amount of time engaged in more private forms of communication. In other, elite-centred sites, such as those described here in the City, the private is, almost exclusively, what constitutes the daily lived relations of participants; whatever the wider consequences of their decisions and actions.

In fact, the elite micro cultures, beliefs and practices generated at many of these sites, can be more culturally cohesive than most subcultures. Partici-pants are more able to isolate themselves from other groups in geographical, material and cultural ways. The social and communication mechanisms for delivering cohesion and consensus, and enforcing rules and practices, are rather more extensive. Processes of globalisation and advances in communi-cation and transport enable increased elite cultural cohesion and invisible practices, not necessarily greater public communication and accountability. Thus there is the potential for such sites, under certain conditions and in relation to particular issues, to become culturally disembedded. In effect, the cultural gap between certain elites and the rest may be just as likely to be growing in some areas as diminishing in others.

# Chapter 6

# Mediated politics

## The mediation of parliamentary politics

## Introduction

This chapter investigates forms of news media influence on political issue agendas and decision-making. It begins with a critical evaluation of media agenda-setting research – the more commonly adopted paradigm for exploring this question in political communication. It then argues instead for a greater adoption of methods and perspectives developed in media sociology. These typically draw on a mix of sociology, psychology and ethnography, to explore how media audiences use, and relate to, media in their everyday cognitive and behavioural processes. In this case the audience is made up of Members of Parliament at Westminster. The question is: how do MPs use and relate to journalists and political news in their efforts to identify political agendas and make substantive decisions?

The general conclusion is that intense media attention on issues can shift political agendas and policy developments, but not according to the simple stimulus–response model of agenda-setting commonly employed. Politicians are usually too sceptical of news content, too media aware and have too many non-news information sources to draw on in policy matters. Instead, news media and reporter influences shape agendas and decision-making in other ways. British MPs, who are both media savvy and media obsessive, consciously shift their policy agendas with future news reporting in mind. Politicians, working either independently or in partnership with journalists, are often the sources behind news campaigns, as they try to anticipate and then ride news coverage in order to influence agendas. Moreover, politicians regularly use news, as well as their daily interactions with journalists, to gauge what other politicians think are the main issues and likely solutions. In other words, journalism and journalists have a significant social and cultural role in helping MPs to reach agreed agendas and positions.

## Investigating the question of news influence on political elites: from media effects to mediation and the social construction of issue agendas

One consistent approach to investigating media influence on politics has evolved directly out of agenda-setting studies in political science and communication (McCombs and Shaw, 1972; Iyengar and Kinder, 1987; Iyengar and Reeves, 1997). Although this paradigm has been applied mostly to public audiences, as opposed to powerful, elite ones, there has been a steady trickle of research projects which have applied the model to elites.[1] Usually, because qualitative and experimental research is difficult with this audience, the methods have tended to rely on quantitative methods that compare news content with political texts or recorded responses. The quantity of news coverage on key topics is tallied up, over time, in one or more key news publications or broadcasts. This is then compared with time-specific, aggregate data, on the number of instances that political elites then communicate on such issues and/or make substantive responses.

Thus, Soroka (2002, 2003) found a link between increased news coverage of foreign affairs and rises in defence spending. He also found that increases in news coverage of environmental issues resulted in more public discussion of these issues in Washington, but found the reverse in terms of reporting on government budget deficits. Pritchard and Berkowitz (1993) compared levels of crime reporting with shifts in criminal justice resourcing in seven cities over a 31-year period. They found a possible causal link in two of the cities but nothing in the other five. Edwards and Wood (1999) found that the President's public pronouncements on foreign affairs and crime seemed to be in response to heightened levels of broadcast news coverage. The results were more mixed in other areas of domestic policy such as education and health care. Brandenberg's (2002) analysis of nine key issues in the British General Election found no data to support a notion of media influences on the political agendas of the two main parties but some instances of the reverse.

A few studies, notably Protess et al. (1991) and Baumgartner and Jones (1993), used a wider range of methods and, consequently, offered more diverse findings on the nature of the relationship between news and political agendas. Each, while underlining the importance of media influences on politics, say as much about the short-comings of the agenda-setting paradigm. Two particular objections come to the fore. First, is the problem of establishing the line of causality from news media stimuli to political response. Effects research has always struggled to isolate media stimuli and separate it from other possible 'real world' stimuli and this is no less a problem when observing political decision-making. The passage of legislation, from policy idea to votes in the legislature, is usually a slow-moving process, involving multiple actors and information sources. These two extensive studies of media influence (see also Cook *et al.*, 1983) found that processes, involving substantive political change, were usually already in motion before news coverage of the relevant issue intensified.

Second, political responses may be tallied up during content analysis but are more likely to be 'symbolic', rather than substantive, in nature (see also Pritchard and Berkowitz, 1993; Walgrave and van Aelst, 2004).[2] That is, politicians may respond to heightened media interest, with more speeches or hearings, but this does not necessarily translate into budgetary, regulatory or legislative action. In each of these case studies, it was clear that politicians discussed the issues with journalists and other interested parties prior to news stories being produced and prepared responses accordingly. Thus, what might be classified as news effects and media agenda-setting by some may, in effect, be reclassified as political news management by others (e.g., Jones, 1995; Stauber and Rampton, 1995; Herman and Chomsky, 2002; Miller, 2004).

There is a third objection concerning the nature of the political elite audience being observed. One conclusion, deducible from several other studies in this field, is that politicians are less likely than most to be influenced by news media (Iyengar and Kinder, 1987; Zaller, 1992, 1997). The indicators are that, if an individual has more education, consumes more news media, has a greater interest in politics or has more knowledge of the topic from non-media sources, he or she is less likely to be subject to media influence on an issue.[3] At the same time, politicians are confronted with multiple topics and conscious choices every day. This differs from the one-off issues or voting choices, made in isolation or at a later date, as tested in much agenda-setting research. It is thus not a matter of looking at news topics and their effects in isolation but, rather, the competition to achieve salience between multiple issues in the social arenas in which politicians exist (see Hilgartner and Bosk, 1988; Ansolabehere, *et al.*, 1997, on this).[4]

Thus, for Gamson (2004: 310), 'the social sciences overall need a more sophisticated social psychology in which cognition, emotion and calculation all play their parts . . . A primitive stimulus-response model still lurks behind many of the key formulations in the study of political communication.' As Walgrave and van Aelst conclude:

> public agenda-setting is a cognitive process while political agenda-setting is essentially a behavioural process. It is not what politicians think or believe but what they do that matters . . . Precisely for that reason we need a specific behavioural theory of political actors and we cannot simply rely on the simple public agenda-setting model. (2004: 15)

There are a number of studies in media sociology and psychology which offer methods and perspectives that might assist in these goals. An alternative media effects tradition has looked at individual media 'uses' and 'gratifications' (Rosengren and Windahl, 1972; Blumler and Katz, 1974). Parallel work in media sociology investigated how audiences actively interpreted their media (Morley, 1980; Ang, 1986; Liebes and Katz, 1990). More recently, enquiry has focused on the 'mediation' of social and political processes (Martin-Barbero, 1993; Thompson, 1995; Livingstone, 1999). This looks at how individuals, in their use of media, inadvertently alter their behaviours and relations. In terms of political decision-making the research question then becomes how do politicians adapt their behaviour and decision-making processes in relation to the evolving news media environment that they are faced with?

In political communication this question has usually been investigated in terms of the efforts of politicians to manage and/or adapt to news agendas. Thus, political parties and governments employ professional marketing and public relations techniques to either 'spin' news media (Ewen, 1996; Herman and Chomsky, 2002; Franklin, 2004; Miller, 2004, see Chapter 4) or adapt and reinvent their brands and policies in ways news journalists and voters will positively respond to (Scammell, 1995; Norris, 2000; Lees-Marshment, 2001). For others, by adapting to an increasingly commercialised media, political processes, including agenda-setting and decision-making, have become driven by a populist media logic (Hallin, 1994; Bennett, 1997; Franklin, 1997; Delli Carpini and Williams, 2001; Underwood, 2001; Altheide, 2004; Entman, 2005). This thesis has been presented at its most extreme in the work of Street (1997) and Meyer (2002). For Meyer, as political elites adapt to the logic of news production requirements so the media 'colonizes' politics. Politics is dominated by an 'iron triangle' of politicians, pollsters and media executives which, in turn, conceive problem definitions and their policy solutions. The unavoidable conclusion is that political processes are being altered as politicians attempt to accommodate and exploit the mediated political environment.

The most significant empirical study that adopts such an interpretive framework is that of Herbst (1998). Herbst asked political staffers such questions as how they regarded news media as a crystalliser of public opinion. Asking these sorts of question leads one to locate journalists and news as significant factors in the long-term research agenda concerned with 'who decides' and why (Mills, 1956; Dahl, 1961, 1989; Bachrach and Baratz, 1962; Lukes, 1974) in political policy spheres or networks?

However, with a couple of notable exceptions, much of the 'mediated politics' work remains speculative when it comes to making assessments of how politicians and agendas are actually influenced. It often tends to conflate the 'public sphere' with the 'policy sphere'. That is, it merges the public presentation of politics, parties and policies with the actual business of politics that takes place largely in private. In total, this work says more about public campaigning, political brand management, and the shaping of news in the public sphere. It says rather less about day-to-day impacts of news media and journalists on elite cognitions, agendas and behaviours in the political private sphere.

A second, alternative approach to the issue of news media influence on politics, concentrates on the nature of the relationships that form between political journalists and politicians. Building on earlier studies (Sigal, 1973; Gans, 1979), recent work in media sociology has renewed its interest in the activities of news sources and media–source relations (Ericson *et al.*, 1989; Schlesinger and Tumber, 1994; Manning, 2000; Davis, 2002). This work suggested that such relationships were fundamental components of the news production process. While the main focus of this research was news construction, it also suggested something about how political elites related to, and were influenced by, their relations with journalists. A key finding of this news sources work, like that of studies of investigative journalism (Cook *et al.*, 1983; Protess *et al.*, 1991; Baumgartner and Jones, 1993), is that politicians and political journalists move in over-lapping spheres (see also Hilgartner and Bosk, 1988; Parsons, 1989; Herbst, 1998; Davis, 2003b).[5] Journalists and politicians, whether in conflict, regular dialogue or working in 'coalitions', contribute to issue agendas and policy debates. These often exclude the wider public sphere and considerations of public opinion (Lang and Lang, 1983; Protess *et al.*, 1991; Davis, 2000b, 2003b; see also Kantola, 2001).

In this scenario it is not a matter of news media, as independent variable, affecting the cognitive processes and behaviours of political elites. Nor is it simply a matter of political elites adapting their thinking and behaviour to accommodate the requirements of journalists and news production. Instead, journalists and politicians regularly have some form of combined role in the identification and selection of issues and their solutions. How that combined role is utilised in agenda-setting, from the point of view of politicians, is something rarely explored in research.

The study presented here is 'audience-centred' and is conceived along these latter lines of 'mediation' and 'social interactionism'. Its starting assumptions are that: politicians consume and make extensive use of news in their daily information gathering and cognitive processes; politicians also have regular interactions with journalists in the course of their work and this also affects their thinking and behaviour. Consequently, journalism and journalists are likely to play a part in the construction of political agendas and political deliberations generally. The study is based on a set of 40 semi-structured interviews with MPs. It also draws on 12 interviews, with parliamentary officials and members of the House of Lords (all former MPs), and two related sets of interviews with political journalists and political support staff.

## Politicians, news and issue agendas: from the stimulus–response model to anticipatory media effects

In some ways the interview material did offer some evidence supportive of a classic political agenda-setting paradigm. The majority of politicians were self-confessed 'news junkies'. On average, MPs consumed four to five different news sources, including three newspapers, each day. Just over two-thirds listened to radio news and the same amount watched television news. A third used online news services. This finding matched up with data from a MORI survey (Duffy and Rowden, 2005: 30). Interestingly, many explained that there was a constant news media presence in their offices; something often observed first-hand when conducting interviews in MPs' offices. A television might be on showing *News 24*, the *Parliament Channel* or *Ceefax* and a desk computer might well display the BBC website and tickertape news headlines.

News media appeared to be a key information source for MPs. Politicians were asked: 'What are your main sources of information when it comes to informing yourself about, and deciding where you stand on, political issues?' The question was put several times in relation to the interviewee's role (back-bench MP, (shadow) minister, committee member), whether they had a special interest/expertise in the issue, and if they were required to vote on the issue. In these circumstances news media was the second most mentioned source by all interviewees with four out of every seven listing it. Significantly, it was the most important source for roughly half the back benchers who listed it. This finding is in line with another MORI survey (summer, 2001). This asked MPs which sources of information 'are most useful to you in your work' and 59 per cent, the top answer, responded 'articles in newspapers or magazines'.

For many interviewees news media was a starting point for their day and gave clues as to what issues needed to be looked at further:

> I guess it's [news] a kind of funnel then, in the sense that you start with awareness of the issue in general terms, and that will probably come from a news source . . . If it's an issue which is then either in one's spokesmanship, or of particular interest, then I would proactively start looking for data or information.
>
> (John Thurso)

> Obviously the newspapers are very important to me. I read habitually . . . and I try to keep up with what the latest thinking is. And then, if something's referred to, I'll go look up the original source . . . So those daily and weekly newspapers and magazines signpost me where to go.
>
> (Sadiq Khan)

A quarter of MPs also suggested that the news, in some way, contributed to setting the political agenda in Parliament for the day. News stories could become the prominent issues and talking points for MPs, journalists and other parliamentarians. For a smaller group coverage was more signifi-cant in that it 'set the context' or 'framework of interpretation' for an issue: (Angus Robertson) 'I read a range of newspapers and websites every day to try and make sure that I know what the issues of the day are . . . that hopefully sets me up for the day'; (Danny Alexander) 'I'm very interested in political commentary . . . in politics, it's very important to understand the context in which you're operating because the context shapes a lot of the way people will see what you're doing'.

Most MPs were also able to think of examples of when the weight of a media campaign had been responsible for initiating or altering new legis-lation and budgetary decisions. Legislation on casinos, alcohol licensing hours, hand guns, dangerous dogs, immigration and asylum, as well as funding decisions on hospitals, schools and rural railways were some of the issues mentioned. Several also talked about media campaigns being the main driving force behind a ministerial resignation or sacking:

> The media can, as it were, suddenly get into its collective head the idea that a particular proposal is wrong . . . you can be involved in the policy-making process, going along in what seems to you an orderly way, publish your proposal, and you can suddenly find that . . . a quiet sea on a quiet day has suddenly whipped itself up into a storm.
>
> (Paul Goodman)

> I think editors can [change political decisions] by the way in which they decide to launch a campaign and sustain it. They have to be prepared to sustain it over a long period. I think once several journalists decide that they have to run together, because they will be picked off separately, and their editors will see them as less competent, less aggressive, less successful, those people then join together. And, once they've joined together then they can have a major impact.[6]
>
> (David Blunkett)

However, the interview material, in many other ways, suggested that news media, in isolation, rarely had such an impact. There was a high degree of skepticism generally about news content in the United Kingdom. When asked about their sources of news not a single MP listed the *Sun* or *Daily Mirror* and only three mentioned the *Daily Mail*; the three most-read news-papers in the United Kingdom. Few MPs talked about the media in terms of its ideal 'fourth estate' roles. Only three believed news was an actual reflec-tion of public opinion and looked to it for that purpose. Just under half, without prompting, described political coverage as overly 'trivial' and dominated by 'personalities' and the 'dramatic'. Just over a third used terms like 'the pack' or 'the herd' to describe political journalists as a group.

Thus, acquiescence to news media did not result because MPs believed political reporting presented reasoned debate or 'the will of the people': 'Well, I don't think many of us would pay very much attention to the media as a gauge of public opinion' (Graham Brady);

> I think that the personalisation of politics has strengthened enormously . . . the media are playing a part in this, of course, because they find it easier to deal with individuals than to deal with collectivities of individuals.
>
> (Robert Maclennan)

> It disturbs me how the media tends to come to issues too late and when they do they treat them in a trivial way. The trouble is, particularly the newspapers now are providers of entertainment and opinion rather than news, and they must titillate and excite their readers rather than inform them.
>
> (Peter Luff)

Similarly, although many MPs listed news media as an important source of information for their jobs, it was not usually so regarded on specific policy matters. It was one of the least (seventh) most mentioned information sources for former government ministers. They prioritised civil servants, personal networks and interest groups well above news media. For backbench MPs it came equal fourth as an information source. For them it was constituents, interest groups and party whips and/or briefings that were more likely to be mentioned. The general impression was that, for most politicians, news media was no more than a general, background information source on policy and legislative matters.

At the same time it was clear that politicians, unlike the typical audience investigated in media effects research, had a very good knowledge of journalism, journalists and news production. Just over four-fifths of those asked had had formal media training and/or previous experience in journalism or public relations/affairs. Many interviewees spoke about the ease of guessing future headlines and slants on the way issues and announcements would be covered. Many appeared to have an extensive knowledge of individual publications and journalists: (Frank Doran) 'But most of the time, for a politician, the way the press will react is fairly predictable'; (Ann Widdecombe) 'You could work out the headline. You could write the headlines for them. You can have a real fun time writing the next day's headlines and you're nearly always right'.

In effect, if news media and journalists play a part in setting and framing political agendas in Westminster it is unlikely to be along the stimulus–response line tested in much agenda-setting research. MPs use alternative sources to inform themselves in policy matters, consume news with caution, have an insider's knowledge of news production and have regular contact with those they read. However, when asked about why they consume, and how they think about, news, further information is revealed about the part played by coverage in setting political agendas and framing policy debates.

One such alternative influence might be termed an 'anticipatory news media effect'. What is clear is that, even when MPs are critical of news media and sceptical about its ability to reflect public opinion, they are still very concerned with its output. The assumption is that reporting has some sort of impact on public opinion. It is that concern that appears to be increasingly influencing the development of policy in a number of subtle ways.

The majority, when asked about media influence, believed that coverage did contribute to public opinion of the parties and individual politicians generally. Almost as many thought MPs were themselves influenced by news. This was usually put down to MPs' general news obsessions and a concern with how constituents would respond:

> I'm not saying the media always has an effect on everything it does. I'm saying . . . if the media can affect public opinion, and politicians have to be sensitive to public opinion, then indirectly they are affected by the media.
>
> (Martin Linton)

> So I think you've got to be careful that you don't get sucked into this goldfish bowl where everything that we – the political classes and the journalists – think is important is necessarily important to most people out there . . . I think it's other MPs, it's other journalists, it's the political classes in here. And I think it does affect the mood music here in terms of the way people think.
>
> (Kevan Jones)

Former government ministers and shadow ministers explained that discussions of policy were frequently linked to the issue of how the policy would play in the media. For many, in fact, this had bordered on media 'obsession'. Almost every interviewee who had served in a cabinet or shadow cabinet since the late 1980s, talked in such terms. As a consequence, an 'anticipatory media effect' can be said to have developed as party leaders now increasingly make policy decisions with future news headlines in mind. Indeed, for many interviewees such media-oriented policy developments were often a cause of future party difficulties. For the Conservatives:

We never discussed a policy without discussing the media impact ever. Because you would be very blind if you just launched a policy and didn't work out exactly what people were likely to make of it.

(Ann Widdecombe)

John Major, on the other hand, cared deeply about what the media said and became obsessed with it . . . William [Hague] would be delivering a major speech. He would understandably want to get coverage and, therefore, he would consult his press secretary . . . and they would say we've got to have something which is newsworthy, and that meant a policy . . . the concern was always how can we get coverage. And the only way you get coverage is by saying something new. And by saying something new you were having to announce something. And that can lead to charges of opportunism – and did clearly – that you are leaping on bandwagons because that's the way to get newspaper coverage.

(John Whittingdale)

For Labour:

Actually they're [the Blair Government] obsessed by it. It's the number one priority. The number one priority [in 1998–99] was the media coverage because at all costs we had to win a second time . . . Never mind about getting reforms.

(Frank Field)

I think where the media has an impact, and where it has a huge impact, is in relation to the question, which is constantly in a minister's mind, which is 'what is the media going to say about this?' Rather than taking information provided by the media as a basis for decision-making it's more that, as you come to make those decisions, the thinking's about 'how's this going to play with media and therefore the public?' . . . It's rare but one of the sins of any government is the 'something must be done' syndrome. That desire to be seen to be doing something normally results in rather bad decisions being made.

(Chris Smith)

Such media-oriented policy-making was supported in accounts given by several political journalists: (Simon Heffer) 'we can write things every day about politicians, be rude about them, and quite often they just shrug their shoulders. But if they sense that the public are really being motivated by something then they get cross'; (George Jones) 'Previously, parties developed policy and then publicised it. But they only considered the publicity at a late stage. But now. . . . what the Labour government has done is to make communications a part of the strategy from the beginning'; (Andy McSmith)

'Politicians have to take note of how a policy will play with the media . . . The need to present policy permeates through the whole way the government does its business.'

If party leaders are extremely sensitive to news media coverage and, in addition, they have an intimate knowledge of how news is produced, it might be argued that the development of policy is inadvertently influenced by prevailing news values. Those issues and policy solutions that are likely to gain media coverage are more likely to be addressed. Those which do not are less likely.

Put all together we are left with a larger picture in which news coverage, or rather anticipation of news coverage, has a shaping effect on the overall policy agenda. Issue saliency is, in part, influenced by anticipation of news media coverage and, therefore, by longer-term news values. As such there appears some evidence in the interview material to support the 'mediated politics' thesis (Hallin, 1994; Bennett, 1997; Franklin, 1997; Delli Carpini and Williams, 2001; Underwood, 2001; Altheide, 2004; Entman, 2005). Although, once again, the evidence could also suggest that politicians may be more prone to keeping certain agendas and discussions within the private policy sphere.

## News and reporters as political process catalysts

The interview material also suggested that news consumption and interaction with journalists had other subtle influences on issue agendas and policy deliberations. Both were used by politicians to get a sense of processes within Parliament and, also, a feeling for what colleagues and opposition MPs themselves thought.

Interviewees were asked why they consumed news media and what kinds of information they were looking for beyond being informed of breaking news. The most common response given, by just over half of MPs, was that they were interested in particular columnists or editorial comment sections. Interviewees explained that they were looking for 'commentary' and/or 'analysis' of issues and events beyond just the reporting of facts: (Tony Wright) 'I would make a point of reading all the commentary columns. News comes from so many sources now . . . and I'm much more interested in hearing what people are saying about something than just reading to know what'. It was also apparent that certain lobby correspondents were taken more notice of and played a more formative role in directing opinion among both journalists and politicians. A number of different commentators and correspondents were named by several MPs without prompting (David Arronovitch, Colin Brown, Matthew D'Ancona, Simon Heffer, George Jones, Trevor Kavanagh, Polly Toynbee and Michael White). Because so many politicians read these columnists or lobby journalists it was assumed that they had a more significant impact on opinion within Parliament itself:

> You have two categories of journalists, some who are influential, others who aren't . . . But there are some journalists that politicians will read regularly and often be influenced by. You know, Peter Riddle in *The Times* or David Arronovich, he's in *The Times* now interestingly, Polly Toynbee, Martin Kettle in the *Guardian*.
>
> (Martin Linton)

> Matthew D'Ancona is useful because he tends to have good sources. So if he's writing something about the Labour Party, he's quite good on it actually, one of the better Conservative columnists at knowing his way around the Labour Party . . . Simon Heffer is always worth reading because if you read Simon Heffer you understand the thinking of what I would call the sort of Conservative majority that exists.
>
> (Iain Duncan Smith)

A quarter of MPs also stated that news was a way of gauging what others, either in one's own party or in rival parties, were thinking on issues. Some also recounted that they often attempted to work out who the political sources of stories were and why they were sourcing the story. In effect, news media aided MPs in their attempts to interpret 'feelings' or trends in opinion within the parties themselves:

> I read the *Daily Mail* to see what my political opponents are thinking and doing, and, to see what the right wing media are saying about us. I don't read it for news . . . if most politicians are honest, if they're speaking to a journalist in a quality newspaper, then they're probably speaking as much to their own MPs and party members as to the public.
>
> (Wayne David)

> I get a lot of my news about what's going on in the Labour Party from the media . . . I'm very interested to know what happened with the PLP and how Blair's speech went down, and what it is that the rebels on the Education Bill are prepared to accept to stop rebelling . . . [that's] how the other political parties would get their information about what was going on. From the newspapers, not exclusively, but in a very large part.
>
> (Julia Kirkbride)

The role of commentary and columnists, as a part of the calculative process of politicians, was also mentioned by some of the journalists:

> Once a policy is out in public and being debated, a paper will write

commentaries on it . . . And there's no doubt that one key issue in Blair's mind, when deciding a new policy, will be the media climate.

(Andrew Grice)

The changes that were made on tuition fees, the changes that were made on trust schools, weren't only shaped by a very sort of feverish debate within Parliament. It was also shaped by the way the leader writers discussed all these subjects. I mean I think it's not necessarily the news stories as much as the way the leader writers of various papers, *The Times*, the *Telegraph*, *The FT*, the *Guardian*, the *Independent*. I would say they all had a huge impact on the shape of legislation.

(Philip Webster)

A similar catalyst/process role for individual reporters was also picked up in the interview material. In the classic literature on media–source relations (Sigal, 1973; Gans, 1980; Tiffen, 1989; Schlesinger and Tumber, 1994; Hess, 2000), there is regular contact between politicians and journalists. The relationship between the two, like that between journalists and public relations advisors (see Chapter 4), is a multi-faceted one. It is a relationship where both sides need each other. Journalists need political information and comment, and politicians need publicity and to promote their policies. But it is also presented as a relationship of tensions that can be extremely damaging to individual careers. However, what also became clear during the interviews was that politicians were not just seeking publicity when talking to journalists. These discussions were themselves part of the political process.

MPs interviewed did, indeed, have a very high level of contact with political journalists and so were well acquainted with the authors of the news they were consuming. Without exception MPs had regular contact with the local and/or regional journalists who covered their electoral constituency. All (shadow) ministers and a slim majority of back-bench MPs talked to national journalists on a regular basis. In all, just over two-thirds talked to journalists, on average, at least once a day, and usually several times a day. At busy periods some said they could have between 10 and 20 conversations with journalists in a single day. The other third talked to journalists once or several times a week. None spoke to journalists less often than this.

Maintaining good relations and gaining publicity were key objectives for the MPs. When asked why they talked to journalists the most common response was that they needed to maintain good relations. There seemed an almost institutionalised relationship on the local level between MPs and their local or regional media. In many cases MPs either wrote for their local papers or virtually constructed the reports that appeared in their local press:

We maintain good relations with our local journalists, newspapers, television station, radio stations . . . You've got to keep them on side. You've got to feed them with stories. You've got to show them you're alive, intermittently alive.

(Austin Mitchell)

You get to know all the local journalists and, of course, you know quite a lot of them before you even get elected . . . Always treat them with a certain amount of caution, be careful about what you say. But, equally, it can be a productive relationship. They're looking for stories and copy. They can help to highlight causes that you're wanting to campaign on and you can help them write their newspaper.

(Jo Swinson)

Just as back-bench MPs talked to local journalists as part of their job so government ministers did the same with national lobby journalists. Every government and shadow minister regarded political reporters at Westminster in much the same way. For all it was essential to talk to key journalists to explain the details of new policy and legislation:

When you're in shadow cabinet, yes, of course, you maintain good working relations with a range of journalists. And you try and help them with their enquiries. You try and offer them good stories.

(John Redwood)

At the end of the day, you know, you want to be able to feed them with your information. You want them to be able to write stories with your information so you want to make contact with them. They're always looking for good stories because, at the end of the day, a journalist himself or herself is judged by what they produce in the main paper . . . it's in their interests also to be alongside you and hope that you will give exclusive rights or feed them stories.

(Iain Duncan Smith)

At the same time, a majority of MPs, regardless of party or position, also appeared to have established relations with national journalists that went beyond the merely functional. Many used terms like 'friend' or 'colleague' and would meet for social as well as professional reasons. Others referred to relationships as part of 'alliances' or 'coalitions'. In all these cases it seemed clear that journalists were very much part of the policy networks that evolved within parliament: 'I would say there's about six or seven journalists that I know and speak to once a fortnight, and feel quite chummy and chatty with' (Chris Bryant);

In any place of work it's best to have reasonably friendly relations with your working colleagues, and they [journalists] are in a sense some of our working colleagues. And I get on with a number of people, some of which work for sympathetic bits of the media, and some of them don't.

(Frank Dobson)

For some MPs, these exchanges with journalists were also a means of gaining more knowledge about what was happening in Parliament. They were a further way of gauging opinion on developments taking place within one's own party or in a rival party. Journalists moved between groups or individuals and carried bits of conversation or opinion with them:

They may well have got wind of a particular emerging story and they ring in order to get a comment . . . And if you know them and trust them then that can be a very fertile process.

(Nick Raynsford)

I would, of course, also be trying to find out from them [journalists], from time to time, in so far as I can, what else is going on in the wider conversation. What Government ministers are saying in policy areas, or political areas I'm interested in . . . dealing with journalists is perhaps not unanalogous to one of these novels about information-gathering in the Cold War. I mean they're trying to find pieces of information from MPs and MPs are trying to find pieces of information from them.

(Paul Goodman)

Several journalists also stated that MPs and ministers actually came to them to try and get their opinions and advice on a range of policy issues and processes:

I mean very few policies, quite rightly, come totally out of the blue . . . people are very keen to talk [to me] about policy when they're sitting there all day wondering how to make their particular department work better.

(Polly Toynbee)

People in the last Conservative administration did so [consulted me] all the time . . . I had friends who were well known to be sympathetic to the Labour party, who were often consulted by Conservative ministers.

(Simon Heffer)

I've had Leaders of the Liberal Democrats asking me what should they ask at PMQs. I've had Conservatives asking me what are the points of vulnerability at the moment in the government. And I've had Labour Ministers asking me what do I think the Tories are going to do over X, Y and Z. And they all do the same, you know, they all want a little bit of your inside info.

(Colin Brown)

These alternative forms of news information suggest that news consumption and engagements with journalists are also relevant as a means of evaluating and relating to the political processes within Westminster itself. MPs read news with a view to asking: how do key columnists and correspondents, who mix with MPs on a daily basis, assess political issues and legislation? What will be the likely talking points around Parliament on any given day, possibly for days to come? What are other MPs saying and thinking and what are the 'moods' within the parties? This seemed to be particularly the case with back-bench MPs who found themselves further removed from decision-making at the top ends of party hierarchies. It might also be suggested that these forms of information and exchange are a key means by which issue agendas and opinions may be agreed upon within the parliamentary political sphere. In Philip Webster's account:

Legislation does get changed a hell of a lot as it goes through Parliament and a lot of that is due to the debate that is sparked off within the press and within Parliament. I think the two go together. I think MPs often take their lead from a [(n) editorial] leader, for example, and sometimes it's the other way round. Sometimes the press might well pick up and say 'these guys have got it right. There should be a change, this is where the government could make a change to legislation'. Sometimes the government might be doing something quite unpopular with Labour back benchers . . . and yet the press, if you like, the Blairite press . . . are pressing him to go further and that has a balancing effect on the debate as it comes out. In the end there is a bit of a compromise.

In many ways the findings among Westminster politicians are similar to those of earlier studies of issue agenda construction in the United States (Cook *et al.*, 1983; Protess *et al.*, 1991; Baumgartner and Jones, 1993; see also Schorr, 1997). Politicians and journalists do have uneasy relations with each other that revolve around an exchange of political information for news coverage. However, the relationships between the two are more multi-faceted than that. Politicians use news and their interactions with journalists to get other sorts of information that are relevant to the political process on a day-to-day level. The two also combine, sometimes consciously in alliances, and sometimes by playing off each other, to influence political agendas and the search for policy solutions.

## Conclusion

As argued here, increased media attention, alone, is unlikely to result in pushing an issue near the top of the parliamentary agenda. At any one time there are multiple issues competing for political attention. Politicians have a lot of alternative sources of information on policy matters that they regard as more authoritative or significant. They are also extremely knowledgeable about the process of news production, are sceptical of media content and have personal contact with the reporters and politicians who construct the news.

What matters more is that a critical mass of MPs, or smaller group of party leaders, come to believe that an issue needs addressing more substantially and, collectively, identify policy solutions. For that, intense and sustained attention and communication among parliamentarians needs to take place. For Hilgartner and Bosk (1988) a process of feedback and amplification is needed. Wolfsfeld (2001) describes this as 'wave amplification' and Edwards and Wood (1999) a 'loop effect'. Widespread and sustained media attention on an issue or individual can sometimes achieve this although, as argued here, not according to a simple stimulus–response model.

More likely, is that this attention is sourced and sustained by MPs themselves, usually in some form of regular exchange or occasional alliance with specific journalists. As also argued here, news media consumption and daily exchanges with journalists can play a less obvious but equally vital role. It contributes to politicians keeping an eye on evolving processes, moods and consensuses on issues among politicians themselves. In effect, news media and political journalists can fulfil a necessary social and cultural function whereby they become one possible means of reaching agreements on issue agendas and policy solution options.

# Chapter 7

# New and alternative media

## The Internet and the parliamentary public sphere

## Introduction

This chapter discusses the part played by new information and communication technologies (ICTs) in social and political processes. In particular it assesses the Internet's potential for restoring the public sphere and tackling the 'crisis of public communications' (Blumler and Gurevitch, 1995). It does so by questioning the conventional research perspective and grounds for evaluation applied in many recent studies. Much work in this area identifies a state of political crisis, caused by the disconnection of ordinary people from institutional politics, and then presents the Internet's new communicative capacities as a potential solution. However, as argued here, this approach has certain drawbacks. It is conceived within a technologically determinist framework. It evaluates the Internet as a force for greater, direct democracy rather than as a means of enhancing representative democracy. Lastly, it conceives, and evaluates, the public sphere according to Habermas's (1989 [1962]) idealised eighteenth-century model, rather than engaging with contemporary politics and communication.

The case material presented here, collected at Westminster, has several alternative conceptual starting points. It takes a 'social shaping' rather than technologically determinist approach. Representative, rather than direct, democracy provides the basis for evaluation. Lastly, Parliament itself is regarded and observed as a public sphere. The findings offer more evidence to support those disappointed about the slow adoption of Internet communication forms to encourage greater politician–citizen exchange. However, as the interview material also reveals, lack of dialogue between MPs and their constituents is not the most likely cause of public alienation from institutional politics. At the same time, as the latter part of the chapter argues, the Internet has managed to enhance the parliamentary public sphere, and its external links, in less obvious ways. New media, used in old ways, has brought additional benefits. The Internet has also aided the ability of parliamentarians to research, organise, deliberate, scrutinise and question government. Using a different accounting system, it might thus be argued that the parliamentary public sphere has been a little more enhanced by the Internet's introduction than might otherwise be concluded.

## The Internet and the rejuvenation of the political public sphere?

A clear thesis has developed regarding the potential of the Internet to restore the health of the public sphere and, with it, faith in British politics. The argument is traced through several steps (Coleman, 2004, 2005b; Coleman and Ward, 2005; Ward et al., 2005; Ferguson, 2006; Lusoli et al., 2006). First, a crisis in the formal political process has emerged. Voting levels and political party memberships have declined significantly. Trust in politicians and government is now extremely low. Thus, institutional politics in Britain, like many other established democracies, is suffering a crisis. The level of crisis and its causes have generated widespread debate,[1] but the key cause identified in this case is the widespread alienation of citizens from parliamentary politics. Citizens are neither cynical about democracy per se nor any less interested in political issues (see Norris, 2002; Hansard, 2004). Rather, they feel disconnected and disengaged from seemingly remote politicians and political institutions.

Like many initial, enthusiastic accounts of the Internet (Negroponte, 1995; Pavlik, 1996; Kahin and Wilson, 1997), new media is juxtaposed with conventional, 'old mass media', and is presented as one potential solution to the issue of public engagement. In the wider comparisons of new and old, old media offers one-to-many forms of communication, is expensive, limited in number, and restricts access to a small number of largely elite sources. The Internet, by comparison, is cheap, easily accessible, offers infinite channels, overcomes barriers of time and space, and is not source restrictive. The potential to fulfil a range of individual needs, such as the reengagement of citizens with their political representatives, is thus clear.

The thesis is given greater theoretical grounding and evaluative capacity, by some (Coleman and Gotze, 2001; Coleman, 2005a), through an adherence to thinking on deliberative democracy and the core ideals of the public sphere (Habermas, 1987, 1989; Bohman, 1996; Dryzek, 2000). Thus a future 'Civic commons in cyberspace', with 'citizen juries', 'citizen panels' and 'E-deliberation' is mapped out. The linking of public sphere theory, deliberative democracy and the Internet has been widely explored in a number of other settings (Dahlberg, 2001; Dahlgren, 2001, 2005; Sparks, 2001; Cammaerts and Audenhove, 2005; Polat, 2005; Wikland, 2005). Each of these studies identifies key components of, and requirements for, the operation of E-democracy. These include: inclusiveness of citizens, open agendas, pluralist balance, rational debate and information presentation, safeguards against over-influence by the state and other powerful actors, and reciprocity.

However, in most cases, where actual research is conducted, the outcome is disappointing. It is the 'usual suspects', those already politically engaged, who make most use of the Internet for further interaction. Significantly, there are clear correlations between higher levels of income and education, new media use and political engagement (see Bonfadelli, 2002; Lusoli *et al.*, 2006). Politicians are more interested in using new media in old ways. So, for example, websites are used to broadcast to the many rather than for two-way exchanges (Gulati, 2004; Jackson and Lilleker, 2004). Online delibera-tion appears costly, poses moderation problems and struggles to attract substantial numbers (Dahlberg, 2001; Dahlgren, 2005; Polat, 2005; Wikland, 2005). The consequence is a series of fragmented and exclusive cyber communities that are dominated by the already engaged and powerful. Thus, there seems substantial evidence to support the claims of cyber-pessimists (Schiller, 1996; Herman and McChesney, 1997; Golding and Murdock, 2000). They argue that new media is just as likely to exacerbate existing socio-economic divides and be used to further concentrate economic and political power.

For many of those focusing on British politics the blame lies most obvi-ously with those same politicians and political institutions which have alien-ated the public. They need to rapidly adopt the necessary hardware, software and political will to make proper use of the Internet's potential.

However, there are some significant, conceptual assumptions underpin-ning the thesis. The first of these is that the political crisis problem and its solutions are conceived within a technologically determinist framework. This puts too much emphasis on technology as a primary, almost revolu-tionary, driver of social change (see objections of Winston, 1998; Lievrouw and Livingstone, 2006; Webster, 2006).[2] Thus, there appears a need to locate 'killer applications' that both differentiate new ICTs from older, mass media forms and direct some form of social advancement. Inevitably, new media, if used in old, mass ways, is discounted. The need to focus on many-to-many and interactive features of new media, as both different from and an advance on old, mass media, are assumed much of the time. Comparisons with traditional cheap, one-to-one forms of communication, such as tele-phones and letters, are ignored entirely. Each of these complaints can be also be applied to much contemporary work on new media.

This is not to argue against technology playing a part in social and polit-ical change. Rather, as recent, strong currents of research on new media and science and technology studies (STS) stress (see MacKenzie and Wajcman, 1999; Lievrouw, 2004; Livingstone, 2005; Lievrouw and Livingstone, 2006: 4) 'recombinant' and 'social shaping' approaches are key. In these, ICTs are 'more of a mutual shaping process in which technological development and social practices are co-determining'. In this case, research approaches that investigate how media is adopted by, and mediates, MPs' existing practices are needed. This means looking at existing political processes and actors and how new media is being adopted and/or mediating activities in the political sphere.

Second, there is an assumption that direct democracy is a clear, and achievable, advance on representative democracy. Failing that, citizens desire maximum access to, and engagement with, their political representatives. However, the ideal principle of direct democracy has never existed outside small, usually exclusive and exclusionary, collectives; a description which applies to both the ancient Athenian polis and eighteenth-century bourgeois public sphere (see, for example, Behabib, 1992; Fraser, 1992). The failings of democracies, as critics and advocates have noted, are not simply reducible to a failure to obtain direct democracy (Miliband, 1969; Habermas, 1977; Offe, 1984; Dahl, 1989; Hirst and Thompson, 1999). Perhaps the issue is not to advocate using new media to achieve an alternative, 'idealised' political system but, instead, to ask how might new media improve the operation of representative democracies? For twentieth-century advocates of representative democracy, or 'deformed polyarchies' (Dahl and Lindblom, 1953; Lindblom, 1977; Dahl, 1989), ensuring parliamentarians are representative of 'the people' is only one concern of many. Other concerns include: the establishment of checks and balances on the executive through the judiciary and the multiple parts of the legislature; the dispersal of state power; and the best conditions in which multiple and competing interests in society can make representations to government. With these other concerns in mind, 'perhaps', as Livingstone suggests (2005: 18) 'we should ask not whether the internet can reinvigorate participation among the many but whether it provides an effective tool for those already committed to participation'.

Third, there is an assumption, implicit in the UK literature, that the public sphere still exists in the communicative space between all political institutions, on the one hand, and private citizens on the other. Thus, the state is one, monolithic force, there is no established and relatively autonomous civil society and media ('mass' and 'new') provides the public sphere space between private individuals and state. However, as Habermas fully concedes in his later work (1996) not much of this is really applicable to contemporary liberal democracies. Therefore, such a conception of media and communication is also outdated (see also Calhoun, 1992; Thompson, 1995). Indeed, for many looking at communication and politics, there exist multiple, linked public spheres (Behabib, 1992; Curran, 2000) or 'sphericules' (Gitlin, 1998). For Habermas the emphasis is less on private individuals, public deliberation and government. Instead it is more on a civil society made up of organisations and interest groups which feed public opinion into the increasingly formalised institutions of government which produce law. 'Communicative power' mobilises public opinion, through interest groups, to influence the processes and participants which enact law.

In these terms, Parliament itself now passes for what might be viewed as a contemporary political public sphere. In fact, it comes rather closer in operation to Habermas's earlier stated ideals (1989) than his eighteenth-century bourgeois template. Opposition MPs, governing party back benchers and peers in the upper chamber may all scrutinise, critique, attempt to amend or oppose government legislation. They do so in the chambers and via a plethora of formal and informal committees and groups supported by extensive clerical and research services.[3] If this claim is accepted, citizen-representative communication is only one part of the political process that may be enhanced by ICTs. Another is the communicative relations that exist between an array of interest groups and the political centre. A third is the parliamentary public sphere itself where public opinion, having been fed into representatives, is then deliberated on during the legislative process. Thus, there is a need to evaluate such things as inclusiveness, pluralist balance, rational debate, safeguards against government influence and reciprocity among the participants and institutions operating within Westminster itself. How then might the Internet enhance or undermine the components and participants of this Westminster public sphere?

The research presented here focused on these first and third communicative processes and how they might be enhanced by the Internet. It began with three alternative starting assumptions to those outlined above. First, Westminster and the actors, practices and institutions contained within, was itself assumed to operate as a political public sphere. Public sphere ideals were evaluated on that basis. Second, it was not judged as a potential facilitator of direct democracy but as an institution of representative democracy. Third, the focus was not on technologically engineered change and potential but, instead, on parliamentary actors and processes and their increasing use of new media in everyday activities. The study, therefore, took a more actor-centred and 'social shaping' approach. It is based on 52 semi-structured interviews with 40 Members of Parliament, six former MPs who were now in the House of Lords, and six officials involved in the administration of media and communication within Parliament. Where possible (in 35 cases) interviewees were also asked their responses to a set of structured questions regarding their use of the Internet and email.

## Evaluating E-exchange and deliberation between MPs and citizens

The Internet offers several new means by which citizens can potentially contact MPs, register their opinions and enter into dialogue. Three obvious forms are email, interactive web logs ('blogs') and E-consultations.

Email has been the simplest and most widely adopted form among politicians. As Table 7.1 shows the use of email has grown consistently. Internal email traffic has almost quadrupled since 2000 to an average of 1.43 million per month. External email traffic, to and from Parliament, has increased

*Table 7.1* Average monthly internal and external email traffic for House of
Commons 2000–06

| | Ja–Jn 2000 | Jl–D 2000 | Ja–Jn 2001 | Jl–D 2001 | Ja–Jn 2002 | Jl–D 2002 | Ja–Jn 2003 | Jl–D* 2003 | Ja–Jn 2005 | Jl–D 2005 | Ja–Jn 2006 |
|---|---|---|---|---|---|---|---|---|---|---|---|
| Av. Internal | 358 | 314 | 366 | 423 | 631 | 640 | 835 | 1,002 | 1,244 | 1,318 | 1,428 |
| Av. External | 378 | 508 | 522 | 606 | 844 | 923 | 1,371 | 1,652 | 1,420 | 1,653 | 2,037 |

Source: PICT (Parliamentary ICT) Unit, 2006.

Notes
Figures in thousands.
*Figures for 2004 missing.

more than fivefold to an average of 2.04 million per month. By 2006, more
than nine out of ten MPs interviewed used email. A few send or receive only
a handful each day (many more are dealt with by assistants). Three-fifths
received and 'took note of' more than 50 'serious' (non-spam and person-
specific) emails a day, with five reading over 100 each day. The majority of
users, four out of every seven, sent less than 20 each day, with two MPs
sending more than 100 per day. Taking out the extremes the average MP
questioned received 65 'serious' and sent 25 emails per day.

In terms of constituency exchanges, MP email addresses have been made
publicly available, going from 50, in 1996, to 412 (almost two-thirds of
MPs) by mid 2002 (Jackson, 2003: 7). Asked in more detail about who they
exchanged email with, just over two-fifths of the MPs stated they emailed
constituents as much, if not more than, other types of correspondent (staff,
other MPs, interest groups, etc.). Among the interviewees there were some
strong advocates for use of E-exchanges with constituents:

> We're pretty E-literate. Because we're a sparse community we took to
> email. I get a tremendous amount of emails now from constituents
> which range from, you know, the passionate argument to a case of 'just
> saw you on Question Time. Well done. You said what I was thinking.'
> (John Thurso)

> I use the Internet all the time for receiving emails from constituents or
> replying to constituents. I live in a very high tech constituency and they
> expect to use the Internet to communicate with me . . . I get about 300
> emails a day . . . I would respond to all the ones that needed responding
> to, so three figures of emails each day I send out.
> (John Redwood)

Websites for individual MPs are also now the norm. By the end of 2004 76
per cent of MPs had individual websites (Lusoli *et al.*, 2006). During the
research period, in 2006, more than nine out of ten MPs had one. There also

seemed to be a slow but steady move towards making greater use of more proactive and interactive website features. During the 2005 UK General Election 65 parliamentary candidates used web logs. In 2006, just over one in ten of those interviewed produced a web log on their website and/or encouraged E-responses in some form from constituents. Derek Wyatt MP, the *New Statesman* 'elected representative', new media award winner of 2006, explained:

> We currently have, this week, 66,000 hits on my website. First time we've gone over 10,000 on a particular page. Christmas we were averaging about 6,500, March and April it went up to 8,500. This week it's gone over 10,000 . . . It's clear that they like large questions, debating. And we send out a weekly blog.

The use of websites for E-consultations was also something being experimented with by individual MPs and, more systematically, by parliamentary select and all-party committees (see HoC, July 2002, June 2004). The Hansard Society has worked closely with Parliament since 1999 (see Ferguson, 2006). They operated eight pilot schemes, between 1999 and 2003, and a further five, using an established template, in 2004. As assessment of these latter consultations concluded that they had been fairly successful in their key aim of expanding public participation. Between 75 and 100 per cent of participants had not given evidence to a parliamentary committee before and 72 per cent said the consultation had been personally stimulating and 'worthwhile'. A small group of interviewees expressed some faith in the potential for such E-consultations to be expanded.

However, the general picture is one in which, although a majority of MPs may have adopted Internet technology in their everyday activities, it is a minority which wants to use it for greater dialogue with constituents. Jackson's survey of MPs (2003: 20) concluded that, with a few exceptions, email had not been used to increase exchanges with constituents. Although MP email addresses had become increasingly publicly available, 86.6 per cent received less than 100 emails per week from constituents and less than 10 per cent used email for any large-scale, proactive communication with them. Things did not appear to have changed much in 2006. While just over two-fifths said they emailed constituents as much, if not more than, any other group, two-fifths said they never emailed constituents and the remainder did so only on a limited basis. If one identifies MP interviewees who both email a lot and regularly email constituents, just less than one out of five MPs is likely to have extensive E-exchanges with constituents (i.e., send more than 20 emails a day and email constituents). Only three of all the MPs interviewed appeared to use email more than traditional communication forms (letter, phone, face-to-face) to engage with their constituents. This is in line with an internal survey of MPs (HoC, June 2004: 48–54), which found that they preferred to inform constituents about parliamentary business via traditional means, such as letters, newsletters and annual reports.

In fact, for each MP who was a constituency email enthusiast, there were several more who voiced strong concerns about it. The strongest objection related to resource constraints:

> You get emails . . . click, click, click and just delete, delete because you just physically can't deal with them and, actually, even though you've got staff, you know, they can't either.
>
> (Kevan Jones)

> It's just a disaster, we can hardly cope with the volume of emails coming on top of postal correspondence . . . There is no rationing on email correspondence and it's growing at an alarming rate . . . We could of course encourage even more email and electronic communication but, to cope with it, we would have to employ staff to respond on our behalf, perversely making us more remote from our correspondents, while appearing to be more responsive.
>
> (Peter Luff)

Many also regarded a large proportion of email, because of its ease and simplicity, to be trivial and unconsidered next to much conventional correspondence. Several noted the fact that a significant proportion of their constituents, often the ones in most need, did not use email (see also Lusoli *et al.*, 2006 on this):

> It's [email] becoming an absolute nightmare to keep up with . . . It's just too easy, and so you will see the same constituents emailing you again and again and again, sometimes repeatedly on the same subject, and sometimes on a variety of subjects . . . I honestly do not know what the answer is. You can't say to people you must not write to me, but when you get 10 or 20 emails in a month from the same person the incentive to reply becomes less and less. I am really not sure that many people appreciate the workload in many MP's offices.
>
> (Neil Gerrard)

> You're only getting a subset, and I worry that if you switch over entirely to email correspondence, you're actually favouring constituents who are not among the most deprived. Mobile phone is the way in which the most disadvantaged tend to contact you because they can't afford the landline.
>
> (Phyllis Starkey)

E-deliberation is avoided rather more. Forms of E-dialogue, from interactive web logs to formal E-consultations, were clearly associated with a small minority of MPs and parliamentary committees. Jackson and Lilleker's analysis of MP websites (2004) found that only 7.1 per cent provided opinion polls, 4.3 per cent surveys and 1.6 per cent used online discussion forums. They concluded that it was only 'a few pioneers' who had really adopted online deliberation and that 'the vast bulk' of such communication was 'asymmetrical.' The research in 2006 suggested some advancement on these figures but nothing significant. Just over one in five had ever engaged in an E-consultation exercise but less than one in ten had done so more than once. In most cases the idea did not generate great interest or a positive response.

Once again, there were some very clear practical objections voiced by the majority of MPs on the issue. Lack of consultation visibility, time and resource pressures, and the digital divide, were all put forward as reasons:

> It's been a sad disappointment. I think all of those people who had blog sites or websites right from the start, and that includes me, have been disappointed by the lack of interest, lack of reaction and lack of replies.
>
> (Austin Mitchell)

> I have consulted. I have listened too. I have given people the chance to get in touch about stuff. I'm yet to be convinced that it is effective at that level . . . Are people seriously suggesting that putting up a website that nobody knows about in cyberspace, with millions of other websites, is a substitute for real and meaningful consultation? I hope not.
>
> (Angus Robertson)

> I'm rather wary of it. We are so time poor and at the mercy of everybody else . . . we're in instant communication. Whether all of that leads to a more participative democracy I think is open for question, because I'm not sure we have a participative democracy. I think we have a representative one.
>
> (John Thurso)

Among the interviewees, there were seven current chairs of select committees in the House of Commons (nearly one in four of the total). Only one of these had engaged in any form of E-consultation and then only once. As he explained, in relation to the notion of E-consultations widening participation:

> The danger I think here is of giving privileged access to those who [already] have access . . . there's still a digital divide . . . So there are E-consultations being toyed with by select committees but you've got to be a bit careful because it can become a self-selecting group at present.
>
> (Peter Luff)

> That actually is in itself a limiting thing. It means you're only dealing with those people who have access to computers and, although it may come as a surprise to you, there are still a section of the community who do not have routine access to laptops.
>
> (Gwyneth Dunwoody)

The issue of costs over benefits was also noted by those who had observed at first hand these initial E-consultations. In Hansard's review (Ferguson, 2006) it was clear that an extensive range of marketing and advertising inputs had been needed to gain a relatively small number of new, registered users. Such efforts, at present, would be hard to justify on a much larger scale. Significantly, the influence of such consultation inputs on select committees also appears marginal. As Coleman, who interviewed some of the officials involved, noted (in Ferguson, 2006: 13): 'Generally speaking, the view was that these particular online consultations had very limited impact.' Three parliamentary officials interviewed, who were involved in such exercises, thought that they had had positive benefits. In the main these were for those members of the public who participated and in terms of widening the consultation process, or at least being seen to do so. However, doubts were expressed about the costs (time, effort, finance) involved and the impacts on the consultation process generally:

> I don't want to sound negative, but . . . What is not yet clear is how much substance, either material or of involvement, they bring to an enquiry. Because they cost quite a lot in staff time and setting up, and so to that extent the jury is out . . . I think the view here is it's not going to change the world, you know, you aren't suddenly going to have thousands of people dialling into every enquiry to give their views. I think there are lots of different ways we can engage . . . more effectively than E-consultation.
>
> (anonymous official)

However, it also became clear during the research that an unwillingness to use email and E-consultations did not mean that MPs were not in regular exchange and dialogue with their constituents. In fact, the evidence suggests that only a small percentage of citizens want to use the Internet to engage with politics and politicians. During the most recent UK General Election, television and newspapers were still the main sources of information for voters. Only 3.3 per cent of the population used the Internet as their main source of information. Most of these consulted news websites, with only 3 per cent looking at political party sites (all figures in Lusoli and Ward, 2005). Ward et al. (2005) found that, despite increasing levels of Internet use generally, only 2 per cent had visited their local MP's website and only 5 per cent had visited the parliamentary website in the last 12 months.

Of those members of the public that did contact their MP, 48 per cent did so by phone, 20 per cent by letter, 11 per cent in person and 12 per cent by email.

Extensive consultation and dialogue does, in fact, take place through other communication media. It certainly seemed very clear from interviews that the vast majority of MPs were in regular contact with their constituents and regarded their opinions highly. When asked about the information sources back-bench MPs consulted most, on policy and legislative matters, the source most often mentioned was 'constituents'. When asked how they 'gauged public opinion' back-bench MPs usually gave a series of answers that equated to engaging with constituents in person or via traditional communication forms such as phone or letter. Interestingly, surveys of the public tend to indicate that contact with politicians has actually increased in recent decades.[4] Although politicians as a class draw little respect, individuals who have had exchanges with their MP more often offer very positive feedback (see Healey *et al.*, 2005).

Clearly, email, as a form of MP–constituent communication, is increasing every year. A small minority of MPs are also embracing the interactive opportunities made possible by the Internet, as a means to engage more fully with their constituents. However, the general majority still prefer traditional forms of communication and very few can see the positive merits of using E-consultation. In most cases this is for very good reasons related to the same practical considerations associated with representative democracies. These include cost and time constraints, public visibility and digital inequalities in society. The majority of ordinary constituents also prefer traditional forms of dialogue and exchange. That extensive exchange and consultation already takes place, and is likely to be going up rather than down, is similarly apparent. Thus, the continuing call for more email exchanges and dialogue, as a means to re-connect citizens with politicians, appears to be more of a technologically determinist 'ideal' than a public demand. A lack of citizen contact with MPs is, therefore, unlikely to be a major reason for perceived alienation of the public from institutional politics.

## An alternative assessment of new media and politics: representative democracy and the parliamentary public sphere

Just as the traditional line of evaluation tends to ignore more mundane forms of communication (phone, mail) in making assessments so, also, there is a tendency to ignore new media used in old ways. Neither does it consider the notion that politicians' use of new media, in their everyday activities, may also enhance certain democratic processes and ideals. As argued here, evaluations of new media and politics should, in addition, be applied to the existing structures of representative democracy. An attempt should be made to evaluate the parliamentary public sphere itself. Observing political use of new media on these grounds offers some useful insights.

First, new media, used in old ways, has benefited the institutional structures of representative democracy at Westminster. It became clear, through a number of internal reviews and enquiries, that Parliament, as an institution, had been generally slow to modernise and invest in ICT use for MPs. It also became clear that Parliament did little to publicise its activities and had little public identity (see HoC, July, 2002, 2004, June, 2004, July 2006; Hansard, 2005; HoL, July 2005, February 2006). Significantly, the public assumed that the government and Parliament were one and the same. For those linked to these committees this issue needed to be urgently addressed:

> This was actually from the Modernisation Select Committee . . . And I thought that lack of connection, that lack of explanation in a parliamentary democracy, was scandalous really, you know. Here we are trying to explain what's happening at the heart of government without any explanation of what is the basic bit of the unwritten British constitution – it's all dependent on Parliament . . . I decided it was time to try and show to people where the entry points were into the legislative process.
>
> (Paul Tyler)

New ICT investment has, accordingly, been focused in two areas: greater investment in ICTs to improve the work of all MPs in Parliament and investment in and development of the parliamentary website. In terms of the website, as the Annual Report (HoC, July 2005: 37) concluded: 'This again demonstrated the extent to which, for many members of the public, the website is the preferred medium for accessing information about the House'. As the most recent business plan noted (HoC December, 2005: 20): 'Our public communications should be focused on the needs and interests of users rather than producers'. To this end there has been extensive development of the website to make it a useful information source for citizens of all kinds.

Since 2003, select committee reports have been published on the web. Commitments were also made to eventually digitalise, and make available, all copies of the Hansard Official Report since 1803 (as of late 2006 they go back to 1988) and all current debates within four hours. Webcasting of all public activities has been initiated. Since October 2004 broadcast coverage of the main chamber has been supplemented by an expanded service which streams further debates in the Commons, Lords and many select and standing committees. Up to 15 meetings at a time were webcast simultaneously in 2005–06. In all, 102 hours of visual webcasts and 45 hours of audio webcasts are provided on the website each week. In 2005–06 average monthly visitor numbers to this part of the website grew to 82,000 (HoC,

July 2006). Similarly, the output of the Parliamentary Research Services has also been made accessible on the website. Research papers and downloads have rapidly increased (see Table 7.2 below). From October 2004 the House of Lords also adopted this strategy to promote its activities and engage more with the public (HoL, July 2005, February 2006). Hits on the House of Lords website have gone up from 775,752 (in 1997) to 12,768,465 (in 2005) (HoL, March 2006).

For those involved in this project the new developments were very positive and reached out to a wide range of actors in civil society, including journalists, interest groups and ordinary citizens. It was not perceived simply as another form of one-to-many, mass-media style output but, rather, as a means of enabling those outside to better observe and potentially intervene in daily parliamentary business:

> Well all our [select] committee work goes onto the net, and the evidence goes onto the net, and as we've gone on, we've used it more and more as a committee.
>
> (Gwyneth Dunwoody)

> It [the website] is essential to distribute to the world information about the House of Lords and what we're doing and how we're doing it, and what our role is in the constitution of our country.
>
> (Kenneth Baker)

> Increasingly, we're putting more of the material onto the web, because the public's interested, journalists are interested, lots of Members are, and their staff or people in their constituency . . . I ought to stress the web as a medium for getting Parliament to the public has suddenly become a very big issue . . . we're actually projecting Parliament out there in ways that people will be able to connect with; it's active rather than passive.
>
> (John Pullinger)

Investing in ICTs, for the use of MPs and a wider range of parliamentary activities, has also enhanced Parliament in public sphere terms. Parliament is made up of a number of balancing parties, groups, committees and institutional structures which attempt to debate, scrutinise and question government legislative programmes and activities. Just as the government is supported by the Civil Service, so each of these other groups looks to an array of parliamentary support services (clerks, research, library, etc.). These groups and institutions are by no means equal in terms of the resources available to them. A key concern of the research was thus to investigate new media use by these different constituents within Parliament. Did new media help to overcome resource inequalities? Was it useful in terms of aiding the

*Table 7.2* Material published and accessed from Parliamentary Website and Intranet 2001–06

| Parliamentary Session | 2001–02 | 2002–03 | 2003–04 | 2004–05 | 2005–06 |
|---|---|---|---|---|---|
| Research papers published on Intranet/Web | 96 | 96 | 91 | 94 | 82 |
| Standard notes published on Intranet/Web | 788 | 1,368 | 1,816 | 2,173 | 2,720 |
| Research papers accessed online | 420,000 | 670,000 | 730,000 | 887,000 | 1,051,000 |
| Standard notes accessed online | 27,000 | 58,000 | 100,000 | 121,000 | N/A |
| Web hits | 7 m | 14.6 m | 24.5 m | 29.4 m | 32.5 m |
| Intranet requests | 800,000 | 3.4 m | 6.8 m | 5.1 m | 5.4 m |

Source: HoC, July 2005: 71–73, July 2006: 95–96.

organisation, interaction and deliberations of those balancing groups and institutional structures within the House?

When interviewees were asked about how new media had changed their working practices it became clear that the most significant advance was being able to use the Internet as a research tool. Nine out of ten said they used it to search for information on a regular basis. This might involve using the Internet to gain access to specific information sources, such as news sites, the House of Commons Library services or interest group websites. It might also involve using the Internet as an encyclopaedia with a view to getting background information on an issue. For many, especially those arguing the direct democracy case, this may appear to be a rather mundane and/or irrelevant finding. But, as many politicians explained, it was an important development.

For all MPs and Peers wanting to engage with constituents and challenge government, lack of research resources is an ongoing issue. For many, the global and encyclopaedic properties of the Internet enabled them to spend hours, rather than days, in researching topics for discussions and policy or legislative challenges:

> I had a very short time to check into this [policy proposal], but I went to the website of the NFU . . . to the website of the Country Landowners' Association and various others. And from what I learnt I was able to look at the DEFRA website and be able, in a relatively short time, to formulate a serious objection to a particular passage in the paper.
>
> (John Thurso)

> I think in years gone by we may not have had the movement that we have had with the free votes had it not been for the instantaneous communication via the web. The information we had, the stuff we had

from overseas, what's happening in Ireland and Europe and stuff. Without the net that would have been very difficult.

(Sadiq Khan)

The Internet's capacity for connecting to parliamentary research facilities and for keeping up to date with news and events was also stated as invaluable by many: (Angus Robertson) 'When I come in, I usually sit in front of the computer for half an hour, three quarters of an hour, and I read a range of newspapers and websites every day'; (Chris Bryant) 'I'm sure the Internet is by far the most useful thing that we use, not least some of the tools that are contained within the Parliamentary Intranet'. This is confirmed by internal research (Clements, 2005) which shows a general decline in MP research requests as more parliamentary material was published online. Through the Parliamentary Intranet they had access to the following legislative-related information in 2005–06: 24,000 research papers, 103,000 'standard notes', 227,000 subject pages, 3,000 constituency profiles, 8,600 'bill information packs' and 4,400 'debate packs'. In that same year members accessed this output on 696,500 occasions. Intranet requests for information, from inside Parliament, rose from 800,000 in 2001–02 to 5.4 million in 2005–06 (see Table 7.2).

In general, dispersed bits of evidence suggest that it is the smaller, opposition parties which have tended to make most use of the Internet as well as the newer ICT support services offered in the Commons. Parliamentary Intranet research services are most frequently used by opposition parties, especially from the front benches. In 2003–04, the average SNP (Scottish National Party) user made 41.2 enquiries. On average, Liberal Democrats made 24.6 enquiries and Conservatives 20.6. The Conservative Shadow Cabinet, on average, made 35 enquiries and the Liberal Democrats 32.2. Labour members, on average, made 13.7 enquiries (Clements, 2005). Interestingly, it was the Liberal Democrats who also led the way in using the Internet for other purposes. In May 2001 four-fifths of the party had publicly available email addresses. Only a quarter of Conservatives and Labour MPs had them (Jackson, 2003: 8). By the end of 2004 92 per cent of Liberal Democrats, 80 per cent of Conservatives and 73 per cent of Labour MPs had personal websites (Lusoli et al., 2006). In interviews, Liberal Democrat MPs were also the most likely, among the three main parties, to engage in greater email dialogues with constituents, in E-consultations, to have developed web pages and so on.

It became apparent in interviews that the Internet had similarly benefited ordinary MPs in terms of their ability to organise and deliberate within Parliament. Internal email traffic, within Parliament, has almost quadrupled since 2000 to an average of 1.43 million per month (see back to Table 7.1). MPs increasingly use emails to log enquiries with the research services of the House of Commons. E-tabling of parliamentary questions was introduced in 2003–04. By the last quarter of the 2005–06 session, 40 per cent of questions were tabled this way and almost half of all MPs had registered to use the service (HoC, July 2006: 30). Since the 2000/01 Parliamentary Session, it has been possible for EDMs (Early Day Motions) to be produced and organised electronically. In that year, on average, 37 EDMs were being produced each week with a total of 1,896 signatures. By 2005–06 this had more than doubled, with 76 being produced, with a total of 4,222 signatures each week (HoC, July 2006: 95–96). In the House of Lords new ICT services were also rolled out in 2004 and a number of electronic services were introduced, including E-tabling of questions, E-delivery of written answers and email alerts (HoL, July 2005).

For many parliamentarians the benefits were of a practical nature and enabled them to spend more time on other business. This was all the more significant for those with finite resources, such as the front bench MPs of smaller parties, back bench MPs and those working in the House of Lords:

> You've got about 250 or so [peers] who are very active, and most of those are computer literate. And they want to receive information, and to pass information by emails and by accessing databases . . . the Commons would tend to have secretaries. In the Lords they don't tend to have secretaries. They do it themselves.
>
> (Kenneth Baker)

> I think that new technology, especially email and the Internet, is going to be an increasingly powerful force in terms of political organisation. You know, how do you provide information to your activists who support us? How do you motivate them to go and do things? How do you raise money?
>
> (Danny Alexander)

For others, new media had actually been very useful as a tool for deliberation and view-taking among ordinary party members and other MPs:

> It's made things like setting up meetings or having a discussion on paper much easier and more efficient and quicker . . . circulating papers before meetings or bouncing ideas or drafts on to people. That all becomes much easier.
>
> (John Maples)

> A group of people across the country drafted an amendment to a conference motion. It was all done on E-groups, and . . . we defeated that, and we'd basically come together and planned this campaign virtually via E-groups.
>
> (Jo Swinson)

All MPs are emailing each other all the time . . . We now email each other if we've got an early day motion. We put it round again and again . . . So, you're sending pressure. There's all sorts of stuff going around in Parliament now to make sure others are aware of issues, have debates about policies, something we're happy about or unhappy about. But that's all grown up in the last five years really.

(Christine McCafferty)

If research perspectives are altered so too are the means of evaluating new media influences on parliamentary politics. An alternative set of measures offers a slightly more positive assessment. First, new media, used in old, mass ways, has actually been significant. Parliamentary websites are increasingly offering more information and choice to those (individuals and organised interests) who want to understand and participate in selected parts of the political process. The Internet also appears to be a means by which oppositional groups, cross-party committees and institutions within Parliament may partly offset their resource inequalities. Lastly, it clearly aids the activities of MPs seeking to organise, deliberate and scrutinise legislation and government activity.

## Conclusion

Ultimately, this chapter has sought to alter the terms on which the Internet should be evaluated as a medium that influences the shape of parliamentary democracies. It has adopted a 'social shaping' approach rather than a technological determinist one. It has evaluated the Internet in terms of its ability to enhance representative, rather than direct, democracy and also focused on Parliament as a self-contained public sphere. In these terms there are grounds for cautious optimism.

According to the findings here email and E-consultation do not appear likely to replace conventional one-to-one forms of exchange and deliberation in the near future. There are very real practical and social reasons for this: resource constraints, digital inequalities and public preferences for other forms of communication. However, there is also little to indicate that the vast majority of MPs are failing to regularly consult their constituents, or that this is a major cause of public alienation from institutional politics. At the same time, new media optimism should not, in its haste, discount traditional communication forms, such as phone or letter, in its calculations. Nor should it discount the advances brought by new media when used in old, mass media ways. Making the workings of Parliament much more accessible through the website is an important development. So is the opportunity for parliamentarians to use the Internet to inform themselves, debate, scrutinise and hold the government to account.

Finally, however, such findings do not mean the perceived crisis of politics is a myth, or, that new media is a simple force for the enhancement of democracy. There still exist significant resource and digital divides between government and its oppositions, both within and outside Westminster. The power of public opinion and Westminster's constituent parts to hold government to account, in an age of large majorities, appears questionable at times. There is still a crisis of public confidence in politicians with many other potential causes identified (see note 1). What is thus to be concluded is that new media forms may well enhance certain democratic processes but may not, in themselves, be an answer to some of the wider problems that confront aging democracies in an era of increasing globalisation.

Chapter 8

# Interest groups and mediated mobilisation

## Communication in the Make Poverty History campaign

*Nick Sireau and Aeron Davis*

## Introduction

This chapter looks at interest group communication focusing, in particular, on the issues affecting new social movement campaigns. The changing political landscape, evolving media environment and widespread professionalisation of campaigning, have presented new campaign opportunities to contemporary interest groups. However, the changes have also left such groups with a number of strategic choices to make which, in turn, present a number of dilemmas and potential pitfalls.

In many ways, the shifting political landscape appears to be increasingly favourable to the growth of new interest groups and social movements (Castells, 1997; Della Porta and Diani, 1999; Grant, 2000; Norris, 2000, 2002; Goodwin and Jasper, 2003; Todd and Taylor, 2004; Amoore, 2005). Formal political parties, attached to traditional ideologies, are in various states of decline. Sectional interests, with their once-privileged access to the political centre, have lost ground. Support for alternative interest groups, especially single-issue social movements, is growing. At the same time the media environment has changed to enable more possibilities for such groups to raise issues more publicly. The quantity and range of old and new media has expanded significantly, as has the professionalisation of campaign communication. Consequently, a range of groups and organisations in society now attempt to influence political and economic processes through a diverse array of communication forms and formats (Davis, 2000a; Cottle, 2003). However, in challenging established parties, political institutions and dominant discourses, interest groups are faced with a number of strategic campaign and communication choices.

There are long-term decisions to be made about the most appropriate means to challenge dominant lines of discourse, policy-evolution and decision-making. Three core dilemmas appear central: the choice of audience priorities, the positioning of a group in relation to government and the decision to use private or mass, public communication. Each of these choices offers potential risks, costs and benefits. Is change better effected by placing a group closer to, or further from, centres of power and decision-making (an 'insider' or 'outsider' approach)? Is it better to orient campaigns towards mass media and mass opinion, or, to focus communication on active memberships and elite decision-makers? The rewards of greater private or public influence may be offset by the threat of institutional or media co-option/assimilation and, possibly, the alienation of group members.

The first part of this chapter discusses these opportunities, dilemmas and choices. It concludes with a broad typological breakdown of group types, audiences and communication forms. The rest of the chapter then illustrates these dilemmas with an extended case study of the 2005 Make Poverty History campaign.

## Selecting communication strategies for social change: choices of audience, political positioning and communication media

One key communication-oriented question for interest groups is: what audiences should a group prioritise to effect change? In terms of communication strategy groups pursue change on two or three fronts, and among quite different audiences. The key audience in most cases is the elite decision-making one; usually political although often also judicial and/or corporate. This seems especially important when contesting specific decisions during the formation of new policy or legislation, or on matters of taxation and regulation.

However, many groups are not simply concerned with decision-making by elites. Much is to be gained by raising media and public awareness of an issue over an extended period. The power of perceived public opinion to change politics is a theoretical and practical necessity for contemporary democracies (see Keane, 1991; Held, 1996; Herbst, 1998). Indeed, the elite audience may be persuaded by an appeal to wider public opinion and culture. Issues such as global warming, gender and racial equality, international debt and trade, have emerged and shifted political issue priorities over lengthy periods. Small-scale campaign victories or losses, over time, contribute to shifts in the larger hegemonic balance of political culture and public discourse.

On the other hand, group membership and mobilisation are central to an organisation's success. New social movements increasingly come together and are sustained because of 'shared collective goals' and a cohesive collective identity (see Klandermans, 1988; Melucci, 1989). Focusing on key issues, which may not necessarily be palatable to decision-makers or the public, similarly serves to cohere and mobilise members of an interest group over an extended period. It also helps to clarify a group's 'master frame' (Snow and Benford, 1992, 2000). For many of these promotional, public interest groups, it is necessary to both raise consciousness among large audiences and also to sustain and motivate members who have little obvious personal reward (Gitlin, 1980; Mansbridge, 1986; Laraña, 1994).

Thus, the choice of audience priorities, and balance between audiences, determine certain aspects of the communication strategy. Each of these audiences may be targeted simultaneously, but at the risk of alienating or encouraging others. There is also a potential cause of conflict and confusion when it comes to prioritising campaign resources and messages.

A second dilemma concerns where an interest group attempts to position itself vis-à-vis government. This influences the way it 'frames' political issues and its choice of public or private communication. For Grant (1978) groups may be located along a scale between 'insiders', close to government, and 'outsiders', on the periphery of the political (and legal) process. Insiders have regular and often institutionalised contact with government and have direct input into policy networks (Marsh and Rhodes, 1992; Marsh, 1998). They may have formal representation on a committee or advisory board. They may be funded, partly or entirely, by government. However, closer access to institutional power also brings associated constraints. Remits and debate frameworks are more likely to be set by government. Challenges must be constrained to what is deemed legitimate by those in power. There is thus a continuing risk of institutional co-option or political assimilation.

Traditionally, insiders were more likely to be corporate and/or established, 'sectional' interests in society, such as professional associations. For critics, new interest groups, social movements and, for much of the time, trade unions, were likely to have at least started as outsiders. Their ability to attain insider status and influence has been hindered by a number of issues. These have included: the inability of large, collective groups to organise effectively (Olson, 1965), the state's propensity to favour the interests of the capitalist class (Miliband, 1969; Poulantzas, 1975) and/or yield to the arguments of business and established institutions to sustain economic prosperity and political stability (Lindblom, 1977; Offe, 1984). Consequently, the concerns of certain groups fail to register at the centre (Bachrach and Baratz, 1962; Lukes, 1974).

However, a perceived shift in institutional politics suggests a positive change in many 'political opportunity structures' (Kriesi, 1991; Gamson and Meyer, 1996); one that raises possibilities for new social movements to make an impact. In many established democracies, political party membership, partisan party alignment and trade union and religious association membership have each declined. In contrast, the number of pressure groups, social movements and business and professional associations continues to grow. Some individual interest group memberships far outstrip those of the main political parties. Many of these new organisations, groups and movements have a less obvious relationship to government but, at the same time, offer potential means for parties to re-engage with voters. For some, the recent evolution of new social movement politics, with its 'multi-level, multi-arena game' (Dudley and Richardson, 1998), mean that such an insider/outsider classification becomes problematic (see also Grant, 2000). Certainly, the traditional views of interest groups and their links to government power have become more complicated by globalisation and cultural and discursive shifts (see Castells, 1998; Nash, 2000; Held and McGrew, 2002). All of which means more flexibility and variety in the relationships between interest groups and decision-making centres.

Interest groups therefore have to make strategic decisions about where they want to position themselves in relation to government. Insider status, with a greater direct input into decisions but with the risk of political co-option, or outsider status, with greater campaigning autonomy but the risk of political exclusion. Accordingly, such a position is also likely to affect the way an organisation attempts to 'frame' key political issues in its campaign communication.

A third dilemma revolves around the choice of whether to use private communication forums, or to go public and take a mass media-oriented approach. Insider groups are more likely to use private, routine and institutionalised forms of communication. This might involve regular consultation with civil servants and ministers in government departments. It might also mean hiring professional lobbyists to make a case and/or gain access. There are also formal written submissions made in response to consultation exercises. For those choosing an outsider path these traditional communication forums are far less available. This leaves a choice between going public and using mass media-oriented strategies, or, making use of alternative private, new media-oriented strategies (not discussed here).[1]

The changing communication environment also offers a mixture of opportunities and potential obstacles to new interest groups. Just as such groups previously appeared to have limited choices in terms of positioning themselves on the insider/outsider scale so it seemed the same with mass media strategies. Mobilisation and campaign communication was limited according to resource constraints (Goldenberg, 1975).[2] In communication terms, groups came to the media with 'organic' media profiles; a set of predetermined cultural and symbolic resources which, in turn, affected how they were presented and their ability to set agendas and interpretive frameworks. They might be perceived as an issue-raising 'arbiter' or a campaign 'advocate' (see Deacon, 2003). A successful campaign organisation could be symbolically positioned as 'legitimate', a reliable supplier of 'information subsidies' (Gandy, 1982) and/or as holding a 'primary definer' status (Hall et al., 1978). Each of these elements was likely to influence how interest groups and their claims were judged by journalists, the public and elite decision-makers. They also made an organisation and its campaigns more or less 'newsworthy' and adaptable to prevailing 'news values' (Gans, 1979; Palmer, 2000). For many resource-poor and outsider groups there was little to be done if an organisation had an illegitimate or 'secondary definer' status or was not deemed newsworthy. Often the only choice then appeared to be between 'commanding attention' and 'securing legitimacy' (Cracknell, 1993).

However, in the contemporary political climate, the symbolic capital of media sources appears far more volatile (Schlesinger and Tumber, 1994). Interest groups have increasingly 'professionalised' their communication operations and personnel (see Davis, 1999, 2002; Deacon, 2003; Cutlip *et al.*, 2004). Professionalisation has brought a range of communication expertise, media contacts and strategic options into the interest group sector. They have recognised the importance of reporter routines and 'news values' in news construction and, accordingly, have managed to gain more sympathetic coverage. The use of celebrities, human interest angles and riding fashionable story lines, are all common approaches (see Kerr and Sachdev, 1992; Anderson, 1997; Davis, 2003a, and also collections in Hansen, 1993; McKay, 1998; Cottle, 2003). They have learnt that forms of 'proxy media access' may negate the need for symbolic capital. They may simply become regular suppliers of expert research and story ideas to journalists, seed anonymous, negative stories about policies or opponents, or go through third parties, such as politicians or scientists, who already have a positive media profile.

However, there are also costs and risks involved in becoming a mass media-oriented campaign group. Just as a group may be co-opted by the political institutions they seek to challenge so they may be co-opted by the demands of the mass media. Challenges may be watered down, messages confused and campaigns distorted by the imperatives of news values and media production requirements (see also Gitlin, 1980; Clarke, 2001; Ross, 2004).

All of which has a bearing on the communication strategies open to interest groups. A table of communication strategies, audiences targeted and group types is drawn up in Table 8.1 (see also Deacon, 1996; Mitchell, 1997, for other strategy comparisons). As suggested in this table, insider groups, including those of a sectional/private interest nature, are most likely to use private, routine or institutionalised communication forms. Business and professional associations and quangos often fall into this category. A greater range of groups and institutions will resort to lobbying and formal written submissions. Any business association, large corporation, trade union, association or promotional/public interest group, with an established organisation and funding, will use such methods.

Almost all kinds of group may make use of mass and alternative media to influence a wider range of audiences, including power elites. However, mass and alternative media are likely to be rather more important to outsider than insider groups. Such groups can make little or no use of the more private communication forms. They are also more reliant on members and the wider public. Many new social movements, particularly promotional/public interest ones, are likely to put a greater emphasis on mass media coverage,

Table 8.1 Interest group typology of communication strategies and audience targets

| Communication forms | Audience target | Group type | Advantages and disadvantages |
|---|---|---|---|
| 1 Routine/institutional Private communication | Power elites Members | Insider Sectional | Exclusive and best access to power elites. High threat of political co-option. Constrained debate/critique. |
| 2 Committee meetings | Power elites Members | Insider Sectional | Good access to power elites. Threat of political co-option and reduced critique. |
| 3 Lobbying/advocacy | Power elites | Insider/outsider Sectional/promotional | Potentially good access to elites. Can be costly. Mixed results. Threat of leaks and public scandal. |
| 4 Formal written submissions | Power elites | Insider/outsider Sectional/promotional | No use for public or members. Limited input to power elites but step to insider status and other forms of access. |
| 5 Alternative/new media | Power elites Members/employees Intermediaries | Outsider/insider Sectional/promotional Communal | Controlled alternative to private or mass media. Best for members. To date, elites and public access more limited. |
| 6 Mass media/direct Journalist relations | Power elites Members/employees Public/intermediaries | Outsider/insider Sectional/promotional Communal | Can also maintain power elite access but risk loss of access. More input into media coverage/framing and public access. Issue of media incorporation. |
| 7 Stunts/protests/strikes (direct action) | Media/journalists Power elites Public/members | Outsider Promotional/sectional Communal | Usually no power elite access. Can get media attention, public access and sometimes frame issues. Potential problem of media incorporation. |
| 8 Illegal acts/violence | Media/journalists Power elites Public/members | Outsider Promotional Communal | Usually no power elite access. Media coverage but little influence on reporting and issue framing. |
| 9 Terrorism/military | Media/journalists Power elites Public/members | Outsider Promotional Communal | Usually no power elite access but may eventually force elite response. Little influence on reporting/issue framing. |

engaging members and raising public awareness. Only outsider groups are likely to use stunts, direct action, illegal activities or violence to make their points. They are likely to be less resourced and less hierarchical. Each of these strategies, except in spontaneous acts, are also consciously aimed at the media and wider public.

It seems clear that powerful, well-resourced and organised interests choose to use the first five, more private forms of communication, but can resort to using others if needed. Weaker, poorly resourced and organised interests are more likely to use the last three and, possibly, mass and alternative media. But, for the majority of organised and reasonably well-resourced, sectional/private and promotional/public interest groups, all but the first and last options are available to a greater or lesser degree. This leaves each interest group with a set of strategic choices to make in terms of: which audiences to prioritise, whether to pursue an insider or outsider policy in the long term and whether to use a private or public communication strategy.

## Case study: Make Poverty History

The Make Poverty History (MPH) campaign of 2005 is an ideal case study with which to explore the issues discussed above. The campaign emerged as a large number of NGOs came together to take advantage of the political opportunities of that year.[3] As 2005 progressed, the campaign grew to 540 member organisations, including leading NGOs such as Oxfam, Christian Aid, Action Aid, Comic Relief, Cafod and Save the Children. The organisations, between them, represented approximately 15 million people in the United Kingdom alone. Well-known public figures and celebrities, such as Bob Geldof and Richard Curtis, took central roles in the campaign and its presentation. The high point was the G8 Summit, in Scotland in July, around which a major MPH rally and the international *Live8* concert were organised. As the campaign grew it was faced with a number of choices to make between competing political strategies and differentiated audiences.

With such a diverse group of actors involved in the coalition it appears inevitable that tensions would develop. These tensions, in turn, influenced the evolution of the campaign's communication and the construction of its public messages. Some organisations in the coalition promoted a more 'insider' strategy that involved a moderate, consensual and supportive campaign approach to government. This strategy dominated the campaign, in the run-up to the G8, and focused on the need to offer aid, cancel debt and alleviate suffering without directing blame at governments. Others took an 'outsider' line that was more critical, and sought to present G8 leaders and corporations as the cause of economic injustice. As a consequence, these conflicting approaches affected communication strategies, membership exchanges and the public framing of the issues through the mass media. Throughout, core messages became blurred. For some there was the constant risk of co-option by the government communication machine. For others the alternative danger was that of campaign isolation and political exclusion.

Just as the threat of political co-option hung over the campaign so did the threat of media co-option. MPH chose to go public and gain mass media attention for the campaign. In so doing it was faced with more uncomfortable choices. For those coalition NGO members with a significant, professional marketing contingent, the goal was to simplify the representation of issues and make extensive use of celebrity endorsement. For those NGOs that were more campaign-led, such strategies threatened to weaken and confuse campaign messages, alienate activist members and hand too much control to the celebrities themselves. All these tensions and divisions came to a head during the *Live8* music event and G8 Summit.[4]

## Framing communication: insiders, outsiders and the problem of political co-option

Throughout the campaign, the positioning of groups in relation to government directly affected attempts to set the communicative frame. There was a constant concern that the campaign would come to be perceived as being too close to, or co-opted by, government. As a result, radical groups pushed for an outsider strategy that involved protest action and intense criticism of the government and the G8. Alternatively, moderates were less concerned with the issue and adopted a more insider strategy of dialogue with the government and G8. As Adrian Lovett explained, both approaches were apparent in the campaign:

> Now in one part of the coalition there is a view that you don't achieve radical, real change by getting into an extended or serious dialogue with decision-makers. That you do so by being wholly detached from that dialogue and sort of speaking a kind of truth to power which, in time, will gather its own power until the world shifts in that direction. There's the other view that says that you go to where the debate is and haul it with all your might on to the territory you want it on. I think one of the great struggles at the heart of Make Poverty History has been between those two quite different views of how change is achieved.

This became more significant as, from the start, the government attempted to associate itself closely with the campaign. Members of the government saw Make Poverty History as a clear opportunity for demonstrating public support for its policies. They frequently referred to the MPH campaign in speeches, took on its key discourse on trade, aid and debt, and even adopted the symbol of the white band. This was particularly a concern for the

MPH image as Comic Relief's market research showed that many thought the campaign was run by Gordon Brown and was the government's idea (Fenyoe and Darnton, 2005). This clearly was an issue for many involved in the campaign: 'We saw from the market research that some of the public thought the government were a leading constituent of the campaign' (Beth Tegg);

> It's a risk and yes we've had to work quite hard to try and not to make it look as if we are co-opted. I mean, genuinely, I think we are not . . . a couple of weeks ago I read an article in the paper that described a Labour party rally on world poverty day as a Make Poverty History rally – that sort of thing is emerging all the time.
>
> (Anonymous)

These concerns were discussed in depth by the Coordination Team early on in the campaign. In its 10 January meeting it debated its public campaign line ahead of the upcoming G7 finance ministers meeting on 4 and 5 February:

PARTICIPANT ONE: I wanted to point out the confusion in some people's minds believing it's a government campaign. In the short term, if it gets into people's minds, that's wonderful. But it's a serious medium-term issue.

PARTICIPANT FIVE: The media group are worried about that too.

PARTICIPANT TWO: If it goes on for too long without us getting in there we're going to struggle to not lose out to a co-optive agenda.

This then led the discussion on to how to do this, with one participant emphasising the need to focus on trade as the main area of difference with the government. It was particularly important to signal this difference early before government members publicly claimed campaign territory for themselves.

PARTICIPANT THREE: Looking at the next phase we really need to hammer home the trade message – and to a certain extent the media have been lazy on this. The government has deliberately ignored it.

PARTICIPANT FOUR: I'm concerned that we will see an exacerbation of this co-option and that we will miss an opportunity to stake out our differences in a concerted way . . . There are times in the year where we have to think – this year we want to hit them hard. We know they're going to say something mollifying on debt or aid but will they say something on trade?

The discussion returned again to the confusion in the public's mind over who was controlling the campaign. Participants then discussed whether to support or denounce the government:

PARTICIPANT SIX: What gets lost here for me is that who wants to be nice to the government, who wants to be nasty? I want to be nasty because I don't think they're putting the political capital they should be putting behind her. Blair went to see Bush after the election and did not mention Africa. We should be very tough both before and after the finance meeting.

The minutes of this meeting summed up the central concerns of the organisers:

> There was a long discussion on whether and when the coalition should clarify its differences with the Government and express its disagreement on some issues like liberalisation and conditionality . . . should the coalition openly criticise the Government on the points of disagreement or just congratulate them for what they have done so far? . . . We should be careful about timing and audience, this might not be the right time for criticising the Government.

It was this latter concern that was foremost in the minds of the more moderate campaigners. For them, the campaign needed to present government actors as potential heroes of the poor, which would then encourage them to take the actions Make Poverty History was calling for:

> We wanted to talk to politicians on their level and say 'Look, millions of people support the aims of Make Poverty History. And now it's up to you. You have the power to make the changes in policy that will make the difference. So please realise how important this is and act' . . . And actually the politicians, who essentially we needed to act on our behalf, felt a little easier with being encouraged to do something great than they did with feverish shouting and screaming that accompanied a lot of campaigning. Although I'm not saying that those methods don't have a place.
>
> (Tom Johnstone)

> [*Live8*] wanted to sort of make leaders feel as though they could be heroes because all the psychology of these leaders is that they want to be returned to office again, and they want people to think well of them, so they go down in the record books as people who've done well for their countries.
>
> (Anonymous)

It was the moderate line that came to dominate the construction of the early message frames in the public campaign. According to the MPH MAC (Messages, Actions and Communications)[5] group exchanges, advertising staff from Abbot Mead Vicker (AMV) said that they had been given instructions to produce non-challenging messages that encouraged government decision-makers. Draft ads circulated to the MAC group in March (MAC, 11.03.05) included phrases such as: 'G8. Make Poverty History.'; 'G8. Do something great.'; 'A few politicians can [written 'can't' but with the apostrophe and 't' crossed out] rid the world of poverty. See how one letter can change everything?' This also came out later in *Live8*'s communication where Comic Relief and AMV played an important role.

Some members of the MAC group were not happy with this approach. They felt that their policy comments on the click ad (shown on several television channels simultaneously at 7.58pm on 31 March 2005) had been ignored (MAC, 03.03.05). The argument within the MAC group that followed was the culmination of months of tension over the framing of the campaign's communication. One of the MAC group's leaders said that he did not feel the campaign was 'in the angry phase yet. It feels like angry comes next.' But for many key members of the coalition, the message frames had been set and this angry and critical phase failed to materialise in the run-up to the G8.

Richard Curtis, vice-chair of Comic Relief and the person who secured the pro bono support of AMV, came to be at the symbolic heart of the moderate–radical struggle and the focus of the radicals' anger. One of the members of the radical faction of the MAC group, Tim Peat, said that he had: 'no doubt that criticism of the UK government within popular public messaging has been vetoed at a very senior level within Comic Relief and that that has significantly weakened our campaigning.' In July, the radical activist *Red Pepper* magazine made a similar point (Hodkinson, July 2005): 'The most destructive aspect of Curtis's involvement, critics argue, has been his intervention in the public communication of MPH . . . "He believes that we should support the efforts of the UK government to bring other G8 countries into its line on aid and debt, and is adamant that Brown and Blair should not be criticised."'

Parts of the coalition clearly felt alarmed by the government's moves to associate itself with Make Poverty History. The co-option issue continued to be raised and discussed in meetings observed throughout the build up of the campaign (11 October and 7 December 2004, 10 January, 7 February, 22 June, 22 July and 8 August 2005). It was the more radical elements who were the most concerned:

> For those campaign groups who see themselves as being more radical it would be very difficult for them to feel like we're following the government's agenda. And, in a sense, what's the point of a protest group if

you're agreeing with the government or if the government's agreeing with you?

(Lucy Cathcart)

I think there's a massive danger of co-option . . . at the first assembly meeting groups were asked to list their concerns. Every table said that there was the danger of co-option. This was written up on the flip chart at the end. Hilary Benn saw this when he came to address the meeting and made a joke about it. Despite this widespread concern amongst MPH core membership, many of the steps you take to avoid co-option have not been implemented, and that's been a deliberate choice.

(Tim Peat)

This fracture within the coalition over whether to support or criticise the government in its communication was evident in the press coverage of tensions within the campaign. On 30 May 2005, the *New Statesman* (Quarmby) argued that members of Make Poverty History were increasingly worried that its messages were being diluted by large NGOs, particularly Oxfam, which were seen as too close to New Labour. Just before the G8 statement was released *The Financial Times* reported (Beattie and Williamson, 08.07.05): 'As of yesterday, the NGOs were still discussing their reaction to whatever is announced today. But whatever their decision, the episode underlines the continual problems of campaigners' relations with governments'. The *Independent* (Hodkinson, 26.10.05, see also 9.11.05) revealed that political disagreements within the campaign had escalated:

between the powerful right-wing grouping of government-friendly aid agencies and charities effectively running MPH (led by Oxfam and including the Catholic Agency for Overseas Development, Save the Children and Comic Relief) and the more progressive yet smaller NGOs such as War on Want and the World Development Movement.

However, interviewees close to Curtis argue that this was not the case. Furthermore, according to the official evaluation of Make Poverty History (Martin *et al.*, 2006: 55), the issue of co-option was 'largely dismissed by those interviewed inside'. In fact, according to the more moderate members of the coalition, any co-option taking place was not necessarily a negative development: (Alison Fenney) 'If the government thinks the same as we do it doesn't mean that we've been co-opted. It means that we think the same. I think that's a really important distinction.' According to Lovett, not only was it strategically wrong to directly attack the government, but the fact that government wanted to appropriate the campaign's discourse was a positive step in itself:

I remember in Jubilee 2000, especially in the earlier days, when Brown would get up and make a speech or even some junior minister or a Labour back bencher or whatever and say 'We want to see the calls of Jubilee 2000 realised', or 'We want a debt-free start for a billion people', which was our catch phrase, we would celebrate in the office. That included some people with good left credentials in the Jubilee 2000 team, who saw that as a great signal of our progress. Immediately we then thought 'Now we're going to make sure that they don't run away with it'. But it's a nice problem to have in my view. This time round it felt right from the start that there's been much more appropriation. Everyone focused on that problem and much less on the fact that that actually is a necessary and desirable stage in a campaign's progress.

As documented here, attitudes towards co-option governed the framing of the campaign's public communication and subsequent evaluations of success and failure. The larger, insider member organisations ultimately had more input into the framing of the issues in the run-up to the crucial G8 Summit. For critics this resulted in a failure to tackle government on the more crucial issue of trade, which became the campaign's focus in the second half of the year. For others there were significant successes. That co-option had taken place was not to be judged as a failing but, in certain ways, the true signifier of success itself.

## Mass media audiences and the problem of media co-option

Just as Make Poverty History had to deal with the problem of political co-option so it was also faced with the parallel problem of media co-option. From the start, the private, government-focused campaign was accompanied by a mass, public-oriented one. Part of this involved widespread use of corporate, mass marketing techniques. Much of this was based on the successful template developed by Comic Relief. This strategy, aided by AMV, combined celebrity endorsement, advertisement, corporate sponsorship and strong branding. However, such an approach also presented further dilemmas and awkward choices. The public campaign suffered its own form of co-option by the news values of the popular media. The complex causes of poverty came to be over-simplified or were lost in an attempt to encourage mass media interest. Celebrities, used to generate media coverage, went 'off message' and inadvertently misrepresented the campaign. All this came to a head as Bob Geldof, and his independently organised *Live8* concerts, over-shadowed MPH's rally and address at the G8 Summit in Edinburgh. Stephen Rand explained the general dilemma:

You can go for mass mobilisation and popularisation, and the price you pay for that is shallowness and opportunism. Every progressive move-ment has always had that tension. And there are the purists who'd rather be right but just have an audience of two – and they never get that audience any further because they can't agree anything together. We had that element. There were people who would argue a policy point to boredom rather than actually agree something that you can get out there. Equally you can go down the celebrity popularisation, mass mobilisation route and realise that . . . you can't expect Kate Moss to click her fingers and also be articulate about trade justice. You can only hope. Make Poverty History was designed to go for the mass mobilisa-tion option. It succeeded, and paid the price. The challenge was to make the most of the mass mobilisation and mitigate the downside as much as possible.

The early strategic choice was for a mass-oriented campaign and, accord-ingly, that meant a certain level of simplification and appeal to common news values. Once again, tensions within the coalition resulted. On the one side were those who argued, from a marketing and mass communication perspective, that simple, short-term, focused messaging was needed to get through to the public:

> You can't have a campaign talking about the economics of trade and trade justice and the importance of governments fulfilling the promises on aid they committed to in 1970 . . . There's a certain extent to which the general public doesn't have the time or the interest for these sort of facts. It's got to be simple for people to get it.
>
> (Ben Ramsden)

> Although they [the campaigners] were worried at times that we were sort of dumbing down Make Poverty History and the causes, I think most of them now realise that actually, as a public awareness campaign, it was a great success in terms of getting as many people as possible engaged.
>
> (Tom Johnstone)

On the other side were the campaigners and policy specialists who argued that more complex messaging and longer-term explanations were needed to educate people about the structural causes of global poverty:

> The tension is between complex policy and how you make complex policy into sound-bites that are interesting enough for people to want to engage . . . it's about that tension between complex policy and making this a massive popular campaign.
>
> (Alison Fenney)

Some of the deeply involved grassroots campaigners had a great under-standing, but I think for most people who followed the campaign issues during the year it was very superficial. Some of the wider public even saw *Live8* as a fundraiser or were even scarcely aware it was a campaign . . . And certainly our analysis at Christian Aid and the more radical and campaigns-orientated organisations . . . is that the core issue that separates rich and poor, the rich world and the poor world, is that we control how they run their economies, and we make them run them in ways that benefit us. If we were seriously going to change the causes of poverty, this is the main message that needed to come across. But the extent to which it received mass profile was abysmal, especially consid-ering the wonderful opportunities available.

(Martin Drewry)

A key part of gaining mass media attention was the use of celebrities to engage news editors and draw public support. Make Poverty History's click advert included a number of celebrities – such as Bob Geldof, Bono, Brad Pitt, Kate Moss, Kylie Minogue and George Clooney – clicking their fingers to symbolise a child dying from extreme poverty every three seconds. Ewen McGregor and Nelson Mandela featured in other adverts and campaign literature. The idea behind all this was that, in a celebrity-obsessed culture, capturing the popular imagination and the popular press had to be done through celebrity endorsement:

I think the general public are so aware and responsive to what they see in the media in terms of celebrities . . . The average celebrity or soap opera star, or someone like that being able to explain what the cam-paign is for and about, well, that will have a much wider impact than any policy expert or charity person.

(Lucy Cathcart)

If Ronan Keating, for example, gets an article in the *Mirror* about Make Poverty History then people are going to read that, because Ronan's featured, and probably learn something about Make Poverty History. And they probably wouldn't have read it otherwise and the *Mirror* probably wouldn't have featured it otherwise unless it had that kind of celebrity hook.

(Adrian Platt)

However, although many interviewees acknowledged the benefits of celeb-rity endorsement, they also expressed concern. The fact that the coalition was made up of numerous organisations, but with no clear central spokes-person, meant that it was the celebrities who tended to capture media and public attention. Consequently, messaging, and the campaign's larger profile, became distorted:

> You can decide what you want in a Make Poverty History committee meeting but then, once it is communicated through major international celebrities and the media, the message that comes across can be very different in tone.
>
> (Martin Drewry)

> In terms of the political impact I don't think it helps and I think, sometimes, celebrities can be more trouble than they're worth because they've all got their own agendas and don't necessarily say the right things at the right time. But I think overall they add weight to the campaign.
>
> (Adrian Platt)

Many of these difficulties came to be typified in the campaign's relationship with Bob Geldof. Geldof's link to the campaign was ambiguous. On the one hand, he was an active campaigner and was supportive of Make Poverty History. On the other hand, he had strong links with the UK government, had instigated and been part of the *Commission for Africa*, and had since had a number of personal meetings with Tony Blair. According to key members of the MPH coalition, this had a distinct influence on Geldof's subsequent messages and was one of the main reasons why many thought that Make Poverty History was a government campaign (see Fenyoe and Darnton, 2005):

> The interventions of Richard Curtis, Bob Geldof and Bono, and their ability to dominate the media space, blurred the line between what MPH was calling for and what the government was calling for . . . for instance, Richard Curtis appeared on a platform at the G8 with Bob Geldof and a couple of other people, and said, 'We have a blueprint, and it's called the Commission for Africa.'
>
> (Steve Tibbett)

The organisation of *Live8* highlighted this conflict of interests. Geldof's independent decision to stage the *Live8* concert during the G8 Summit directly clashed with the 2 July Edinburgh rally that the coalition had been organising for months in advance. Geldof did put his ideas to the MPH Coordination Team, some time ahead, arguing that *Live8* would generate enough world-wide public pressure to force the G8 leaders to act. For organisers, whatever their reservations, it was also clear that *Live8* would provide a major publicity boost:

> The fact that it had such a high recognition factor amongst the general public, I think, comes from *Live8* predominantly because everyone thought *Live8* was organised by Make Poverty History.
>
> (Anonymous)

I think *Live8* elevated the thing to stratospheric levels in a way that it's quite hard to imagine what it would have been without it really . . . it was after *Live8* was announced that Make Poverty History really had massive power in terms of brand profile.

(Martin Drewry)

Nevertheless, *Live8* rapidly began creating communication problems. Any public sense of consecutive events building up to the G8 was compromised and concern was raised over messaging around *Live8*. It was decided that, since the Edinburgh Rally was the only place to guarantee MPH messaging, it should be where the political voice of the campaign came through (MAC, 13.06.05). As the event day moved closer, serious concerns arose about the messages promoted by *Live8* and how these were becoming confused with those of Make Poverty History:

*Live8* was on the same day, so we weren't able to get the message out in the way that we wanted to . . . People didn't see a difference. Even people who are very close to the campaign didn't see a difference between *Live8* and Make Poverty History.

(Steve Tibbett)

*Live8* may have inspired new people to activism, and that's obviously great, but it introduced them to activism in the context of political messaging that was at times horrific. You know, the sense of you've done it all, you've succeeded in making poverty history, and the sense that somehow, just by watching *Live8*, we were contributing to the end of poverty.

(Martin Drewry)

A particularly difficult moment came during the press conference just after the G8 Summit. Following the announcement of the G8 package on international development Geldof gave an enthusiastic assessment. He spoke of a 'great day', gave the G8 Summit '10 out of 10 on aid, eight out of 10 on debt', and concluded that 'never before have so many people forced a change of policy onto a global agenda' (BBC, 09.07.05). According to reports Bono was less satisfied but did not want to criticise the G8 (BBC, 08.07.05). NGOs approached Geldof to make a more restrained statement about the G8, but he refused, claiming that it was 'the most important summit there had ever been for Africa' (BBC, 08.07.05; see also Simonson, 2005).

It soon became clear that this was not the message that the MPH campaign wanted to convey. As one member of the Coordination Team explained:

Crunch moment, I think, was press conference time immediately at the end of the G8. I don't need to tell you that what Bob said is famous and keeps getting repeated. And what Bob said was not what Bob had been briefed to say and was a reaction to having just read the press release of the Global Call to Action Against Poverty, primarily, rather than the Make Poverty History one, I think, which we'd spent a week crafting down to the last letter.

Many members of the coalition were furious with this. The more radical elements of Make Poverty History publicly criticised Geldof through the press. An article in the activist *Red Pepper* magazine, reproduced in the *Independent*, reflected the more radical criticism of *Live8* and the involvement of celebrities. Under the headline 'Do Stars Really Aid the Cause?' (Hodkinson, 26.10.05), it claimed that:

> there has been little coverage of how bitterly most MPH members feel about the concerts, which were organised separately by Geldof and Curtis but with the full knowledge of Oxfam, Comic Relief and the Treasury. This is not just because they overshadowed MPH's rally in Edinburgh on 2 July . . . Their focus was not on global poverty, but Africa. And their demands were not those of MPH, but of the Commission for Africa, a Government-sponsored think-tank committed to free-market capitalism.

Even more moderate members of the coalition expressed concerns. Oxfam Policy Advisor, Max Lawson, said that there was 'an incentive on the part of Number 10 and even Bob Geldof to portray these announcements as a huge deal' (*Financial Times*, 05.07.05). The World Development Movement (WDM) published a press release criticising Geldof's 'unwarranted praise for the dismal deal' and concluding that 'Mr Geldof has become too close to the decision makers to take an objective view of what has been achieved at this summit'.

However, in Stephen Rand's assessment, much of the coverage of the anti-Geldof reaction was itself just another reflection of the media's obsession with celebrities, rather than its interest in the deeper issues:

> The *Independent* published the piece that Stuart Hodkinson had written weeks earlier, straight from *Red Pepper* . . . They weren't bothered to report what we were saying to MPs about the campaign [when we gave evidence to a select committee] . . . They ran the article because there was a row about celebrities. So I think we just live in a world where celebrities get media attention, even from broadsheets.

Clearly campaigners knew that they needed to simplify the issues and get celebrities such as Geldof to gain access to the international media and the support of the wider public. Yet, they also felt frustration at the simplistic explanations of poverty and the lack of control they were able to exercise when the issues were relayed through such high profile figures. The media then focused on this disagreement between Geldof and the more radical elements of the coalition. However, yet again it was the presence of Geldof at the centre of this dispute, rather than the substance of the dispute, that made it newsworthy.

## Conclusion

The shifting political and communication environment appears to offer more opportunities to new interest groups and social movements to influence elite decision-making. However, as demonstrated here, the adoption of corporate-style lobbying and media-friendly campaign strategies may also be detrimental to a group's long-term goals. Greater political access and mass media coverage may result in forms of political and news media co-option. This may or may not be a negative outcome depending on short- and long-term campaign goals.

One way of understanding Make Poverty History, a prominent example of a new global social movement, is as a coalition of organisations with different identities and strategies. Some occupied a more 'insider' position in relation to government and others a more 'outsider' one. Some embraced commercial communication techniques and others not. These differences became more problematic, leading to conflict within the coalition's leadership and its message frames. Outsider groups promoted public protest and criticism of the UK Government and G8. Insiders wanted gentler and more supportive messages designed to encourage them even at the cost of perceived political assimilation.

Just as political co-option hung over the campaign so did the threat of media co-option. In an attempt to engage and mobilise mass opinion, campaign organisers found themselves having to accede to mass news values: simple sound-bites over complex policy, short-term events over long-term issues, and celebrity endorsement over NGO pleas. As the campaign evolved so Make Poverty History lost control of its frames, messages, celebrity spokespersons and news coverage. The campaign lost support among a number of its activist members and struggled to compete with the media's more traditional 'primary definers': politicians and celebrities.

One year later (autumn 2006), consensus over the campaign's achievements remains elusive. Many members of the coalition stress the campaign's success as a mobilising tool. Activist recruitment is rising and public interest in development issues is on the increase. For others there remains general pubic confusion over what MPH was about. Significant numbers believe it was simply part of *Live8* and have little understanding of what was accomplished at the G8 Summit. Some argue that the campaign built up the international development sector and brought it together in an unprecedented way. But one interviewee asked whether the sector would ever be able to come together in such a way again after all the tensions and fall-outs. On the policy front, the moderates tend to point to the decisions taken at the G8 as a sign of success, while the more radical elements see it as a missed opportunity for challenging world leaders more critically. All this shows the difficulties in assessing the impact of a social movement as it tries to break into a public and policy arena dominated by powerful political and media institutions.

## Chapter 9

# Media audiences and effects

## The question of the rational audience in the London Stock Exchange

### Introduction

This chapter suggests an alternative perspective on the media effects debate. Early work on media influence assumed a causal link between mass media and mass behaviour. Conservative elite fear of the malleable masses focused on the 'magic bullet' effect of the media. Critical elites, in turn, argued that conservative elites kept the 'unconscious' masses in check via control of mass media and culture. In contrast, decades of effects and audience research has established the inadequacy of this 'strong effects' paradigm. The main thrust of this counter research is the realisation that audiences actively consume and use the media for self-serving purposes. They are, in effect, independent individuals, capable of deciding how to use the media to fulfil their own personal interests and pleasures.

The alternative perspective presented here, based on speculative research on an elite audience with high levels of media consumption, is that: individuals can respond actively to media and in ways that appear to be in their own best interests; but, collectively, the results can be both self-defeating and on a mass scale. In this scenario, media and communication, audiences and mass behaviour are all linked. However, individuals do not have to be ignorant nor act irrationally to contribute to media-instigated, collective irrationality.

The research used to support the discussion comes from a study of fund managers operating in the London Stock Exchange. Fund managers are considered to be an elite, rational audience par excellence. Every day, they make conscious, well-thought-out decisions, based on the information gained from media and communication sources that are widely circulated and consumed. And yet, there is evidence of regular occurrences of mass behaviour at work. The evidence presented here is a mixture of interview material with fund managers and an accumulation of secondary findings gathered from industry surveys and financial academic research.

## Audiences and effects: dominant paradigms

Fear of the ignorant masses and the power of new mass forms of media drove early thinking on media effects. Observation of totalitarian regimes in Europe, which used mass propaganda techniques, combined with instances of media-inspired mass behaviour in the United States, gave rise to 'magic bullet' theories of strong media effects (Lippman, 1922; Lasswell, 1927; Cantril *et al.*, 1940). These in turn set the parameters for the mostly US-based research that took place in the cold-war period. Research, from studies of voting to violence (Lazarsfeld *et al.*, 1944; Bandura and Walters 1963), sought to link the stimuli of media depictions and/or information with mass behavioural responses. The implicit assumption was that the public, or vulnerable constituent groups of the public, could be persuaded to act irrationally, that is, contrary to their own best interests, as a consequence of media consumption.

From a critical perspective, the fears were different but the mechanisms and assumptions concerning the ignorant masses, were the same. In this case, media and culture worked more to subdue the masses and prevent them from realising, let alone acting in, their own best (class) interests. In critical cultural theory (Adorno and Horkheimer, 1979 [1947]; Hall, 1980; Althusser, 1984 [1971]), and media political economy (GUMG, 1976; Murdock and Golding, 1977; Garnham, 1979) power over the masses came through power over the production of media and cultural texts. The mass of individuals were not conscious of their true conditions and could not, there-fore, act in their own best interests.

The counter-thesis to the 'mass media stimuli–mass unthinking response' position has really been built upon demonstrating that audiences consume media actively and respond individually, that is, in their own self interests. Hence, empirical research on audiences in the United States concluded that audiences, far from being media-influenced, instead used media for gratifi-cation or reinforcement purposes (Rosengren and Windahl, 1972; Blumler and Katz, 1974). A second, later body of work, developed in the United Kingdom, was audience research within cultural studies (Morley, 1980; Ang, 1986; Radway, 1987). Here, the focus was on consumption of popular cul-ture. Similarly, far from being subjected to media, audiences were deemed to actively consume it, for pleasure, reinforcement and identity construction.

Both bodies of work, although separated by matters of method and polit-ical perspective, had a similar impact on the effects tradition. Their conclu-sions indicate that audiences do not simply react to media, but reason over and/or choose to be stimulated by its contents. By the same token, audiences are not homogenous masses but, rather, collections of individuals. Indi-viduals may choose between texts which are polysemic and emanate from many competing sources. Patterns of media consumption are thus extremely varied, subject to wide demographic variations and immersed in processes of social interaction. In a post-industrial world of new media and consumer choice, audience fragmentation and pluralist diversity are continuing apace. The logical conclusion is that, because audiences are made up of conscious individuals, mass unconscious behaviour, in response to mass media, is unlikely.

To sum up, three generalised positions on audience effects have emerged. The first, in both conservative and critical forms, links the behaviour of mass, unthinking audiences to mass media and culture. This now appears to be an increasingly marginalised position in mainstream effects work and draws few advocates. The second position, directing most research in the media field, continues to emphasise the conscious, rational, self-serving individual, in all her or his guises: voter, fan and consumer of popular culture. The third argues that the media is largely irrelevant. The homogenous audience does not exist as anything more than the creation of the audience researcher (Hartley, 1988; Ang, 1991). The empirical evidence consistently fails to find a link between media and behaviour in any context (Barker and Petley, 1996; Gauntlett, 1998; Norris, 1999). Other social factors are the most significant influences on people's thinking and behaviour.

In recent work, the most sophisticated audience research sidesteps the third position and seeks to chart a way through the first two, in that it offers perspectives which seek to combine the autonomous audience with a number of media factors that can limit and guide cognitive interpretation and understanding. One such approach follows the line that the media has no strong single effect but, rather, has a series of minor effects that, in aggregate, have a significant influence. Agenda-setting, framing, priming, demobilisation and partisan reinforcement each have an influence on how people make sense of media (Jhally and Lewis, 1992; Iyengar and Reeves, 1997, Part IV). Another approach emphasises the activity of audiences, but similarly acknowledges the limits of interpretation and the possibilities for shared mainstream interpretation, when confronted by repetitive and relatively closed texts (Kitzenger, 1999; Livingstone, 1999). In most cases, the link between media consumption and mass, unconscious behaviour has been intellectually dispensed with.

There is, however, an alternative perspective worth exploring; one that draws on the syntheses that have emerged in such recent work. That is, that individuals can each respond actively to media and with their own needs in mind, but that their responses can, in aggregate, be both mass and irrational. Thus, individuals may all consume the same information in individual contexts. They may also respond in ways that they think are in their own best interests. But, collectively, the results may be on a mass scale and in a form that may not benefit those individuals at all. In other words, mass media is implicated in mass behavioural responses, without denying the existence of active and conscious media consumers.

To explain the logic of the argument I now turn to research into an audience hitherto ignored in audience and effects research: financial elites. Traditionally, the whole thrust of audience research has been to look at those individuals considered vulnerable in society and susceptible to media influence and irrationality (children, deviants, the marginalised, the 'ignorant masses'). Researchers have then sought to establish the autonomy and individuality of such groups. By contrast, I have spent some time looking at an audience considered powerful in society, immune to media influence and acutely logical: institutional fund managers, operating in the London Stock Exchange. Indeed, their job is to actively consume large quantities of information with a view to making multiple rational investment decisions that benefit themselves and their clients. In looking more closely at this 'interpretive community', it becomes clear how often such active media consumption results in financial shifts that could be considered both mass and irrational.

## Locating the empirical study: financial elites, communication effects and rationality

Instead of the 'active audience' in media/communication studies, the focus has been the 'rational individual' in economics and finance. But, when it comes to looking at individual information responses and actions, work on markets and finance has had a quite opposite trajectory to that in audience studies. Work on media audiences began by assuming individuals were unthinking, passive and mass and came to adopt an opposing view. Work on economics and markets, particularly in the area of financial market theory, has for several decades been built on assumptions of rationality and the notion of the rational, profit-maximising individual. Such individuals, in their very autonomous behaviours, absorb and respond to all price-relevant information in the market and, collectively, produce perfect, rational markets. However, since the 1980s, doubts about the rationality of both individuals and markets have come to the surface.[1] The emergence of 'behavioural finance' theory, coupled with greater attention to the volatility of markets, has led to many questioning the assumptions of information dissemination and rational investor responses that lie at the base of finance theory. Ironically, just as audience theory was establishing the active independence of individuals, so behavioural finance began to investigate instances of just the reverse.

The issue of rationality quickly became a major theme of my elite audience-centred research. My study of the investment audience consisted of 34 interviews, 22 with experienced fund managers and 12 with other elite participants in the equities market of the London Stock Exchange (LSE). Fund managers control the flow of investment in the 'City' and, therefore, make decisions about the allocation of the majority of surplus capital in the country (see Chapter 5 for details). As most observers of the LSE are aware

(Holland, 1997; Chapman, 2002; Golding, 2003) it is the decisions of this elite group (no more than a few thousand), not the millions of individual shareholders, that determine prices and investment trends more generally.

From an outsider's view it appears that media and communication are somehow implicated in frequent and large-scale shifts that take place in financial markets. The regular, and often quite dramatic, rises and falls of individual share prices, market sectors and whole markets, appear to signify evidence of mass behaviour. Such spectacular shifts, indeed, must relate directly to large numbers of individuals buying or selling simultaneously and, therefore, acting on shared, widely available information. If: a) an elite group is responsible for most share price shifts, b) shifts in share prices and markets are often extreme, and c) shared information is implicated in the process of evaluation and trading, then the logical conclusion is that some kind of communication-induced, elite form of mass behaviour frequently occurs. The aims of the research have thus sought to enquire into the valuation and decision-making processes of fund managers, the part played by the 'information environment' in that evaluation and the causes of volatility in markets.

Before continuing, it is worth clarifying the use of media and communication in Stock Markets. On the one hand it is debatable how important mainstream news media is to professional fund managers. The financial press is always a day behind and financial journalists are considered of secondary importance in the financial communication strategies of quoted companies. Fund managers have access to instant electronic sources of financial information. They, and their research teams, also spend much of their time looking directly at company information and research, and talking directly to company managers and analysts. In effect, electronic and privately generated sources of information are as important to fund managers as mass media sources (see Holland, 1997; Davis, 2000b, 2005; Golding, 2003, on each of these points).

On the other hand, there is also a substantial amount of evidence, within the finance sector itself, to suggest some degree of news media influence. A MORI (summer, 2000) survey of 104 institutional investors (professional fund managers) asked 'What various sources of information would you say are most useful to you in your job?' The second highest answer, at 51 per cent, was newspapers, and the third highest, at 38 per cent, was news/wire services. There are also several studies, in banking and finance journals, which have looked for links between financial news and share price movements. All 11 that I located, without knowledge of, or reference to, audience/effects debates, found significant statistical correlations between the publication of financial information in newspapers and abnormal trading volumes and share price shifts.[2] For others, researching instances of volatility in markets generally (Shiller, 1989, 2001; Cassidy, 2002), the media must play a central role in order for mass trading activity to occur.

The interviews also suggested two further interpretations to support a mass media/communication effects paradigm in the LSE. First, although there were many rival information sources to news every interviewee, without exception, read *The Financial Times*. Everyone had instant access to and followed the same price-sensitive information relayed directly through the Regulatory News Service (RNS) of the LSE, either directly or via a news wire service. In effect, the consumption of certain news sources is more prevalent among fund managers than almost any other audience studied. Second, many 'private' information sources are actually available to, and consumed by, a very high proportion of professional investors. All have access to the same analyst research reports and recommendations and to electronic services summarising market/analyst information. All have access to the same company information published in multiple forms. As one interviewee explained: (Gordon Midgley) 'This is a market where everyone can see everything all the time because everyone is competing all the time and selling all the time. Everyone puts their brokers circulars or sell-side notes out via email lists all the time.'

Private information sources of this nature thus take on a mass media function for this interpretive community. Indeed, this electronically enhanced 'information environment' has a greater dispersion and saturation level among the relevant audience than any mass media form does for a general audience. Arguably, this intense 'information environment' (in traditional and electronic forms), in combination with a number of common, rational and individually pursued investment strategies, can and does lead to irrational and mass forms of behaviour.

## Rational and irrational calculation in response to market information

As stated, the rational, profit-maximising individual who responds to price-sensitive information lies at the heart of most finance theory that has been produced since the 1950s. The Efficient Markets Hypothesis (EMH), which is part of any textbook on finance (e.g., Reilly and Brown, 2000; Bodie *et al.*, 2003), relies on rationality for the efficient functioning of financial markets. Prices and market equilibrium are reached by the absorption of all market-relevant information by large numbers of self-serving individuals competing to buy and sell shares (or other products). Each participant knows what they want and applies rational calculations to the valuation and trading process. According to the EMH, even if some individuals act irrationally – that is, not in their own best interests or not using calculative rationality – there are enough rational buyers and sellers to cancel out irrational actions and outcomes. Moreover, if that fails to happen, 'arbitrageurs' (professional, short-term profit-seekers) in the market will move in to take advantage of the irrationalities of others and then make a profit. In so doing, all relevant information will come to be reflected in market prices, market equilibrium will be restored and irrational participants, because of their losses, are traded out of the market altogether. Thus, the market is assumed to be populated by active individuals who, for their own survival, must respond rationally to market-wide information. Consequently the market always finds its rational equilibrium.

In the process of interviewing fund managers they did indeed appear to be rational individuals: highly educated, very focused, calculating examples of 'homo economicus'. Each was very computer literate and communication-oriented and able to collect and collate large amounts of data relevant to their investment strategy. Every fund manager had an investment philosophy, or 'style' (informing that strategy), that they must be able to explain to their clients and assessors. Each was highly numerate and able to use a number of accounting tools and measures. Interestingly, many were aware of their own potential irrationalities and failings, and took steps to counter them. As two fund managers explained in relation to their valuation process: (Tony Dye) 'You are always a bit worried that it's your own cognitive dissonance that's leading you to that opinion rather than a rational assessment of what they are saying'; (Michael Rimmer) 'Lots of things un-level the playing field and mean that you are not being totally objective. No-one can claim to be totally objective but we try and improve the odds in our favour by having the system that we do.'

However, a closer inspection of the calculative process itself frequently reveals it to be dependent on non-calculative or irrational bits of information. In other words, those involved may be rational in their approach but reliant on non-rational data and cognitive processes. Since the 1980s the subdiscipline of 'behavioural finance' has slowly emerged within the finance field. The work of Kahneman and others (Kahneman *et al.*, 1982; Kahneman and Tversky, 2000; Shleifer, 2000) has sought to explore the heuristic devices used by individuals when calculating risk. Their findings have identified a number of elements which influence calculations contrary to simple rules of probability and, thus, lead to systematic errors. Many of these elements have similarly been identified in psychological approaches to media effects research (Iyengar and Kinder, 1987; Iyengar and Reeves, 1997). They include 'cognitive dissonance' (akin to partisan reinforcement), 'framing', 'loss aversion' and the use of anchoring (akin to cognitive shortcuts). As a result, market participants, including so-called arbitrageurs, may act with a rational thought process but not necessarily according to their own best interests. As several observers note, these calculative processes, when widely reproduced, can lead to quite volatile and irrational trading patterns (Kindleberger, 2000; Shleifer, 2000; Shiller, 2001). As Kahneman and Tversky argue (2000: xvi): 'A growing body of findings support a radical challenge to the assumption, central to much economic theory, that stable profits exist. The image of a decision-maker who makes choices by consulting a preexisting preference order appears increasingly implausible.'

A closer look at the calculation process also shows it to be based on a number of subjective assumptions. Essentially, participants in financial markets are making decisions based on estimates of how a company or industry will do in the future. However, identifying what is the most current relevant information for extrapolating future profits is never sure. No matter what measures are adopted there is no accounting for the impact of macro economic or political shifts, or natural disasters or as-yet-unknown competition. In my interviews it also became clear that 'investment fashions' and 'styles' frequently changed. For example, in the 1970s conglomerates were thought to be good. By the 1990s demergers and 'focus' were good. Until the 1990s inflation was generally thought to be good for stock markets. Since the 1990s the reverse has been true. As one investment manager explained, there is no real agreement on approaches even within investment firms:

> I have worked at a number of institutions in the past, including XXX for six or seven years. From my experience there, and everywhere else . . . within any large company with lots of fund managers you have an entire spectrum of opinions on how it should be done. That was undoubtedly the case at XXX where you had people like AAA at one end who was very much contrarian, very much value, BBB, very much value, CCC, when he was there, more growth than surprise, DDD, maybe growth, earnings surprise. . . . to define exactly what was the common trigger to a buy or a sell for any stock I always felt we didn't do very well.
>
> (anonymous fund manager)

It also became apparent that valuation tools regularly changed as different parties adjusted and presented their accounts in more favorable ways. Everyone interviewed said that the valuation tools they used had changed at least once during their career:

> The concept of value has changed. If you go back 30 years people were putting much more emphasis on asset values. They then put much more emphasis on dividend yields. They then put much more emphasis on P/Es. So . . . the definition of value has changed at least three times in the 30 years.
>
> (Michael Hughes)

Many also indicated that they thought several traditional measures had been corrupted by companies manipulating the presentation of data:

I think just now, it's almost a fashion for people to just report what the companies give off the headline earnings, which are often not the true accounting earnings per share . . . they do within their accounts but it's buried in a footnote really. What they report instead is earnings per share that are adjusted to add back exceptionals, add back depreciation. And for acquisitive companies the difference can be two, three or more times what the actual earnings are.

(Colin McLean)

The interviews thus add further evidence to what some critical economists have highlighted for years, that accounting and financial data are regularly subjected to rhetoric, change and manipulation (McCloskey, 1985; Smith, 1996; Miller, 1998).

Interestingly, the issue that tops many fund manager agendas, when making value judgements of a company, has little to do with rational calculation at all. In survey after survey, the view of the chief executive and senior management of a company are either considered the most important or second most important factor in making investment decisions (see also Holland, 1997; MORI, *Captains of Industry*, 1998; Golding, 2003). A MORI (summer 2000) poll of institutional investors and City analysts asked, without prompting, 'What are the most important factors you take into account when making your judgment about companies?': 77 per cent of investors and 70 per cent of analysts said 'quality of management'. Fifty per cent of investors and 31 per cent of analysts said 'financial status/balance sheet'.

The survey data was clearly supported by the interviews. Many fund managers talked of the 'cult of the CEO' and said it was very common for professionals to follow the careers of managers, meet them regularly, and include an assessment of management in the company valuation process:

And if you were to think about quality of management, well clearly . . . it's going to have an impact on the success of the company and that'll be measured through its own share growth.

(Rick Lacaille)

Meeting with companies' management teams is very important for fund managers. We often have between 15 and 20 companies coming into our offices each week . . . Unlike the number-crunching part of a fund-manager's job, management meetings are very subjective – it is very much down to your personal judgement of them as individuals and as a team. In this regard there is no substitute for experience.

(Edward Bonham-Carter)

Such issues have led a vocal minority in finance theory to question the 'rational' basis of financial information, finance theory and the EMH generally. Indeed, for many (Soros, 1994; Shiller, 2000; Shleifer, 2000), 'sentiment', 'emotion' and psychological factors are as core to responses in markets as rationality. As one interviewee put it:

> Mr Market is a moving animal. And its mood swings will change and passion swings change but you've got to be alert to those. The mood music changes. Then you have to. You can't, as the Americans say, 'Fight the tape'. You've got to change and be flexible and say yes, that something's changed, something fundamental has changed and your attitude's got to change.
>
> (anonymous fund manager)

In effect, the investment process is presented as one informed and guided by 'formal rationality' but, in practice, is much closer to Weber's (1968 [1922]) description of 'substantive rationality'.

## Communication, rational calculation and mass behaviour

If the basis of individual rational calculation in stock markets may, in part, be based on irrational premises, individuals acting in stock markets may, in response to the information environment, also have a tendency to behave in mass-like ways. The reason is that many aspects of stock market trading rely on making calculations based, not on the values of businesses in isolation but, instead, in relation to what the mass of other traders are doing. The information environment in markets facilitates and even encourages such reflexive calculative behaviour. An abundance of such information enables individuals to continually monitor both prices and the behaviour of others. In effect, individuals are in a position where they may respond to information by rationally choosing to follow or avoid 'the herd' as a strategy for increasing individual profits. As such the information environment, from financial news to electronic data transmission, is implicated in mass behavioural tendencies.

To explain further, this reflexive, mediated environment is central to the valuation process. The experience of those involved in markets is that valuations and trades are rarely divorced from knowledge about the consensus views of traders generally. For outsiders and amateur investors, traders simply value and pick stocks according to the estimated accounting value of a company in isolation – in terms of assets, sales, industry share and so on. However, many professional trading strategies rely on valuing and picking stocks purely in relation to other company shares traded in the market, that is, according to what others do. The first method looks at the actual accounting value of a company and attempts to make decisions based on possible future profits. The second looks at the company purely as a commodity to be speculatively bought and sold in relation to other company-commodities within the market. An oft-cited description (in the finance world) of the market by JM Keynes (1936) sums up this situation. Keynes compared professional investment to a beauty contest in which:

> the prize [is] awarded to the competitor whose choice most nearly corresponds to the average preferences of the competitors as a whole . . . It is not a case of choosing those which, to the best of one's judgment, are really the prettiest, nor even those which average opinion genuinely thinks the prettiest. We have reached the third degree where we devote our intelligence to anticipating what average opinion expects the average opinion to be.

According to many observers, this 'reflexive' form of valuation and investment decision-making, which assumes others have access to and respond to the same information, dominates real trading decisions in most stock markets (Pratten, 1993; Soros, 1994; Golding, 2003). As such, the more saturated and extensive the information environment, the more such reflexive valuation and behaviour can occur.

This 'reflexive investment' approach, including the need to know what others think, what the consensus beliefs are, and how the market is likely to react, as well as the role of information in such, became very clear when discussing valuation processes with fund managers. No matter the investment 'style' or belief in the companies traded, there was a constant eye on 'the market' in evidence:

> And the emphasis here is that it's a score for the stock not the company. In other words he [the fund manager] is making an assessment of what he thinks the stock price is going to do, not whether he likes the company or not. Now, the influence on his stock price judgement may be whether or not he likes the company, but sometimes you get a good stock performance on a company you don't like. So it is much more about stock scoring than it is about companies really.
>
> (Michael Hughes)

> To say 'This is a good company. It will outperform over five years. I am going to buy it and just forget about it' is unlikely to be a defensible approach these days. Because if the share under-performs sharply for the first 12 months of holding it your client is going to be extremely unhappy. So . . . you have to be realistic.
>
> (anonymous fund manager)

In seeking the consensus opinion investors continually monitor market movements and information about consensus figures; and here financial media and communication are a vital part of the consensus seeking. Many stories in the financial media are built around the presentation of what the general feeling is of a company or trend according to what 'analysts', 'the City', 'the Market' or 'major shareholders' think as a group. And, although fund managers did not want to admit to being overly influenced by media stories, they did seem very aware of consensus opinions appearing there:

> I think the media don't set the agenda there. But they can reinforce it. They reinforce what the common view is . . . They reflect a general consensus that has built up already.
>
> (Colin McLean)

> They may not agree with the consensus opinion but it's not hard to see that consensus emerging. You may not be part of that consensus but you may be aware of it. . . . I think the meeting will be the start of the process. It's reinforced by the newspapers talking to analysts who have been at the meeting. Ones they trust and think know their industry. The meeting becomes reinforced in the press later.
>
> (Tony Golding)

Most importantly, investors seek to locate consensus opinions among research analysts. There may be thousands of investors but only a handful of analysts for any company. The very largest companies have no more than 20–30 analysts following them and producing research and trading recommendations; most have rather less. Not only do professional fund managers have access to the same analysts' output, they also have access to the same electronic database services which collate all this output. Such services can summarise analyst forecasts for any company and its history, as well as offering statistical summaries of the forecasts. Every fund manager I interviewed referred to the process of checking their estimates against the 'analyst consensus' figures. So, as one fund manager explained in detail:

> So let's say you have got five analysts covering the stock and they have all got different levels. Where is the average? It's a simple calculation, the average of all forecasts . . . it comes from Multex earnings revision data. It's a database. For Multex you can pick up for any stock forecasts for this year and next year. You can then dig into that and see all the brokers who have contributed to that consensus and can see the distribution of the estimates. Some will be really high, some really low, lots closer to the middle. Then you can see over time how individual analysts have changed their numbers and therefore have a consensus for change.
>
> (Michael Rimmer)

This reflexive, communication-linked investment process encourages many traders to pursue a number of trading strategies which simply respond to information signals in the market. When large groups pursue similar strategies, or 'investment styles', herd-like behaviour follows and prices can surge up or down with some regularity. 'Indexing', 'quant' styles, 'momentum investing' and 'hedge funds' all rely on making use of widely available, internally generated market information. All are individual profit-maximising strategies that, at the same time, can generate mass-like and potentially damaging results.

One low-cost alternative to active fund management is index tracking or passive fund management. Such tracker funds are run by computer programs and automatically buy and sell shares in an index, such as the FTSE 100, as they enter or leave the index. It is difficult to estimate the proportion of such funds that exist in the market, but all concerned are sure that proportion is rising. Golding (2003: 156) estimated that 20–30 per cent of funds were either trackers or 'closet indexers' (i.e., they stuck closely to the index numbers). Myners (2001: 81) estimated passive management to be in the order of 20–25 per cent. Clearly, indexing and passive management encourage herd-like activity. The more funds are bound by investment indices and computer programs the more potential there is for mass shifts in investment to occur. Similarly, as Woolley (May 2002) argues, the consequences are quite detrimental to investors generally and, therefore, irrational. If too many people move to passive investment and indexing then there is less competition over prices, sellers can take advantage of automatic, herd-like trading responses and instability results. As he concludes, index-tracking may be a logical choice for individuals but, if too many use them, index returns become worse for everyone.

Two further forms of investment, that are internally focused, offer the same potential problems: 'momentum investing' and 'hedge funds'. Momentum investing is a strategy where fund managers simply buy shares which are rising rapidly and sell those which are not. Advances in computer-aided information dissemination and trading has made this strategy all the easier. Hedge funds rely on complex computer programs and follow a strategy of buying and selling opposite products in great quantities, so both ensuring one's risks are 'hedged' and making automatic profits on the differences. Much of the time this strategy is considered low risk but, on occasion, has resulted in some extreme losses. When hedge funds deal with derivatives (betting on future movements), and excessively leverage their deals (deal on borrowed capital), the potential for large-scale breakdowns increases. The collapse of Barings and the Long Term Capital Management hedge fund, in the 1990s, are examples of such catastrophes, when markets did not behave according to expectations or computer models (see MacKenzie, 2003).

Similarly, like passive investing and indexing, both momentum investing and hedge funds can operate automatically and blindly and, when a number of funds are acting in unison, can have potentially dramatic effects on market volatility. As Paul Woolley explained:

> It is very appealing for individual investors to use momentum, either standalone or in conjunction with other strategies. From the point of view of collective utility, however, their use is damaging because in certain conditions they can trigger (or fuel) bubbles and implosions in individual stocks, industry sectors or entire equity markets . . . Hedge funds serve to aggravate the problem. They offer a number of apparent advantages to investors, not least the benefits of diversification. However, hedge funds have a very short investment horizon and are consequently more inclined to adopt momentum. Though representing less than 2 per cent of assets under management in equities, their leverage, ability to ignore index weights and frenetic turnover accord them a hugely disproportionate influence on share prices. The paradox of individual gain yet collective cost, therefore, becomes magnified when hedge funds are brought into account.

Passive management, momentum investing and hedge funds were regarded as recent investment trends that had strongly influenced the shape of the market. Each follows a sort of self-interested 'free-rider' (Olson, 1965) logic that also, simultaneously, threatens to break down for all concerned if too many partake.

These reflexive, heavily mediated investment processes are also key to the way fund manager performance is evaluated and, consequently, similarly encourages herd-like responses. Fund managers are often judged in relation to how well they do relative to an index – such as the FTSE AllShare. They all aim for, but rarely achieve, results which get better returns than the average of shares quoted on their index (their 'alpha'). Increasingly, fund managers are also compared to each other relative to 'benchmarks' – specially constructed indices of certain shares. But, the obvious consequence, for critics (Myners, 2001; Golding, 2003), is that fund managers feel bound to stick closely to their index or benchmark, in order to be validated and lower their personal risks. If a majority are close to the index when things go wrong, none can be singled out, but if someone breaks ranks and things are going wrong they can be blamed personally. Therefore, regardless of what an investor thinks of a particular company, if it is part of the benchmark and its shares are rising, they feel bound to buy into the shares – to keep a 'full' or 'neutral weighting'. The results are that a number of fund managers will automatically buy into or sell certain shares which, in turn, moves the value and encourages abnormal trading.

One well cited recent example was the rapid rise in value of Vodaphone (see Woolley, May 2002; Golding, 2003). The company's share price rose far in excess of its assets or possible future returns largely because of indexing pressures. In fact, one of the main conclusions of a Treasury-sponsored investigation into the industry (Myners, 2001: 2; see also Davis, 1995; Blake and Timmermann, 2001) was that:

> many objectives are set which give managers unnecessary and artificial incentives to *herd*. So-called 'peer group' benchmarks, directly incentivising funds to copy other funds, remain common. And risk controls for active managers increasingly set in ways which give them little choice but to cling closely to stock market indices, making meaningful active management near impossible.

As many of my interviewees explained, the pressures to follow the herd are often greater than those encouraging the reverse. If it all goes wrong it does so for the majority and no-one gets blamed. But if it goes wrong for someone following a different strategy the business is jeopardised:

> There has been a feeling that too many managers are index huggers. So, they are not necessarily passive managers but if they are told to beat the index they do not necessarily bother because it was seen as too big a risk to their business. And you wouldn't get sacked for modestly underperforming. You would only get sacked for significantly underperforming.
>
> (Hugh Sergeant)

> You've heard of the so-called herd instinct. Over the last 10 years, by and large, there has not been much to choose between the approaches of many of the big managers in their portfolio management styles. Also, there is not a great performance differential between the top and bottom performers . . . the moral of the story is that it's a lower risk strategy for a fund manager to follow the herd rather than being in the more risky position of an outrider.
>
> (John Rogers)

In effect, there are very logical reasons why fund managers, encouraged by the shared and intense information environment, adopt the investment strategies they do. Observing the consensus, indexing/passive management, hedge funds and momentum investing, all have their rationales for self-interested profit-maximising individuals. In each case a widely shared communication environment is essential. However, each of these strategies, combined with the insular, reflexive nature of the investment process more generally, encourages herd or mass-like behaviour. Cumulatively a lot of such actions can also have quite self-defeating (irrational) consequences.

## Irrationality meets mass behaviour: manias, panics, bubbles and crashes

Nowhere is mediated mass behaviour and irrational activity more visible than during stock market bubbles and crashes. At such points investor optimism and share price values rise and fall in quite dramatic ways. All markets encounter such bubbles and crashes periodically. Between 1970 and 1999, 21 different national financial markets experienced increases in value of over 100 per cent in a year and 17 of those same markets experienced drops of over 50 per cent in a subsequent year (Shiller, 2000: 119–20). The United States and United Kingdom have both experienced two relatively recent large bubbles and crashes, in 1987 and 2000.

Observers of bubbles and crashes in history (Shiller, 1989, 2000; Kindleberger, 2000; Cassidy, 2002), tend to find the same elements present in each. For all observers, while economic factors provide an initial impetus (e.g., easy bank credit, an economic shift), bubbles and crashes then become driven by 'psychological factors', 'herd behaviour' and the 'media'. For each bubble and crash markets are very inefficient and participants, in aggregate, do not behave rationally. For Kindleberger (2000: 31):

> yet euphoric speculation, with stages or with insiders and outsiders, may also lead to manias and panics when the behavior of every participant seems rational in itself . . . The action of each individual is rational – or would be, were it not for the fact that others are behaving in the same way.

Shiller (1989, 2000) and Cassidy (2002) both devote some attention to the part played by media and communication in bubbles and crashes. Shiller (1989) looked at news before and during crashes in 1929 and 1987. In both he concluded there were no external social or economic news stories that triggered the crash. The significant stories, that investors remembered, were those about very recent drops in the market itself. His survey of professional investors in 1987 found that, on the first day, they checked prices an average of 35 times. 'Symptoms of anxiety' were reported by 43.1 per cent of them, 'a contagion of fear from other investors' was experienced by 40.2 per cent and 31.1 per cent of them changed their holdings that day.

The most recent TMT (Telecommunications, Media, Technology) boom and bust in 2000, as most interviewees referred to it, followed a similar pattern. From 1995–2000, the New York Dow Jones effectively tripled in value – from below 3,500 points to just under 12,000. The London Stock Exchange went from just over 3,000 points to almost 7,000 points. According to Shiller (2000) and Smithers and Wright (2000), historical measures of these stock markets showed them to be over-priced beyond all financial logic in 2000. Prices of companies in the market were so high that they bore no relation to the actual profits or asset values of these companies when valued by traditional accounting measures (see figures in Chapter 2)

For Cassidy (2002) and Shiller (2000) media and communication were deeply implicated in this period of 'irrational exuberance'. For both, the *Wall Street Journal*, the new financial news channels (CNBC, CNNfn, Bloomberg), the rise of new financial journals, and the Internet itself, all fed the boom. They provided a speculative forum in which financial information and opinion were circulated on rises/trends and helped to hype new TMT stocks and the rhetoric of 'new economy'. According to Cassidy (2002: 123), the rising prices and media speculation meant it seemed too great a risk not to join the boom:

> Many mutual fund managers carried on buying stocks even though they believed them to be over-valued, which was not necessarily irrational . . . Trapped in this logic, the vast majority of fund managers tend to keep buying stocks regardless of their prices, which makes the market even more overvalued.

The rational decision was thus to follow what many believed was an irrational path. All interviewees were asked about their experience of the TMT bubble and why they chose to invest or not. None singled out the UK media for specific blame. But all spoke of the intense, self-reflexive nature of communication during the bubble, and of the pressures to participate, regardless of their own views. Two high-profile fund managers I talked to were well known for resisting the majority decision to invest in TMT stocks and had consequently suffered at the time. For Woolley:

> The TMT bubble offered a classic example of the bandwagon effect. Unrealistic expectations were the main culprit, but the share price explosion was undoubtedly fuelled by demand from managers concerned to protect their portfolios against benchmark risk by staying close to index weights in the sector.

Tony Dye is well known in the City (every interviewee cited his case) for having publicly defied the boom and, consequently, lost his job just before the crash. For Dye, the internal, reflexive elements of investment also played a part:

> Most of our heuristics are based on observing what other people do and if they don't get hurt by it then they follow and do it themselves. That's why these things, if they really get some social momentum behind them, they can be absolutely powerful phenomenon – massively powerful phenomenon. And that's what happened in the dot.com boom. Companies that didn't have anything, no capital, no prospects, as it

happened, could be worth hundreds of millions, or in America, tens of billions, or even hundreds of billions of dollars. That's pretty frightening in this supposedly rational world in which we live. Those things can and do happen . . . And that's what tends to happen in financial markets. All you can do is look at the history of booms and busts and see that they don't get any smaller. They may in fact get bigger.

All other interviewees explained similar influences and pressures, which meant that the logical course of action was to invest, in the short term, in stocks that could not possibly meet long-term expectations. According to John Davies's experience of events:

Racey stories combined with a lack of knowledge. You then start to see real share price performance . . . You then start to worry because you haven't got any and you pile in. As everything keeps going up that gets worse and worse, especially if you are underweight. Investors start chasing their tales then. They feel they've got to be exposed to it. The odd investor who stood back from it – Tony Dye being the supreme example – actually gets the sack before he's proved right. . . . If you look at an index that doesn't do anything but 10 per cent of it doubles in a year, the index would have gone up 10 per cent. If you didn't have any exposure there you would have under-performed by 10 per cent even though it's relatively small. If that happens for four years on the trot. Most will forgive one year's performance, maybe two. But then by the third year you must have made a mistake . . . It really didn't matter what the company did. That's no different from tulip bulbs or Australian mines . . . 'momentum' was the only thing that was working and that's a very dangerous investment philosophy to use.

Ultimately, the costs to the City and those professionally involved in the London Stock Exchange were high and immediate. The market lost almost 50 per cent of its value over the next three years. At the time of writing (autumn 2006) it has yet to recover its 2000 peak level. The most severe job losses in any sector of the UK economy at the time were in the City itself. Many of the largest investors in the market, such as pension funds and insurance companies, have since withdrawn a large proportion of their funds from the equities market (IMA, 2004) and/or invested in passive funds. The costs to the wider economy were equally large (or larger) but less immediately visible (see Chapter 5). What thus becomes clear is that short-term, logical and rational decision-making by fund managers, has resulted in long-term irrational losses on a mass scale.

# Conclusion

The evidence presented here offers an alternative account of the links between mass media/communication and mass behaviour. Instead of focusing on 'vulnerable' or general 'mass' groups this study has looked at elite, specific ones. Instead of identifying instances of individual interpretation and difference in media consumption the topic has uncovered examples of collective behaviour in response to media consumption. This alternative focus has helped present a quite different perspective on the media effects question.

Quite clearly the members of the financial audience studied act individually and are in direct competition with each other. They also quiet clearly consume their media actively, with conscious purposes in mind, and respond rationally, that is, in ways that follow a clear logic and with self-interest in mind. However, the basis upon which rational calculations are made may have little to do with rational calculation at all. The reflexive nature of the investment process, which encourages all participants to observe and react according to what they think their rivals might do, encourages similar responses to information. Investment strategies, such as momentum investing or passive investment, which rely on the communication environment of the market, automatically create herd-like tendencies. The need to assess and compare performance creates yet more of thé same. All these tendencies mean that mass, irrational acts, such as volatile trading patterns, bubbles and crashes, are frequent occurrences. In effect, rational and individually competitive responses to widely available information can, under such circumstances, create mass behaviour of an irrational nature. In other words, rational, self-interested individuals can, collectively, behave in mass, irrational ways; and in response to common sources of media and communication.

# Chapter 10

# Conclusions

This final chapter identifies some of the themes that link the diverse case examples presented in the book. Although the discussions, professions and elite sites of power observed vary, there are some common, identifiable themes that appear and reappear through these chapters. These say much about elites, their relations to power, culture and communication at elite-centred sites, and mediation and journalist–elite relations at those sites.

## Inverted political economy and mediated power

Most of the case research in this book has been conceived within a conceptual framework I have labelled an 'inverted political economy of communication'. This has involved locating specific sites of economic and politico-legal power where localised or networked actions and decision-making have wider social impacts. In this book the main networks/sites investigated were Parliament at Westminster, the London Stock Exchange and an NGO-centred international development policy network. Research has then attempted to explore the cultures, beliefs, discourses, practices and processes of mediation at these sites.

Such an approach has naturally lead to several enquiry lines being developed. One of these has been to identify those specific groups that inhabit these network/sites, and to investigate their relationship to power. The logic is not simply to identify a cohesive elite group or class unit which knows its interests and has worked to maintain its position and material benefits through the exercise of power. Such groups were, instead, selected on the basis of their inhabiting such sites of power and the assumption that their decisions or actions have a greater impact on power relations in society. The principal groups investigated in this book were professional public relations practitioners, national journalists, fund managers, elected politicians and senior NGO activists.

Another line of enquiry has involved observing the forms of culture that are present and evolving at such sites; culture in the 'whole way of life', rather than the 'culture as art', sense. The assumption is that discrete, localised cultures develop at these sites and with some autonomy from the outside world. Within such elite subcultural sites or networks a number of elements can be documented depending on the theorists and tools utilised. Observations here tended to be at the level of norms, values, ideologies and discursive practices. The point of investigation was not to distinguish 'higher' forms of culture or greater cognitive capacities. Rather, interest was directed by a belief that such cultures, cognitions and practices have a greater influence on wider power and inequality by virtue of the positions of individuals within those sites of power.

A third level of enquiry has focused on exploring processes of mediated power. How do elites, elite institutions and networks use media and communication and, conversely, how do media and communication shape elites, elite institutions and networks? How, in other words, do individuals, in their use of media, inadvertently alter their behaviours, relations and discursive practices? Hitherto, the question has generally been applied to non-elite groups in society, but is just as applicable to elite actors and sites of power. Indeed, such actors may not have greater cognitive capacities than others but they do have distinctive relationships with journalists and media. They are prominent information sources for news media, are often the subject of news stories and are frequently scrutinised and evaluated through the media. Moreover, their professions require that they follow the news media closely and, in fact, many are avid consumers of it. They also have regular, personal relations with media producers and many others who appear in media coverage. These differences are significant when exploring contemporary processes of mediation.

It is these lines of enquiry which have directed the research and determined the interview questions. Thus, enquiry has sought to ask what is the nature of the social relations of those that inhabit such sites – with each other and with other professions? How much autonomy or influence do they feel they have and how are they rewarded or disciplined? What are the daily discursive practices that engage them and have a potential bearing on those in wider society? What are the significant terms and concepts that are specific to their sites or networks? How do they use news media in their daily practices and as a means for achieving strategic objectives? How do they relate to it during their evaluative and decision-making processes?

In perusing these lines of enquiry a number of themes and passing observations have tended to surface across the different sites investigated. Some might argue that deducing generalised patterns of behaviour and understanding from series of interviews is problematic. In which case making more generalised claims about elites and sites of power is more problematic still. That should be borne in mind when reading the following sketched-out thoughts.

## Elites and elite relations to power

The first set of observations relate to those groups which operate in the selected sites of power. In most studies of media, politics and power the traditional lines of interpretation tend to follow (post) Marxist or liberal pluralist lines. These either assume that elites (or classes) are cohesive enough to disseminate consistent and self-sustaining discourses, or that elite and non-elite groups are too fragmented and conflictual for such dominant lines of communication to be sustained. However, a feature identified in many of the studies here is one of inter-elite conflict in which non-elite majorities are excluded altogether.

As observed, NGO campaigners, politicians and fund managers are frequently involved in internal competitions to set organisational goals and frameworks. This is in addition to involvement in external conflicts with rivals, or clashes with larger groups in society. The outcome is that certain elite groups, networks or sites of power do prevail and are rewarded in economic, political and status terms. Indeed, the concentration of capital in international financial centres, the economic rewards bestowed on certain corporate elites and the levels of national (and international) inequality, all continue to rise at rapid rates. In many cases there are still identifiable, socially cohesive groups that are able to maintain and pass on their positions of privilege and reward. Thus, the outcome of conflict and negotiation, between elite groups, may often be to benefit all sides to the detriment of those excluded from the exchanges altogether. All of which does suggest that a necessary way forward involves developing some form of 'competitive elite' theory of power and communication.

However, there is also much to complicate the picture beyond both the early, 'classic elite' accounts, and, many of the later, critical, 'power elite' studies. What often struck me during the research was the dislocation between perceived, symbolic power and actual power. Most MPs appear to be relatively powerless in comparison to public perceptions. Many work extremely long hours, balance conflicting roles and usually have negligible input into, or influence over, government policy and legislation. City fund managers are the people that company CEOs are answerable to and so set the terms for company success. Despite this, they are themselves rarely in the public eye and appear completely detached from the power they wield over the mass of employees working for the companies they control. In turn, financial actuaries, whose all-important assessments of fund managers are crucial in the City, have relatively low levels of status and financial reward in the LSE.

Ironically, many seemed to be strongly affected by the pressures of market competition. Journalists, politicians and fund managers all feel forced to become 'more productive' with their time and resources. Fund managers repeatedly have their performances checked, compared and evaluated. Their financial decisions have measurable outcomes that are scrutinised by their companies, peers or rivals, financial actuaries and investing institutions. Backbench MPs have to continually account for their decisions and non-decisions to constituents, local journalists and party hierarchies. Ministers are continually watched by civil servants, rival ministers and national journalists. Journalists are constantly aware of being tracked by editors, powerful sources and rival publications. What was striking was how often so many of the interviewees, regardless of their occupation or political outlook, expressed anti-market concerns. Some, while being pro-market, had grave doubts about the unfettered influences of market forces on their own profession. Others were critical of the almost ideological application of blunt market solutions to problems.

Clearly, many of the 'elite' groups investigated appear to have a rather insecure and pressured existence. One decision or indiscretion can potentially end some of these careers. The average FTSE 100 company CEO holds his or her position for less than three years. MPs, on average, have a career span in Parliament of nine years. Industry listings of individual fund managers and other City professionals become virtually outdated within a year. In response, elites are forced to take short-cuts, make conservative choices and follow the mainstream when it comes to using information sources and decision-making; even if that means being part of a herd movement they do not agree with. As such, the rational actor, who makes reasoned choices according to self-interest, is as much a myth in elite sites of power as among the mass of consumer-citizens.

In effect, personal rewards, economic power, political power, status and security may not be located in the same hands. Those with perceived power may have relatively little. Those with more significant levels of power may operate quite invisibly and may not understand its operation, let alone be aware of wielding it. They may make self-interested decisions without being able to comprehend the repercussions for themselves and others. They may feel very insecure in their positions. It might be concluded that those considered to be part of the 'power elite' may well have professional lives that are 'nasty, brutish and short'. Consequently, elites may have more political power or economic capital than before, but, they are also more fragmented, transitory, insecure and less connected by social class elements. As such, the cultures and organisational processes of such elite sites of power are likely to be playing an increasingly significant part in achieving elite cohesion and informing elite cognitions and practices.

## Elite communication and cultures at sites of power

This last point naturally leads on to a second set of observations. These relate to the cultures present in sites/networks of power. What is immediately clear is that the communication environments within such sites are extremely intense. Fund managers, politicians, journalists and professional communicators have numerous formal meetings and informal, personal exchanges every day. Each consumes large quantities of news, specialist media outputs and electronic datasets. Working hours are long and dialogues continue in shared social spaces and through electronic exchanges. Under pressure, information has to be accumulated, opinions gathered and important decisions made – sometimes several times a day. Accordingly, such professionals become immersed in their intense and rapidly evolving communication environments. Observing the multiple, shifting norms, values, trends and points of consensus at elite sites is, thus, the cultural studies equivalent of following genetic shifts in fruit fly populations.

Elites must, therefore, develop procedures and strategies for doing business in the environment, processing information, making quick decisions and calculating personal risks. So they employ a range of intermediaries to collect and summarise information for them. They seek out trusted expert sources (their personal 'primary definers') in important decision-making areas. They develop cognitive short-cuts and other heuristic devices for collecting and digesting information and then making decisions. Thus, they tend to focus on individual leaders, rely on past experiences and try to spot prevailing trends in order to hasten decision-making. All these strategies can be found beyond such sites of power but are rarely so intense, institutionalised and consequential.

What also became apparent was how often such professions looked to and followed their peers and rivals. Journalists, politicians and fund managers all continually watch each other and are aware of being watched. Conversations, news reports, financial data streams and databases, and even physical observation, are all used to try and estimate what others are thinking and doing. Such knowledge may be a means of getting 'an edge' or, equally, a means of reducing one's personal risks and the threat of failure. Journalists cover stories that other papers cover because those stories are more likely to be accepted by editors. MPs and ministers need to assure themselves of political support before making political manoeuvres, statements or policy announcements. Fund managers invest because they think others are investing too. Such tendencies, as in other shared cultural settings, become fashions and can often result in significant 'mood swings', 'moral panics' and herd-like behaviour.

Under such circumstances it is quite possible that such sites of power may develop quite exclusive elite cultural and discursive networks. The practices and beliefs within them may become quite 'deviant' or 'disembedded' from wider public cultures, practices and beliefs. Perhaps more significant, are those elite networks which have come to exclude journalists altogether – as appears increasingly the case in many financial, international trade and diplomatic networks. Such disembedded tendencies are implicated in stock market crashes in 2000, the push to invade Iraq in 2003 and the continuing failure of corporate and political elites to fundamentally engage with global inequalities and climate change. The crucial issue for outsider groups, such as campaigning NGOs, then becomes one of how best to influence such intense and exclusive/exclusionary discourse networks: join the network, maintain critical distance or apply wider social, mediated pressure?

## Mediated power and elite source–journalist relations

In much of the classic literature on media–source relations the nature of the exchange is usually defined as a competition between two sides who need each other. Journalists get access and sources get a media platform. Power balances vary, according to a number of factors, and the two sides, accordingly, renegotiate the terms of their relationship.

Arguably, in recent decades, relations have become much more complex and multi-faceted, and not simply because one side has become more or less powerful than the other. In large part this is because media relations and sensitivities have come to play a fundamental part in elite employment practices and even promotion prospects. Established sources increasingly undergo media training and have an almost professional knowledge of how news is produced. They talk to journalists regularly, build up long-term relations with some and try to maintain links with others. They are also avid news consumers and see their own images, as well as others they know personally, projected into larger, public or private, professional media spheres.

Consequently, the source–journalist relationship serves a number of other purposes for elites. For them, talking to journalists is not simply about self-promotion and giving information. It is about receiving information. Journalists give away information about what other individuals, organisations and institutions are doing. Elite sources attempt to use such forms of information to work out the answers to a number of their occupational concerns. Is there is a growing consensus about an investment area or a policy solution? Which individuals or investments are rising and which are falling? What is the opposition or personal rival going to do next? Or, how is a decision or policy initiative likely to be reported and received by the key audiences? Journalists, therefore, are not simply reporting on political and economic processes and sites of power. They are immersed in them. They are a physical component of the information networks that form in elite sites of power. In constantly going between sources, who are also key media subjects and audiences, they are part of the elite circuits of information exchange and dialogue.

By the same token news texts may also become a part of the political or economic process. They act as a 'proxy' for, or 'consensus indicator' of, significant elite opinion. Those in the City tend to take more notice of key journalists or columns such as the *FT*'s *LEX* column. Politicians are more likely to read certain political correspondents or columnists with a view to getting much more than a personal opinion on an issue. Such columns are deemed to be reflective of a key, constituent group, within the City or Westminster. When a column refers to 'analysts think', 'reaction in the City', 'the feeling in the party', 'the mood at Westminster', there is a sense of broader, collective opinion even if, as is often the case, it is gauged from a handful of conversations. Even without such signifiers experienced news consumers judge those columns and writers – either to reflect the views of a significant audience or to make an impact on that audience. In some cases there are coded references or clues which only really make sense to the audience within the elite site. In this respect news texts act as 'elite consensus indicators' or 'crystallisers of elite opinion'. Thus, news has an information function in elite discourse networks that goes well beyond being a source of breaking news stories.

At the same time the way sources deal with journalists and news has shifted. Because of their intimate knowledge of news production, and regular exchanges with journalists, many consciously make news media part of their political or corporate strategies. Fund managers may anticipate market reactions to news stories and alter their investment decisions accordingly. Politicians and NGO campaigners look for big news stories that they can then 'ride' to publicise themselves or their positions. Each of these groups, as well as the professional communicators that work for them, are also far more proactive in using the media as a political or investment tool. Journalists are monitored, assessed and selectively targeted. Companies manage the earnings expectations of their investors by carefully (and often illegally) releasing specific bits of financial information. Allied and rival politicians, parties and interest groups 'leak stories' and 'fly kites' to test ideas, undermine opponents and push new policies. Speeches and events are trailed, selectively leaked and pre-spun.

Quite clearly journalists and news media have had a strong mediating influence on those elites who operate in sites or networks of power. Such elites have oriented a proportion of their information gathering, decision-making and behaviour around media. Consequently, media has also indirectly shaped elites and elite sites of power.

However, news media have also had more direct influences on elites and sites of power. Among all the groups interviewed there was a consistent anxiety about the larger media entity itself. While many tried to ride it or use it there was also a sense of dealing with a powerful, unmanageable and unpredictable force. MPs, interest group campaigners, CEOs and their professional communicators attempt to take advantage of news values and routines, court journalists, set reporting agendas and frames. At the same time, however, such actions involve compromises and risks.

Compromises are made because, in all areas of reporting, news values, news gathering techniques and consumer interest may conflict with elite communication objectives. One obvious consequence is a continuing media focus on individual personalities. Company CEOs and top directors, political party leaders and (shadow) ministers, and celebrity spokespeople acting for interest groups, are elevated in the media. As such, they come to represent a whole organisation; a short-hand for its brand, a signifier of its qualities or its inadequacies. The organisation is evaluated by the charisma and fashionability of its celebrity representative rather than its products, policies and arguments. News values and news gathering limitations also elevate the sensational, the short term, the single event, the financial bottom-line, the negative and the personal scandal or clash. Demoted or excluded are the chronic, the long term, the technical, the complex, the historical context, the rounded or positive assessment and the inconclusive or mixed picture. Story selection and presentation must appeal to a perceived, simplistic demographic cut-out of an audience.

The risk, always present, is that the media will turn on its rider. Many, including experienced journalists, spoke about the force of the media 'pack' or 'herd' as publications and journalists would unite around a position and push it for extended periods. Companies, markets, political parties, campaigns, political issues, individual CEOs and politicians, could all suddenly be promoted or undermined by the pack. The media are integral to the evolving fashions and moods that evolve within political or financial spheres. When moods change, or the pack decides to attack a decision or individual, personal relations with individual journalists became irrelevant. As soon as a source or journalist loses his or her position most access is cut and relations dry up.

# Appendix I

## A short note on research methods

This section offers a short overview of the research methods employed in the case study parts of each chapter. In the studies drawn upon the research aims were to document the uses and influences of media, communication and culture in specific settings and among particular professions. Such objectives, which necessitated gaining access to elite participants and restricted sites, both guided and limited the choice of methods used. The difficulties of gaining research access and cooperation in such circumstances are well documented (e.g., Moyser and Wagstaffe, 1987; Abercrombie *et al.*, 1990). Surveys and experimental cognition work is expensive, time-consuming and often impossible. Other, more qualitative methods, such as focus groups or ethnographies, are not usually realistic options either. The most practical approaches therefore include the use of interviews, content analysis, some participant observation and secondary analysis of existing industry or government survey data.

The most common method chosen was interviewing. The research material draws on studies involving over 220 interviews. The majority of those cited in the book were interviewed over a two-year period (September 2004 to September 2006). The largest constituent groups of interviewees were: Members of Parliament (MPs) at Westminster (40 interviews); fund managers from large investment institutions in the City of London (22); and senior NGO workers (22). In some of the chapters material is also taken from interviews conducted over an earlier three-year period (August 1998 to August 2001). The largest occupational group in that period were public relations professionals in the corporate and political party sectors (52). Across both time periods other groupings include: national news journalists (33); officials (e.g., civil servants, independent regulators) in state and professional bodies (17); and a variety of analysts (14). Further interviewees included members of the House of Lords, CEOs and others with a professional link to the issues researched. Some interviewees are not clearly identifiable as a professional in only one of these sectors.

The vast majority of interviews were conducted face to face, at work locations around London, many taking place at Westminster or London's

'Square Mile' financial district. Interviews lasted on average 35–40 minutes and generated just over 5,500 words of transcript material. A few were as short as 20 minutes. Many lasted over an hour and a few lasted two hours.

Interviews fell into two categories. In certain professional sectors an attempt was made to select a 'sample' and present each individual with a similar list of semi-structured questions. Three of the largest sets (public relations professionals, fund managers and MPs) were 'theoretically sampled' (Strauss and Crobin, 1998), according to quotas, from professional, industry or government publications. MPs were selected to reflect the current balance of the UK Parliament in terms of party and gender. Thus, 23 Labour, 11 Conservative and six Liberal Democrat and Independent MPs were selected. The sample was also made up of 32 men and eight women. In other cases 'sampling' was more difficult. Industry lists of organisations and representatives were used to select a list of possible interviewees on the basis of organisational characteristics; for example, large, medium and small firms, or categories of institution as designated by industry listings. In the case of journalists selection was based on gathering a balance across the left–right political spectrum and between broadsheet and tabloid publications.

There was also an element of snowballing in gaining several of the interviews (although still guided by quota considerations). This did lead to certain biases in the sample. Using industry lists often lead to a tendency to interview those in more senior or high-profile positions. In the case of MPs a conscious attempt was made to seek out those who had (shadow) ministerial or select committee experience. In all, two of the interviewees had been party leaders, 13 had government ministerial experience, 17 had shadow ministerial experience and eight were, or had been recently, chairs of parliamentary select committees. It was also likely that snowballing led to a greater proportion of interviewees having some form of media experience or interest.

Each set of interviewees was asked for responses from a list of semi-structured and open questions. Questions were slightly altered for each interviewee in line with their specific position and experience. There was not always time to put all questions to all participants although, in some cases, longer time periods allowed for more follow-up questions.

The second category of interviewee was selected because of their ability to offer a specific account of an event and/or their alternative accounts could be used to cross-reference the interview material of others. They were interviewed, therefore, in the tradition of an 'oral historian' or biographer, or as a simple means of achieving 'triangulation'. In the Make Poverty History case study (Chapter 8) it is an insider's view of particular events which is being sought. The research material in this chapter is based on 27 semi-structured interviews with 22 leading actors involved in the campaign during the course of 2005 and early 2006 (five were repeat interviews after the campaign ended). For cross-referencing purposes, financial analysts, CEOs, government and Parliamentary officials, were usually interviewed to broaden the picture offered by fund managers or MPs. Similarly, the recollections of journalists are matched with those of public relations professionals or MPs. Some of the interviewees were selected on both bases, that is, they were part of a 'theoretical sample' and they could, in addition, offer accounts of specific events. Former (shadow) ministers, senior fund managers and journalists often fell into this duel category. They would be questioned about the events surrounding a particular resignation or appointment, piece of legislation, investment decision, market crash or campaign issue.

Other, qualitative, forms of data were gathered in an effort to further inform the theory. Thus, there was an element of participant observation. Notes were usually taken about the interviewees and the interview settings. Having made over 80 separate visits to Westminster, and another 80 to offices in the City, a number of cultural and procedural issues became more apparent. In Chapter 8 participant observation was a significant part of the process as Nick Sireau attended many campaign group meetings. In many cases, written texts were collected and used to supply supporting evidence. These included (private and public) industry, NGO and government reports, surveys, meeting minutes and emails.

The qualitative material was used to produce a comprehensive, triangulated account of a specific event and/or build general 'grounded theory' (Glaser and Strauss, 1968) about cognitions, behaviours and practices at sites of elite power.[1] At each site, and with each sample set of interviews, theory developed inductively and incrementally. Thus, the interview protocol, in each case, shifted after the initial interviews, as certain topics and question lines proved more productive than others. Periodically, certain 'patterns' would be identified in the way interviewees understood their environment, used common terms, participated in particular professional practices or related to information sources and journalists. As such, many of the points made in these chapters are representative of the answers given by a majority of respondents. In some cases a point is deduced indirectly from a number (not necessarily a majority) of similar descriptions or opinions volunteered on an issue. In the case of MPs, in particular, the semi-structured interview responses were used to develop small quantitative summaries, such as the most commonly used information sources. Thirty-five of the MPs were also asked their responses to a set of relatively closed questions, with quantifiable responses, such as the quantity of news sources they used or the number of exchanges they had with journalists each week.

The speculative assumption at the core of all the research presented is that regular patterns of individual-level understanding, decision-making and practice are linked to larger political and economic consequences. Micro-level behaviour, when aggregated within elite sites of power, is likely to feed into macro-level outcomes in wider society. Where possible, quantitative and macro-level data was also gathered in an attempt to suggest these links. Many industry and government surveys and reports, some private and some public, were collected and, at times, offered useful related data. However, proving such lines of cause and effect definitively is difficult. Those who might already be critical of the methods employed here are likely to object more vociferously to attempts to establish such connections.

# Appendix II

## List of interviewees

Only those interviewees directly cited in the text are listed here. The majority of interviews took place 'on-the-record' and most citations are referenced. However, a proportion of interviewees, as well as particular parts of on-the-record interviews, were recorded 'off-the-record'.

Martin Adeney, Managing Director of Group Public Relations at ICI, 17 December 1998.

Danny Alexander, Liberal Democrat MP for Nairn, Badenoch and Strathspey, 28 February 2006.

David Bailey, Chairman of Datacash, former Partner at Philips and Drew, 16 August 2004.

Lord Kenneth Baker of Dorking, former Conservative cabinet minister 1985–92, 2 March 2006.

Paul Barber, Group Corporate Affairs Director of Inchcape, 20 August 1998.

Lord Tim Bell, Chairman of Bell Pottinger, former communications advisor to Conservative Party and Margaret Thatcher, 20 November 2001.

David Blackwell, Business Correspondent for the *FT*, 17 May 1999.

Rt Hon David Blunkett, Labour MP for Sheffield Brightside, former shadow minister 1992–97, government minister 1997–2004, 20 March 2006.

Tim Blythe, Director of Corporate Affairs at WH Smith, former government communications advisor, 15 September 1998.

Edward Bonham-Carter, Chief Investment Officer and Joint Chief Executive Officer of Jupiter Asset Management, 1 October 2004.

Graham Brady, Conservative MP for Altrincham and Sale West, 8 December 2005.

Andy Brough, Co-Head of UK and European Small and Mid-Cap, Schroders, 28 September 2004.

Colin Brown, Deputy Political Editor of the *Independent*, 1 August 2006.

Alex Brummer, Financial Editor of the *Guardian*, 16 June 1999.

Chris Bryant, Labour MP for Rhondda, 12 December 2005.

Lucy Cathcart, Membership Coordinator at the Catholic Institute for International Relations, 14 January 2005.

Nick Chaloner, Director of Corporate Affairs at Abbey National, 16 September 1998.

William Claxton-Smith, Director of UK Equities, Insight Investment, 25 January 2005.

Nick Clegg, Liberal Democrat MP for Sheffield Hallam, Shadow Home Secretary, 14 March 2006.

Barrie Clement, Industrial Correspondent of the *Independent*, 25 May 1999.

Tim Collins MP, former Director of Communications and Senior Vice Chairman at the Conservative Party, 7 November 2001.

Jeremy Corbyn, Labour MP for Islington North, 24 April 2006.

Mike Cunnane, Ex-Broker and Investment Analyst, 8 October 2004.

Wayne David, Labour MP for Caerphilly, 10 January 2006.

John Davies, ex-Managing Director of Asset Management for 3i UK, 13 May 2004.

Alistair Defriez, Director General of the Takeover Panel, 22 December 1998.

Rt Hon Frank Dobson, Labour MP for Holborn and St Pancras, former shadow minister 1983–97, former cabinet minister 1997–99, 29 March 2006.

Frank Doran, Labour MP for Aberdeen North, former shadow minister 1988–92, select committee chair 2005–, 15 May 2006.

Martin Drewry, Head of Campaigns at Christian Aid, 16 March 2005 and 17 January 2006.

Rt Hon Iain Duncan Smith, Conservative MP for Chingford and Woodford Green, shadow minister 1997–2001, party leader 2001–03, 25 April 2006.

Gwyneth Dunwoody, Labour MP for Crewe and Nantwich, chair of select committees 1997–, 8 May 2006.

Tony Dye, founder and Director of Dye Asset Management, 7 April 2004.

Jonny Elwes, Account Manager at Infopress, 31 July 1998.

Clare Ettinghausen, Chief Executive Officer of Hansard Society, 9 May 2006.

Alison Fenney, Director of Advocacy and Communications at CAFOD, 8 April 2005.

Rt Hon Frank Field, Labour MP for Birkinhead, former government minister 1997–99, former chair of select committees 1987–97, 19 April 2006.

Neil Gerrard, Labour MP for Walthamstow, 10 May 2006.

Jeremy Goford, Principal at Tillinghast Towers Perrin, Immediate Past President of the Institute of Actuaries, 29 September 2004.

Tony Golding, ex-fund manager, author and consultant, 6 April 2004.

Paul Goodman, Conservative MP for Wycombe, shadow minister 2003–, 27 March 2006.

Chris Grayling, Conservative MP for Epsom and Ewell, Shadow Secretary of State for Transport, 14 June 2006.

Bob Gregory, Director at Bell Pottinger, 21 August 1998.

Roland Gribben, Business Editor of the *Daily Telegraph*, 21 May 1999.

Andrew Grice, Political Editor of the *Independent*, 5 September 2001.

Simon Heffer, Political Columnist and Associate Editor of the *Daily Telegraph*, 30 August 2006.

David Hill, Director of Good Relations Group, former and current Head of Communications for the Labour Party 1993–98, 31 August 2001.

Chris Hopson, Director of Corporate Affairs at Granada Media Group, 13 October 1998.

Michael Hughes CBE, Chief Investment Officer, Barings Asset Management, 26 August 2004.

Simon Hughes, Liberal Democrat MP for North Southwark and Bermondsey, party leadership contender 1999, 2006, Party President and Shadow Secretary for Constitutional Affairs and Attorney General, 4 July 2006.

Rt Hon Michael Jack, Conservative MP for Fylde, former government minister 1992–97, shadow minister 1997–98, chair select committee 2002–, 12 June 2006.

Tim Jackaman, Chairman of Square Mile, 8 October 1998.

Joy Johnson, freelance journalist, former Labour Director of Campaigns, Elections and Media, 23 January 1997.

Tom Johnstone, Planner at Abbott Mead Vicar, 20 December 2005.

George Jones, Political Correspondent at the *Daily Telegraph*, 7 August 2001.

Kevan Jones, Labour MP for North Durham, 8 February 2006.

Trevor Kavanagh, Political Editor of the *Sun*, 28 August 2001.

Sadiq Khan, Labour MP for Tooting, 1 March 2006.

Lord Neil Kinnock, former shadow minister and Leader of the Labour Party 1983–92, 4 May 2006.

Julia Kirkbride, Conservative MP for Bromsgrove, former shadow minister 2003–04, former journalist, 3 February 2006.

Andrew Kirton, Head of UK Mercer Investment Consulting, 22 December 2004.

Richard Krammer, Founder and MD of Arete Research Ltd, 26 April 2004.

Rick Lacaille, Chief Investment Officer Europe, State Street Global Advisors Ltd, 11 October 2004.

Charles Lewington, Managing Director of Media Strategy, former Director of Communications at the Conservative Party 1995–97, 18 September 2001.

Martin Linton, Labour MP for Battersea, 24 February 2006.

Adrian Lovett, 2005 Project Director at Oxfam, 14 October 2005.

Peter Luff, Conservative MP for Mid-Worcestershire, party whip and chair of select committees 1997–2000, 2005–, 29 March 2006.

Christine McCafferty, Labour MP for Calder Valley, 3 May 2006.

Colin McClean, Managing Director of SVM Asset Management, 3 September 2004.

Lord Robert Maclennan of Rogart, former Labour government minister 1974–79, former leader of Social Democratic Party 1987–88, former Liberal Democrat shadow minister 1988–98, 8 February 2006.

Andy McSmith, Chief Political Correspondent of the *Daily Telegraph*, 14th November 2001

Kevin Maguire, Chief Reporter of the *Guardian*, 6 November 2001.

Angus Maitland, Chairman of the Maitland Consultancy, 17 September 1998.

John Maples, Conservative MP for Stratford on Avon, Deputy Chairman 1994–95, former shadow cabinet minister 1997–2000, 28 Mar 2006.

Gordon Midgley, Director of Research, Investment Managers Association, 12 March 2004.

Nick Miles, Chief Executive Officer of Financial Dynamics, 17 August 1998.

Austin Mitchell, Labour MP for Great Grimsby, former journalist, 15 February 2006.

Richard Northedge, Deputy Editor of *Sunday Business*, 25 May 1999.

Richard Oldworth, Chief Executive Officer of Buchanan, 26 August 1998.

Tim Peat, Senior Campaigns Officer at War on Want, 3 June 2005.

Adrian Platt, Campaigns Assistant at Christian Aid, 25 May 2005.

John Pullinger, Head Librarian, House of Commons Library, 29 March 2006.

Ben Ramsden, Projects and Fundraising Officer at Jesuit Missions, 18 March 2005.

Stephen Rand, Co-chair of Jubilee Debt Campaign, 24 November 2005.

Rt Hon Nick Raynsford, Labour MP for Greenwich and Woolwich, former shadow minister 1993–97, former government minister 1997–2005, 2 May 2006.

Rt Hon John Redwood, Conservative MP for Wokingham, former cabinet minister 1990–95, shadow cabinet minister 1997–2000, 2004–05, party leadership candidate 1995, 1997, 20 February 2006.

Lord Chris Rennard, Director of Campaigns and Communications for the Liberal Democrats, 13 November 2001.

Peter Riddell, Chief Political Commentator for *The Times*, 30 August 2006.

Michael Rimmer, Senior Portfolio Manager at Investec Asset Management, 5 May 2004.

Angus Robertson, Scottish National Party MP for Moray, former journalist, 17 January 2006.

John Rogers, Chief Executive Officer of the UK Society of Investment Professionals, 11 March 2004.

Paul Routledge, Chief Political Commentator of the *Daily Mirror*, 19 September, 2001.

Roland Rudd, founding Partner at Finsbury, 15 October 1998 and 23 November 1998.

Hugh Sergeant, Head of UK Equities, SG Asset Management, 27 August 2004.

Jan Shawe, Director of Corporate Affairs at the Prudential, 7 October 1998.

Lord Chris Smith of Finsbury, former Labour MP, former shadow minister 1992–97, former cabinet minister 1997–2001, 6 February 2006.

Andrew Smithers, ex-fund manager, Director of Smithers and Company, 20 April 2004.

Raymond Snoddy, Media Correspondent of *The Times*, 17 May 1999.

Phyllis Starkey, Labour MP for Milton Keynes South West, chair select committee 2005–, 16 May 2006.

Jo Swinson, Liberal Democrat MP for East Dunbartonshire, 21 March 2006.

Mark Tapley, ex-fund manager at JP Morgan, West LB, American Express, 31 March 2004.

Beth Tegg, Communications Manager at Comic Relief, 18 January 2006.

Lord John Thurso, Liberal Democrat MP for Caithness, Sutherland and Easter Ross, shadow minister 2003–, 7 December 2005.

Steve Tibbett, Director of Policy and Campaigns at Action Aid UK, 17 March 2005 and 12 January 2006.

Polly Toynbee, Political Columnist for the *Guardian*, 25 August 2006.

Lord Paul Tyler, former Liberal Democrat MP, chief whip and shadow minister 1997–2005, 2 Mar 2006.

John Underwood, Director of Clear, former Director of Campaigns and Communications at the Labour Party, 6 November 2001.

Michael Walters, Deputy City Editor of the *Daily Mail*, 19 October 1998.

Philip Webster, Political Editor of *The Times*, 9 August 2006.

Michael White, Political Editor of the *Guardian*, 18 October 2001 and 1 August 2006.

John Whittingdale, Conservative MP for Malden and East Chelmsford, former shadow minister 2001–04, select committee chair 2005–, 28 February 2006.

Rt Hon Ann Widdecombe, Conservative MP for Maidstone and the Weald, former government minister 1994–97, former shadow minister 1997–2001, 9 March 2006.

Graham Williams, Director of External Affairs at the Investor Relations Society, 26 October 1998.

Paul Woolley, Chairman of GMO UK Ltd, 29 April 2004.

Tony Wright, Labour MP for Cannock Chase, chair of select committee 1999–, 15 March, 2006.

Derek Wyatt, Labour MP for Sittingbourne and Sheppey, 23 May, 2006.

# Notes

## 2 Media policy: communication and the economic inefficiencies of market liberalisation

1 See public sphere-oriented discussions in Calhoun, 1992; Dahlgren and Sparks, 1992, and also Thompson, 1995; Goldsmiths Media Group, 1999; Sparks, 2001; Dahlgren, 2001, 2005.

2 For some work questioning the economics benefits of market reforms in the media and communication industries see: Leys, 2001; Doyle, 2002; Price, 2002. For some questioning privatisations, on economic grounds, in other utilities areas, see the work of Shaoul, Froud and others at Manchester School of Accounting and Finance (e.g., Shaoul, 2000; Froud and Shaoul, 2001).

3 Please note that criteria associated with 'efficiency' in markets generally are not the same as those applied in financial market theory. A market may operate efficiently according to Efficient Markets Hypothesis (EMH) criteria but still be inefficient in other ways. See Fama, 1970, for a description of the EMH. For Fama (1970: 387), ideal market conditions are those where:

> (i) there are no transactions costs in trading securities, (ii) all available information is costlessly available to all market participants, and (iii) all agree on the implications of current information for the current price and distributions of future prices of each security.

See also von Hayek, 1945; Coase, 1952; Arrow, 1979, for similar descriptions of the role of information in markets generally.

4 By 2003, 2,488 pages of regulations had been produced to guide companies through: the Companies Act (1985), the Companies Act (1989), the Criminal Justice Act (1993), the Listings Rules ('Purple Book') FSMA 2000 and Code of Market Conduct (COMC), and the Combined Corporate Governance Code (Cadbury, Greenbury, Hampel, Higgs).

5 For most market theorists the idea that market prices are accurate or inaccurate is not a question to be contemplated. Prices are simply set by supply and demand and relative to measures set within the market itself and regardless of the conditions in which information is created. One can only suggest that markets are more or less 'accurate' on the basis of historical and accounting measures – but many market theorists are also sceptical of their applicability.

6 The P/E or price-earnings ratio of a company or market is the total price of the share(s) divided by the actual annual earnings of the company or market. The higher the ratio the smaller the returns and the riskier the investment.

7 See also Smithers and Wright, 2004, for another long-term market measurement:

Talbot's Q. This compares stock market prices, in aggregate, with accountant valuations of companies, in aggregate. This too showed the stock market to be significantly over-priced.

8 On these issues see, for example: Ingham, 1984; Strange, 1986, 1998; Hutton, 1996; Hirst and Thompson, 1999; Myners, 2001; Shiller, 2001; Cassidy, 2002; Golding, 2003; Davis 2007.

9 See Susan Strange, 1998 and Shiller, 2001 for overviews. In terms of the NYSE see Shiller, 2001 and Smithers and Wright, 2000, 2004, who have calculated the extreme over-valuation of the NYSE up to 2000 and since. Cassidy, 2002 and Swedberg, 2005, pointed out similar conflicts of interest and corrupt information in the US media and brokerage industries.

### 3  Media production: discursive practices, news production and the mobilisation of bias in public discourse

1 Kovach *et al.* (2004: 28) recorded that the period 1985 to 2004 saw a drop in network news correspondents of 35 per cent but an increase in story output of 30 per cent per reporter. Radio Newsroom staff were down by 57 per cent in the period 1994 to 2001 and newspaper staffers down 4 per cent between 2000 and 2004. According to the Pew Research Centre (2004) survey of journalists: 66 per cent believed 'increased bottom-line pressure' and the emergence of 'the 24-hour news cycle' is hurting news coverage – up from 41 per cent in 1995; 45 per cent think reporting is 'increasingly sloppy and error prone' – up from 30 per cent in 1995; 86 per cent were most concerned that 'the media was paying too little attention to complex stories'; 48 per cent said staff numbers had decreased over the previous three years; 52 per cent said there was more repackaging of stories.

### 5  Culture, discourse and power: the rediscovery of elite culture and power in media studies?

1 Defining the terms 'culture' and 'ideology', and relations between the two, is not a chapter-sized task. For some of the more comprehensive overviews on the subject see Larraine, 1983; Thompson, 1990; Eagleton, 1991; McLellan, 1995.

2 Clearly, such critical elite studies have been regularly produced: e.g., Mills, 1956; Domhoff, 1967; Useem, 1984; Scott, 1997. However, these have focused on economic classifications and social networks rather than culture, communications, practices and beliefs. Such elements are also largely absent in the more ethnographically oriented studies of economic sociology: e.g., Grannovetter and Swedberg, 1992; Abolafia, 1996; Callon, 1998.

3 Observation and awareness of elite culture and ideology also has a long history in (post-) Marxist literature. Marx and Engels's much cited *The German ideology* (1938) originally spelled out its arguments in relation to German intellectual elites. See also Lenin (1970 [1902]); Miliband (1969); Lukes (1974); Abercrombie *et al.* (1984). However, much of this tradition's close attachments to elements of class, the state, the material determination of culture and consciousness, is unlikely to be deemed useful to current media and cultural studies research.

### 6  Mediated politics: the mediation of parliamentary politics

1 For a very useful summary and analysis of work in this area see Walgrave and van Aelst, 2004.

2 See Boorstin, 1962; Edelman, 1964 for early observations of public political communication being more symbolic than substantive.

3 At the same time there are indications that news media may have greater priming and reinforcement effects on these same individuals. Such might be deduced from Iyengar and Kinder, 1987; Zaller, 1992, 1997 and also in MacKuen, 1984; Miller and Krosnick, 1997. For MacKuen (1984: 383) 'Short-term public responsiveness to events on the public stage is concentrated only at the upper stratum of political involvement'.

4 For a range of other objections to agenda-setting forms of research see also studies in media and cultural/audience studies (Ang, 1986; Morley, 1992), election studies and behavioural psychology (Gauntlett, 1998; Norris et al., 1999). See Ruddock, 2001; McQuail, 2000, for overviews here.

5 In Parson's account, Keynes, Galbraith and Freedman succeeded in getting their economic policies adopted by governments in large part because of their extensive journalistic outputs.

6 There are also several documented case studies where media campaigns appeared to change substantive policy or legislative decisions. See for example: Nelson, 1989; Manheim, 1994; Stauber and Rampton, 1995; Anderson, 1997; Davis, 1999.

## 7 New and alternative media: the Internet and the parliamentary public sphere

1 For a range of discussions and causes see, for example: Blumler and Gurevitch, 1995; Norris 2000, 2002; Putnam, 2000; Meyer, 2002; Bromley et al., 2004; Franklin, 2004; Todd and Taylor, 2004; Lewis et al., 2005.

2 Earlier examples of technological determinism include: Bell, 1976; Meyrowitz, 1985; Sola Pool, 1990; and, arguably, Castells, 1997.

3 For example, in 2004–05, 44 Government bills and 95 Private Members' bills were put forward, to which 7,668 new amendments and clauses were tabled. There were 421 standing committee meetings to discuss these. There were 1,286 Select Committee meetings which produced 190 reports. Fifty-four thousand written questions and 14,500 oral questions were put to the government by MPs. An average of 16 EDMs were tabled each day and drew over 100,000 signatures in total from MPs (all figures HoC, July 2005). In that same year, members of the House of Lords proposed 3,306 amendments to legislation, 913 of which were accepted. They also put 1,877 written and 228 oral questions to government and defeated government legislative proposals 36 times (all figures HoL, March 2006).

4 The percentage of enquiries made to the Library Research Services by MPs on behalf of constituents has also steadily increased, between 1995–96 and 2003–04, from 26 per cent to 44 per cent (Clements, 2005).

## 8 Interest groups and mediated mobilisation: communication in the Make Poverty History campaign

1 The growing importance of 'alternative' (Couldry and Curran, 2003), 'radical' (Downing, 2001) or 'citizens' (Rodriguez, 2001) media in oppositional activity has become apparent. New media technologies present an array of other communication methods: camcorders, streaming, mobile phones, the Internet, greater radio and television broadcasting capacity and alternative publishing. They potentially offer new means for communicating with public and elite audiences.

Although for many, their most useful function to date has been in networking, exchanging information and campaign organisation between interest groups and their members (Livingstone, 2005).

2 On 'resource mobilisation' approaches to social movements see McCarthy and Zald, 1977; McCarthy, 1997.

3 A sympathetic Labour Government, the G8 summit in Scotland, the upcoming UK presidency of the European Union, the twentieth anniversary of Live Aid, Comic Relief's tenth Red Nose Day, the UN millennium summit in New York and the WTO meeting in Hong Kong.

4 The research material in this chapter is based on 27 semi-structured interviews with 22 leading actors in MPH during the course of 2005 and early 2006 (five were repeat interviews after the campaign ended). Material was also gathered from participant observation notes of key MPH working group and Coordination Team meetings, meeting minutes, emails and campaign documents and research.

5 The MPH MAC group was one of the main working groups set up by the leading member organisations of the campaign.

## 9 Media audiences and effects: the question of the rational audience in the London Stock Exchange

1 Work on new economic sociology in the United States established itself on the back of its critique of mainstream economic theory. See, for example, Grannovetter and Swedberg, 1992; Swedberg, 2003; Smelser and Swedberg, 2004.

2 Some of the better cited include: Lloyd-Davies and Canes, 1978; Beneish, 1991; Sant and Zaman, 1996; Barber and Odean, 2002.

## Appendix I

1 Herbst's (1998) work proved extremely useful when constructing the research design used in many of the studies. The strengths and weaknesses of a 'grounded theory' approach, using semi-structured interviews with elite participants selected from established professional sectors, is discussed in some detail in her book.

# Bibliography

Abercrombie, A, Hill, S and Turner, B (1984) *The Dominant Ideology Thesis*, London: Allen and Unwin.

——(1990) *Dominant Ideologies*, London: Unwin Hyman Ltd.

Abolafia, M (1996) *Making Markets: Opportunism and Restraint on Wall Street*, Cambridge, MA: Harvard University Press.

Adorno, T and Horkheimer, M (1979 [1947]) *The Dialectic of Enlightenment*, New York: Herder and Herder.

Allan, S (2004) *News Culture*, 2nd edn, Maidenhead: Open University Press.

Allan, S, Adam, B and Carter, C eds (2000) *Environmental Risks and the Media*, London: Routledge.

Altheide, D (2004) 'Media Logic and Political Communication' in *Political Communication*, vol. 21, no. 3, pp. 293–96.

Althusser, L (1984 [1971]) *Essays on Ideology*, London: Verso.

Amoore, L ed. (2005) *The Global Resistance Reader*, London: Routledge.

Anderson, A (1997) *Media, Culture and the Environment*, London: UCL Press.

Ang, I (1986) *Watching Dallas*, London: Methuen.

——(1991) *Desperately Seeking the Audience*, London: Routledge.

Ansolabehere, S, Iyengar, S and Simon, A (1997) 'Shifting Perspectives on the Effects of Campaign Communications' in Iyengar, S and Reeves, R eds, *Do the Media Govern? Politicians, Voters, and Reporters in America*, Thousand Oaks, CA: Sage.

Arrow, K (1979) 'The Economics of Information' in Dertouzos, M and Moses, J eds, *The Computer Age: A Twenty-Year View*, Cambridge, MA: MIT Press.

Atton, C (2004) *An Alternative Internet*, Edinburgh: Edinburgh University Press.

Bachrach, P and Baratz, M (1962) 'Two Faces of Power' in the *American Political Science Review*, vol. 56, no. 4, pp. 947–52.

Bagdikian, B (2004) *The Media Monopoly*, 7th edn, Boston, MA: Beacon Press.

Baker, D, Gamble, A and Seawright, D (July, 1999) *Mapping Changes in British Parliamentarians Attitudes to European Integration*, Colchester, Essex: UK Data Archive.

Baker, R (1997) *Information Flows Between Finance Directors, Analysts and Fund Managers*, WP 16/97, Judge Institute of Management Studies, Cambridge: Cambridge University Press.

Bandura, A and Walters, R (1963) *Social Learning and Personality Development*, New York: Rinehart and Winston.

Barber, BM and Odean, T (2002) *All that Glitters: The Effect of Attention and News on the Buying Behavior of individual and institutional investors*, Graduate School of Management, Working Paper, Davis, University of California.

Barker, M and Petley, J eds (1996) *Ill Effects: The Media Violence Debate*, 2nd edn, London: Routledge.

Barnett, S and Gaber, I (2001) *Westminster Tales: the Twenty First Century Crisis in Political Journalism*, London: Continuum.

Bauman, Z (1997) *Work, Consumerism and the New Poor*, Milton Keynes: Open University Press.

Baumgartner, FR and Jones, BD (1993) *Agendas and Instability in American Politics*, Chicago, IL: University of Chicago Press.

BBC Broadcast (08.07.05) 'Mixed Reaction over Blair G8 Deal' and 'Half Full or Half Empty?'

——(09.07.05) 'Government Defends G8 Aid Boost' and 'African Head Defends G8 Agreement'.

Beattie, A and Williamson, H (08.07.05) 'NGOs Divided Over G8's $50bn Global Aid Proposal' *Financial Times*.

Beesley, M (1996) *Markets and the Media*, London: Institute of Economic Affairs.

Behabib, S (1992) 'Models of Public Space: Hannah Arendt, the Liberal Tradition and Jurgen Habermas' in Calhoun, C ed. *Habermas and the Public Sphere*, Cambridge, MA: MIT Press.

Bell, D (1976) *The Coming of the Post-Industrial Age*, 2nd edn, Harmondsworth: Penguin.

Beneish, MD (1991) 'Stock Prices and the Dissemination of Analysts' Recommendations' in *Journal of Business*, vol. 64, no. 3, pp. 393–416.

Bennett, WL (1990) 'Towards a Theory of Press–State Relations in the United States' in *Journal of Communication*, vol. 40, no. 2, pp. 103–25.

——(1997) 'Cracking the News Code: Some Rules that Journalists Live By' in Iyengar, S and Reeves, R eds, *Do the Media Govern? Politicians, Voters, and Reporters in America*, Thousand Oaks, CA: Sage.

Bennett, WL and Paletz, DL (1994) *Taken By Storm; The Media, Public Opinion, and U.S. Foreign Policy in the Gulf War*, Chicago, IL: University of Chicago Press.

Bennett, WL and Entman, RM eds (2001) *Mediated Politics: Communication in the Future of Democracy*, Cambridge: Cambridge University Press.

Bennett, WL and Manheim, J (2001) 'The Big Spin: Strategic Communication and the Transformation of Pluralist Democracy' in Bennett, WL and Entman, RM eds, *Mediated Politics: Communication in the Future of Democracy*, Cambridge: Cambridge University Press.

Berkman, R and Kitch, W (1986) *Politics in the Media Age*, New York: McGraw-Hill.

Bird, SE (2000) 'Audience Demands in a Murderous Market: Tabloidization of U.S. Television News' in Sparks, C and Tulloch, J eds, *Tabloid Tales: Global Debates Over Media Standards*, Lanham, MD: Rowman and Littlefield.

Blake, D and Timmermann, A (2001) *Performance Benchmarks for Institutional Investors: Measuring, Monitoring and Modifying Investment Behaviour*, London: Birkbeck College/Pensions Institute.

Blumler, J and Katz, E eds (1974) *The Uses of Communications*, Beverly Hills, CA: Sage.

Blumler, J and Gurevitch, M (1995) *The Crisis of Public Communication*, London: Routledge.

—— (2000) 'Rethinking the Study of Political Communication' in Curran, J and Gurevitch, M eds, *Mass Media and Society*, 3rd edn, London: Arnold.

Blumler, J and Kavanagh, D (1999) 'The Third Age of Political Communication: Influences and Features' in *Political Communication*, vol. 16, no. 3, pp. 209–30.

Blunkett, D (2006) *The Blunkett Tapes: My Life in the Bearpit*, London: Bloomsbury.

Bodie, Z, Kane, A and Marcus, A (2003) *Essentials of Investment*, 5th edn, London: McGraw Hill.

Bohman, J (1996) *Public Deliberation: Pluralism, Complexity, and Democracy*, Cambridge MA: MIT Press.

Bonfadelli, H (2002) 'The Internet and Knowledge Gaps: A Theoretical and Empirical Investigation' in *European Journal of Communication*, vol. 17, no. 1, pp. 65–84.

Boorstin, D (1962) *The Image*, London: Weidenfeld and Nicolson.

Boswell, J and Peters, J (1997) *Capitalism in Contention – Business Leaders and Political Economy in Modern Britain*, Cambridge: Cambridge University Press.

Bourdieu, P (1979) *Distinction*, London: Routledge.

—— (1993) *The Field of Cultural Production*, Cambridge: Polity Press.

Brandenburg, H (2002) 'Who Follows Whom? The Impact of Parties on Media Agenda Formation in the 1997 British General Election' in *Harvard International Journal of Press/Politics*, vol. 7, no. 3, pp. 34–54.

Brazier, A, Flanders, M and McHugh, D (2005) *New Politics, New Parliament? A Review of Parliamentary Modernization Since 1998*, London: Hansard.

Brittan, S (1983) *The Role and Limits of Government*, Hounslow: Temple Smith.

Bromley, C, Curtice, J and Seyd, B (2004) *Is Britain Facing a Crisis of Democracy?*, London: University College London.

Brookes, R, Lewis, J and Wahl-Jorgensen, K (2004) 'The Media Representation of Public Opinion: British Television News Coverage of the 2001 General Election' in *Media, Culture and Society*, vol. 26, no. 1, pp. 63–80.

Bryant, J and Zillman, D (1994) *Perspectives on Media Effects*, New York: Lawrence Earlbaum Assoc.

Calhoun, C ed. (1992) 'Introduction' in *Habermas and the Public Sphere*, Cambridge, MA: MIT Press.

Callon, M (1986) 'Some Elements of a Sociology of Translation: Domestication of the Scallops and the Fishermen of St. Brieuc Bay' in Law, J ed. *Power, Action and Belief: A New Sociology of Knowledge*, London: Routledge and Kegan Paul.

—— ed. (1998) *The Laws of the Markets*, Oxford: Blackwell.

Cammaerts, B and Audenhove, L (2005) 'Online Political Debate, Unbounded Citizenship and the Problematic Nature of a Transnational Public Sphere' in *Political Communications*, vol. 22, no. 2, pp. 179–96.

Cantril, H, Gaudet, H and Hertzog, H (1940) *The Invasion from Mars*, Princeton, NJ: Princeton University Press.

Cassidy, J (2002) *Dot.Con: The Greatest Story Ever Told*, London: Penguin/Allen Lane.

Castells, M (1996) *The Rise of the Network Society*, Oxford: Blackwell.

—— (1997) *The Power of Identity*, Oxford: Blackwell.

—— (1998) *End of Millennium*, Oxford: Blackwell.

CBI and Abbey Life Assurance Co. Ltd (1981) *The Headline Business: A Business-man's Guide to Working with the Media*, London: CBI.

Chalaby, J (1996) 'Journalism as an Anglo-American Invention' in the *European Journal of Communication*, vol. 11, no. pp. 303–26.

Chan, L, Karceski, J and Lakonishkok, J (2003) *Analysts' Conflict of Interest and Biases in Earnings Forecasts*, Working Paper 9544. Cambridge, MA: National Bureau of Economic Research.

Chapman, C (2002) *How the Stock Market Works*, London: Random House.

City Business Series (2003) *Fund Management*, London: International Financial Services.

Clarke, J (2001) 'Ethical Globalization: The Dilemmas and Challenges of Internationalizing Civil Society' in Edwards, M and Gaventa, J eds, *Global Citizen Action*, Boulder, CO: Lynne Rienner.

Clegg, S (1989) *Frameworks of Power*, London, Sage.

Clements, R (2005) unpublished internal House of Commons Report, *Research Statistics for 2003–04*, London: House of Commons.

CMD (Centre for Media and Democracy), website: www.prwatch.org.

Coase, R (1952) 'The Nation of the firm' in Stigler, G and Boulding, K eds, *Readings in Price Theory*, Homewood, IL: Irwin.

Cockerell, M, Hennessey, P and Walker, D (1984) *Sources Close to the Prime Minister: Inside the Hidden World of the News Manipulators*, London: Macmillan.

Coleman, S (2004) 'Connecting Parliament to the Public via the Internet: Two Case Studies of Online Consultations' in *Information, Communication & Society*, vol. 7, no. 1, pp. 1–22.

——(2005a) 'New Mediation and Direct Representation: Reconceptualising Representation in the Digital Age' in *New Media and Society*, vol. 7, no. 2, pp. 177–98.

——(2005b) 'The Lonely Citizen: Indirect Representation in an Age of Networks' in *Political Communications*, vol. 22, no. 2, pp. 197–214.

Coleman, S and Gotze, J (2001) *Bowling Together: Online Public Engagement in Policy Deliberation*, London: Hansard Society.

Coleman, S and Ward, S eds (2005) *Spinning the Web: Online Campaigning in the 2005 General Election*, London: Hansard Society.

CommunicateResearch, (February 2004) 'The East Lothian Question', *CommunicateResearch Parliamentary Panel*, London.

——(September 2004) 'Voluntary Euthanasia', *CommunicateResearch Parliamentary Panel*, London.

Connell, I (1992) 'Personalities in the Popular Media' in Dahlgren, P and Sparks, C eds, *Journalism and Popular Culture*, London: Sage.

Cook, FL, Tylor, TR, Goetz, EE, Gordon, MT, Protess, D, Leff, DR and Molotoch, HL (1983) 'Media and Agenda Setting: Effects on the Public, Interest Group Leaders, Policy Makers and Policy' in *Public Opinion Quarterly*, vol. 47, no. 1, pp. 16–35.

Corner, J and Pels, D eds (2003) *Media and the Restyling of Politics: Consumerism, Celebrity and Cynicism*, London: Sage.

Cottle, S (1993) *Television News, Urban Conflict and the Inner City*, Leicester: Leicester University Press.

——ed. (2003) *News, Public Relations and Power*, London: Sage.

Couldry, N and Curran, J eds (2003) *Contesting Media Power: Alternative Media in a Networked World*, Oxford: Rowman and Littlefield.

CPJ (Committee to Protect Journalists), website: www.cpj.org.

Cracknell, J (1993) 'Issue Arenas, Pressure Groups and Environmental Issues' in Hansen, A 'Greenpeace and Press Coverage of Environmental Issues' in Hansen, A, ed. *The Mass Media and Environmental Issues*, Leicester: Leicester University Press.

CRE (Commission for Racial Equality) (2005) *Why Ethnic Minority Workers Leave London's Print Journalism Sector*, London: Commission for Racial Equality.

Crewe, I and Gosschalk, B eds (1995) *Political Communications: The General Election Campaign of 1992*, Cambridge: Cambridge University Press.

Crewe, I, Gosschalk, B and Bartle, J eds (1998) *Political Communications: Why Labour Won the General Election of 1997*, London: Frank Cass.

Curran, J (1978) 'Advertising and the Press' in Curran, J ed. *The British Press: A Manifesto*, London: Macmillan.

——(2000) 'Rethinking Media and Democracy' in Curran J and Gurevitch, M eds, *Mass Media and Society*, 3rd edn, London: Arnold.

——(2002) *Media and Power*, London: Routledge.

Curran, J and Seaton, J (2003) *Power Without Responsibility*, 6th edn, London: Routledge.

Curran, J and Gurevitch, M eds (2005) *Mass Media and Society*, 4th edn, London: Hodder Arnold.

Curtice, J and Semetko, H (1994) 'Does it Matter What the Papers Say?' in Heath, A, Jowell, R and Curtice, J eds, *Labour's Last Chance*, Aldershot: Dartmouth.

Cutlip, S, Center, A and Broom, G (2004) *Effective Public Relations*, 9th edn, Englewood Cliffs, NJ: Prentice-Hall.

Dahl, R (1961) *Who Governs? Democracy and Power in an American City*, New Haven, CT: Yale University Press.

——(1989) *Democracy and its Critics*, New Haven, CT: Yale University Press.

Dahl, R and Lindblom, C (1953) *Politics, Economics and Welfare: Planning and Politico-Economic Systems Resolved into Basic Social Processes*, New York: Harper and Row.

Dahlberg, L (2001) 'The Internet and Democratic Discourse: Exploring the Prospects of Online Deliberative Forums Extending the Public Sphere' in *Information, Communication and Society*, vol. 4, no. 4, pp. 615–33.

Dahlgren, P (1995) *Television and the Public Sphere*, London: Sage.

——(2001) 'The Public Sphere and the Net: Structure, Space and Communication' in Bennett, W and Entman, R eds (2001) *Mediated Politics: Communication in the Future of Democracy*, Cambridge: Cambridge University Press.

——(2005) 'The Internet and the Public Sphere' in *Political Communications*, vol. 22, no. 2, pp. 147–62.

Dahlgren, P and Sparks, C eds (1992) *Journalism and Popular Culture*, London: Sage.

Davis, A (1999) 'Public Relations Campaigning and News Production: The Case of New Unionism in Britain' in Curran, J (ed.), *Media Organisations*, London: Arnold.

——(2000a) 'Public Relations, News Production and Changing Patterns of Source Access in the British National Press' in *Media, Culture and Society*, vol. 22, no. 1, pp. 33–59.

——(2000b) 'Public Relations, Business News and the Reproduction of Corporate Elite Power' in *Journalism: Theory, Practice and Criticism*, vol. 1, no. 3, pp. 282–304.

——(2002) *Public Relations Democracy: Public Relations, Politics and the Mass Media in Britain*, Manchester: Manchester University Press.

——(2003a) 'Public Relations and News Sources' in Cottle, S ed. *News, Public Relations and Power*, London: Sage.

——(2003b) 'Whither Mass Media and Power? Evidence for a Critical Elite Theory Alternative' in *Media, Culture and Society*, vol. 25, no. 5, pp. 669–90.

——(2005) 'Media Effects and the Active Elite Audience: A Study of Media in Financial Markets' in *European Journal of Communications*, vol. 20, no. 3, pp. 303–26.

——(forthcoming, 2007) 'Spinning Money' in Miller, D and Dinan, W eds, *Thinker, Faker, Spinner, Spy: Spin and Corporate Power*, London: Pluto.

Davis, EP (1995) *Institutional Investors, Unstable Financial Markets and Monetary Policy*, Special Paper no. 75, London: LSE Financial Markets Group.

Dayan, D and Katz, E (1992) *Media Events*, Cambridge, MA: Harvard University Press.

de Certeau, M (1984) *The Practice of Everyday Life*, Berkeley, CA: University of California Press.

de Sola Pool, I (1983) *Technologies of Freedom*, Cambridge, MA.: Harvard University Press.

——(1990) *Technologies Without Boundaries: On Telecommunications in a Global Age*, Cambridge, MA: Harvard University Press.

Deacon, D (1996) 'The Voluntary Sector in a Changing Communication Environment' in the *European Journal of Communication*, vol. 11, no. 2, pp. 173–99.

——(2003) 'Non-governmental Organisations and the Media' in Cottle, S ed., *News, Public Relations and Power*, London: Sage.

Deacon, D and Golding, P (1994) *Taxation and Representation*, London: John Libby Press.

Della Porta, D and Diani, M (1999) *Social Movements: an Introduction*, Oxford: Blackwell.

Delli Carpini, MS and Williams, BA (2001) 'Let Us Infotain You: Politics in the New Media Environment' in Bennett, WL and Entman, RM eds, *Mediated Politics: Communication in the Future of Democracy*, Cambridge: Cambridge University Press.

Deloitte and Touche (April 2004) *Assessment of the Economic Impact of Implementation of the Proposals Contained within FSA Consultation Document CP 176 with Reference to Incumbent Fund Managers' Ability to Compete in the UK Market*, London: Financial Services Authority.

Deuze, M (2005) 'What is Journalism?: Professional Identity and Ideology of Journalists Reconsidered' in *Journalism*, vol. 6, no. 4, pp. 442–64.

Domhoff, G (1967) *Who Rules America?* Englewood Cliffs, NJ: Prentice-Hall.

Downing, J (2001) *Radical Media: Rebellious Communication and Social Movements*, London: Sage.

Doyle, G (2002) *Media Ownership: The Economics and Politics of Convergence and Concentration in the UK and European Media*, London: Sage.

Dreier, P (1988) 'The Corporate Complaint Against the Media' in Hiebert, R and Reuss, C eds, *Impacts of Mass Media*, 2nd edn, New York: Longman.

Dryzek, J (2000) *Deliberative Democracy and Beyond: Liberals, Critics, Contestations*, Oxford: Oxford University Press.

du Gay, P ed. (1997) *Production of Culture/Cultures of Production*, London: Sage/Open University.

du Gay, P and Pryke, M (2002) 'Cultural Economy: An Introduction' in du Gay, P and Pryke, M eds, *Cultural Economy*, London: Sage.

Dudley, G and Richardson, J (1998) 'Arenas without Rules and the Policy Change Process: Outsider Groups and British Roads Policy' in *Political Studies*, vol. 46, pp. 727–47.

Duffy, B and Rowden, L (April 2005) *You Are What you Read?*, London: MORI.

Eagleton, T. 1991 *Ideology: An Introduction*, London: Verso.

Edelman, M (1964) *The Symbolic Uses of Politics*, Urbana, IL: University of Illinois Press.

Edwards III, GC and Wood, BD (1999) 'Who Influences Whom? The President and the Public Agenda' in *American Political Science Review*, vol. 93, no. 2, pp. 327–44.

Eldridge, J (1995) *Glasgow Media Group Reader, vol. 1: News Content, Language and Visuals*, London: Routledge.

Entman, R (2005) 'Media and Democracy Without Party Competition' in Curran, J and Gurevitch, M eds, *Mass Media and Society*, 4th edn, London: Arnold.

Entman, R and Herbst, S (2001) 'Reframing Public Opinion as We Have Known It' in Bennett, WL and Entman, RM eds, *Mediated Politics: Communication in the Future of Democracy*, Cambridge: Cambridge University Press.

Ericson, RV, Baranek, PM and Chan JBL (1989) *Negotiating Control: a Study of News Sources*, Milton Keynes: Open University Press.

Evans, G and Norris, P eds (1999) *Critical Elections: British Parties and Voters in Long-Term Perspective*, London: Sage.

Ewen, S (1996) *PR! A Social History of Spin*, New York: Basic Books.

Fairclough, N. (2000) *New Labour, New Language?* London: Routledge.

Fallows, J (1996) *Breaking the News: How the Media Undermine American Democracy*, New York: Pantheon.

Fama, E (1970) 'Efficient Capital Markets: A Review of Theory and Empirical Work' in *Journal of Finance*, vol. 25, no. 2, pp. 383–417.

Fenyoe, A and Darnton, A (November 2005) *Public Perceptions of Poverty, Qualitative Research Findings: Wave 2*, London: Synovate.

Ferguson, R ed. (2006) *tellparliament.net Interim Evaluation Report 2003–05*, London: Hansard Society.

Fidler, J (1981) *The British Business Elite – Its Attitudes to Class, Status and Power*, London: Routledge and Kegan Paul.

Field, J (2002) *The Story of Parliament in the Palace of Westminster*, London: Politicos.

*Financial Times* (05.07.05) 'NGOs Grow Weary of World Leaders' and 'Empty' Initiatives', London.

Finn, D (1981) *The Business–Media Relationship: Countering Misconceptions and Distrust*, New York: AMACOM.

Fishman, M (1980) *Manufacturing News*, Austin, TX: University of Texas Press.

Fiske, J (1989) *Understanding Popular Culture*, London: Unwin Hyman.

——(1996) *Media Matters: Everyday Culture and Political Change*, Minneapolis, MN: University of Minnesota Press.

Flynn, P (1997) *Commons Knowledge: How to be a Backbencher*, Bridgend: Seren Books.

Forgacs, D ed. (1988) *An Antonio Gramsci Reader: Selected Writings 1916–1935*, London: Lawrence and Wishart.

Foucault, M (1975) *Discipline and Punish: The Birth of the Prison*, Sheridan, A trans., London: Penguin.

——(1980) *Power/Knowledge: Selected Interviews and Other Writings 1972–77*, Gordon, C ed., Hemel Hempstead: Harvester Wheatsheaf.

——(2000) *Power, vol. 3 of Essential Works of Foucault, 1954–1984*, Faubion, J ed., New York: New Press.

Fowles, J (1996) *Advertising and Popular Culture*, London: Sage.

Franklin, B (1994 and 2004) *Packaging Politics: Political Communications in Britain's Media Democracy*, 1st and 2nd edns, London: Arnold.

——(1997) *Newzak and News Media*, London: Arnold.

——(2005) 'McJournalism: the Local Press and the McDonaldization Thesis' in Allan, S ed., *Journalism: Critical Issues*, Maidenhead: Open University Press.

Franklin, B and Parton, N eds (1999) *Social Policy, the Media and Misrepresentation*, New York: Routledge.

Fraser, N (1992) 'Restructuring the Public Sphere: A Consideration of Actually Existing Democracy' in Calhoun, C ed., *Habermas and the Public Sphere*, Cambridge, MA: MIT Press.

Freedman, D (2005) 'GATS and the Audiovisual Sector: An Update' in *Global Media and Communication*, vol. 1, no. 1, pp. 124–28.

Froud, J. and Shaoul, J (2001) 'Appraising and Evaluating PFI for NHS Hospitals' in *Financial Accountability and Management*, vol. 17, no. 3, pp. 247–70.

Froud, J, Johal, S, Leaver, A and Williams, K (2006) *Financialization and Strategy: Narrative and Numbers*, London: Routledge.

FSA (Financial Services Authority) Report (July 2002) *DP 15 Investment Research: Conflicts and Other Issues*, London: FSA.

——(February 2003) *CP 171 Conflicts of Interest: Investment Research and Issues of Securities*, London: FSA.

——(April 2003) *CP 176 Bundled Brokerage and Soft Commission Arrangements*, London: FSA.

——(October 2003) *CP 205 Conflicts of Interest: Investment Research and Issues of Securities: Feedback on CP 171*, London: FSA.

——(March 2004) *PS Conflicts of Interest in Investment Research*, London: FSA.

——(May 2004) *Feedback on CP 176 Bundled Brokerage and Soft Commission Arrangements*, London: FSA.

FSA/Deloitte and Touché (April 2004) *Assessment of the Economic Impact of Implementation of the Proposals Contained within FSA Consultation Document CP 176 with Reference to Incumbent Fund Managers' Ability to Compete in the UK Market*, London: FSA.

FSA/OXERA (April 2003) *An Assessment of Soft Commission Arrangements and Bundled Brokerage Services in the UK*, Oxford: OXERA.

Fukuyama, F (1992) *The End of History and the Last Man*, Harmondsworth: Penguin.

Galtung, J and Ruge, M (1965) 'The Structure of Foreign News' in the *Journal of International Peace Research*, vol. 1, pp. 64–90.

Gamson, W (2004) 'On a Sociology of the Media' in *Political Communication*, vol. 21, no. 3, pp. 305–07.

Gamson, W and Meyer, D (1996) 'Framing Political Opportunity' in McAdam D, McCarthy J and Zald M eds, *Comparative Perspectives on Social Movements: Political Opportunities, Mobilizing Structures, and Cultural Framings*, Cambridge: Cambridge University Press.

Gandy, O (1982) *Beyond Agenda Setting: Information Subsidies and Public Policy*, Norwood, NJ: Ablex Publishing Corporation.

Gans, HJ (1980) *Deciding What's News: A Study of CBS Evening News, NBC Nightly News, Newsweek and Time*, New York: Pantheon.

Garnham, N (1979) 'Contribution to a Political Economy of Mass Communication' in *Media, Culture and Society*, vol. 1, no. 2, pp. 123–46.

——(1990) *Capitalism and Communication: Global Culture and the Economics of Information*, London: Sage.

Gauntlett, D (1998) 'Ten Things Wrong with the Effects Model' in Dickinson, R, Havindranath, R and Linne, O eds, *Approaches to Audiences: A Reader*, London: Arnold.

Gavin, N ed. (1998) *Economy, Media and Public Knowledge*, London: Cassells/University of Leicester Press.

Gelder, K and Thornton, S eds (1997) *The Subcultures Reader*, London: Routledge.

Gitlin, T (1980) *The Whole World is Watching*, Berkeley, CA: University of California Press.

——(1994) *Inside Prime Time*, 2nd edn, London: Routledge.

——(1998) 'Public Sphere or Public Sphericules?' in Liebes, T and Curran, J eds, *Media, Ritual and Identity*, London: Routledge.

Glaser, B and Strauss, A (1968) *The Discovery of Grounded Theory*, London: Weidenfeld and Nicolson.

Glasser, T ed. (1999) *The Idea of Public Journalism*, London: Guildford Press.

Glassman, J and Hassett, K (1999) *Dow, 36,000: The New Strategy for Profiting from the Coming Rise in the Stock Market*, New York: Random House.

Goldenberg, E (1975) *Making the Papers: The Access of Resource-Poor Groups to the Metropolitan Press*, Lexington, MA: D.C. Heath.

Golding, P and Murdock, G (2000) 'Culture, Communications and Political Economy' in Curran, J and Gurevitch, M eds, *Mass Media and Society*, 3rd edn, London: Arnold.

Golding, T (2003) *The City: Inside the Great Expectations Machine*, 2nd edn, London: FT/Prentice-Hall.

Goldsmiths Media Group (1999) 'Media Organisations in Society: Central Issues' in Curran, J ed., *Media Organisations in Society*, London: Arnold.

Goodwin, J and Jasper, J eds (2003) *The Social Movements Reader: Cases and Concepts*, Oxford: Blackwell.

Goodwin, P (1998) *Television Under the Tories*, London: British Film Institute.

Gordon, M (1997 [1947]) 'The Concept of the Sub-Culture and Its Application' in Gelder, K and Thornton, S eds, *The Subcultures Reader*, London: Routledge.

Gould, P (1998) *The Unfinished Revolution*, London: Abacus.

Grannovetter, M and Swedberg, R eds (1992) *The Sociology of Economic Life*, Boulder. CO: Westview Press.

Grant, W (1978) *Insider Groups, Outsider Groups and Interest Group Strategies In Britain*, Department of Politics Working Paper no. 19, Warwick: University of Warwick.

——(1995) *Pressure Groups, Politics and Democracy in Britain*, New York: Harvester Wheatsheaf.

——(2000) *Pressure Groups and British Politics*, London: Macmillan.

Gray, A and McGuigan, J (1993) *Studying Culture: An Introductory Reader*, London: Arnold.

Grossberg, L, Nelson, C, Treichler, P and Baughman, L eds (1992) *Cultural Studies*, London: Routledge.

Gulati, G (2004) 'Members of Congress and Presentation of Self on the World Wide Web' in *Harvard Journal of Press/Politics*, vol. 9, no. 1, pp. 22–40.

GUMG (Glasgow University Media Group) (1976) *Bad News*, vol. 1, London: Routledge and Kegan Paul.

——(1985) *War and Peace News*, London: Routledge.

——(1993) *Getting the Message*, London: Routledge.

Habermas, J (1977) *Legitimation Crisis*, Cambridge: Polity Press.

——(1987) *The Theory of Communicative Action*, Cambridge: Polity Press.

——(1989 [1962]) *The Structural Transformation of the Public Sphere: An Inquiry into a Category of Bourgeois Society*, Burger, T trans., Cambridge: Polity Press.

——(1996) *Between Facts and Norms*, Cambridge: Polity Press.

Hall, S (1973) *Encoding and Decoding in Media Discourse*, Stencilled Paper no. 7, CCCS, Birmingham: University of Birmingham.

——(1980) 'Cultural Studies: Two Paradigms' in *Media, Culture and Society*, vol. 2, no. 1 pp. 57–72.

——(1982) 'The Rediscovery of "Ideology": Return of the Repressed in Media Studies' in Gurevitch, M, Bennett, T, Curran, J and Woollacott, J eds, *Culture, Society, and the Media*, London: Methuen.

——(1983) 'The Problem of Ideology: Marxism Without Guarantees' in Matthews, B ed., *Marx: 100 Years On*, London: Lawrence and Wishart.

Hall, S, Critcher, C, Jefferson, T, Clarke, J and Roberts, B (1978) *Policing the Crisis – Mugging, the State, and Law and Order*, London: Macmillan.

Hallin, D (1994) *We Keep America on Top of the World – Television Journalism and the Public Sphere*, London: Routledge.

——(2000) 'Commercialism and Professionalism in the American News Media' in Curran, J and Gurevitch, M eds, *Mass Media and Society*, 3rd edn, London: Arnold.

Hall Jamieson, K (1996) *Packaging the Presidency: A History and Criticism of Presidential Campaign Advertising*, 3rd edn, Oxford: Oxford University Press.

——(2006) *Electing the President: The Insiders' View*, Philadelphia, PA: University of Pennsylvania Press.

Hansard (2004) *An Audit of Political Engagement*, London: Hansard Society and Electoral Commission.

——(2005) *Members Only: Parliament in the Public Eye*, London: Hansard Society.

Hansen, A ed. (1993) *The Mass Media and Environmental Issues*, Leicester: Leicester University Press.

Hartley, J (1988) 'The Real World of Audiences' in *Critical Studies in Mass Communication*, September, pp. 234–38.

Healey, J, Gill, M and McHugh, D (2005) *MPs and Politics in Our Time*, London: MORI and Hansard Society.

Heath, A, Jowell, R and Curtice, J (2001) *The Rise of New Labour: Party Policies and Voter Choices*, Oxford: Oxford University Press.

Hebdige, D (1979) *Subculture: The Meaning of Style*, London: Sage.

——(1988) *Hiding in the Light*, London: Comedia.

Held, D (1989) *Political Theory and the Modern State*, Cambridge: Polity Press.

——(1996) *Models of Democracy*, 2nd edn, Cambridge: Polity Press.

Held, D and McGrew, A (2002) *Globalization/Anti Globalization*, Cambridge: Polity Press.

Held, D, McGrew, A, Goldblatt, D and Perraton, J (1999) *Global Transformations: Politics, Economics and Culture*, Cambridge: Polity Press.

Herbst (1998) *Reading Public Opinion: Political Actors View the Democratic Process*, Chicago, IL: University of Chicago Press.

Herman, E and McChesney, R (1997) *The Global Media: The New Missionaries of Global Capitalism*, London: Cassell.

Herman, E and Chomsky, N (2002) *Manufacturing Consent*, 2nd edn, New York: Pantheon.

Hess, S (2000) 'The Washington Reporters Redux, 1978–98' in Tumber, H ed., *Media Power, Professionals and Policies*, London: Routledge.

——(2003) *Organising the Presidency*, 3rd edn, Washington DC: Brookings Institute.

Hess, S and Kalb, M (2003) *The Media and the War on Terrorism*, Washington DC: Brookings Institute.

Hilgartner, S and Bosk, C (1988) 'The Rise and Fall of Social Problems: A Public Arenas Model' in *American Journal of Sociology*, vol. 94, no. 1, pp. 53–78.

Hill, S (1990) 'Britain: The Dominant Ideology Thesis After a Decade' in Abercrombie, A, Hill, S and Turner, B eds, *Dominant Ideologies*, London: Unwin Hyman.

Hirst, P and Thompson, G (1999) *Globalization in Question: The International Economy and the Possibilities of Governance*, 2nd edn, Cambridge: Polity Press.

Hodkinson, S (July 2005) 'Make the G8 History' in *Red Pepper*, London.

——(26.10.05) 'Do Stars Really Aid the Cause?' in the *Independent*, London.

——(09.11.05) 'Geldof 8 – Africa Nil: How Rock Stars Betrayed the Poor' in *New Internationalist*, website: www.newint.org/features/geldof-8/index.html.

Hoge, J (1988) 'Business and the Media: Stereotyping Each Other' in Hiebert, R and Reuss, C eds, *Impacts of Mass Media*, 2nd edn, New York, Longman.

Hoggart, R (1958) *The Uses of Literacy*, London: Penguin.

Holland, J (1997) *Corporate Communications with Institutional Shareholders: Private Disclosure and Financial Reporting*, The Institute of Chartered Accountants of Scotland, Glasgow: Bell and Bain.

Hollingsworth, M (1986) *The Press and Political Dissent*, London: Pluto Press.

HoC (House of Commons) Report (July 2002) *Digital Technology: Working for Parliament*, House of Commons Information Committee, London: HMSO.

——(2004) *House of Commons Liaison Committee: Annual Report for 2004*, House of Commons, London: HMSO.

——(June 2004) *Connecting Parliament with the Public: First Report of Session 2003–04*, Select Committee on Modernisation of the House of Commons, London: HMSO.

——(July 2005) *Twenty-Seventh Annual Report – Financial Year 2005/2006*, House of Commons Commission, London: HMSO.

——(December 2005) *House of Commons Corporate Business Plan 2006*, House of Commons Commission, London: HMSO.

——(July 2006) *Twenty-Eighth Annual Report – Financial Year 2005/2006*, House of Commons Commission, London: HMSO.

HoL (House of Lords) Reports (July 2005) *House of Lords Annual Report 2004/05*, House of Lords, London: HMSO.

——(February 2006) *House of Lords Business Plan 2006*, House of Lords, London: HMSO.

——(March 2006) *The Work of the House of Lords 2004–05*, House of Lords, London: HMSO.

Hutton, W (1996) *The State We're In*, London: Vintage.

——(2001) *On the Edge: Living with Global Capitalism*, London: Vintage.

IMA (Investment Management Association) (2003, 2004) *Survey of Members*, London: IMA.

Ingham, B (1991) *Kill the Messenger*, London: Fontana.

Ingham, G (1984) *Capitalism Divided: The City and Industry in British Society*, London: Macmillan.

Investor Relations Society (1998) *Investor Relations in the UK: Current Practices and Key Issues*, London: Business Planning and Research.

Iyengar, S and Kinder, D (1987) *News that Matters*, Chicago, IL: Chicago University Press.

Iyengar, S and Reeves, R eds (1997) *Do the Media Govern? Politicians, Voters, and Reporters in America*, Thousand Oaks, CA: Sage.

Jackson, N (2003) *Vote Winner or a Nuisance: Email and British MPs Relationships with their Constituents*, paper presented to Political Studies Association, 17.04.03, Leicester.

Jackson, N and Lilleker, D (2004) 'Just Public Relations or an Attempt at Interaction?: British MPs in the Press, On the Web and "In Your face"' in *European Journal of Communication*, vol. 19, no. 4, pp. 507–33.

Jhally, S and Lewis, J (1992) *Enlightened Racism: the Cosby Show, Audiences, and the Myth of the American Dream*, Boulder, CO: Westview Press.

Jones, N (1995) *Soundbites and Spin Doctors: How Politicians Manipulate the Media and Vice Versa*, London: Cassell.

——(1999) *Sultans of Spin: the Media and the New Labour Government*, London: Orion.

——(2002) *The Control Freaks: How New Labour Gets its Own Way*, London: Politicos.

Jowell, R, Brook, L and Davids, L eds (1992) *International Social Attitudes: The 9th BSA Report*, Aldershot: Dartmouth.

——(1993) *International Social Attitudes: The 10th BSA Report*, Aldershot: Dartmouth.

Kahin, B and Wilson, E eds (1997) *National Information Infrastructure Initiatives: Vision and Policy Design*, Cambridge, MA: MIT Press.

Kahneman, D and Tversky, A (2000) *Choice, Values and Frames*, Cambridge: Cambridge University Press.

Kahneman, D, Slavic, P and Tversky, A eds (1982) *Judgement Under Uncertainty: Heuristics and Biases*, Cambridge: Cambridge University Press.

Kantola, A (2001) 'Leaving Public Places: Antipolitical and Antipublic Forces of the Transnational Economy' in *Javnost/The Public*, vol. 8, pp. 59–78.

Katz, E and Lazarsfeld, P (1955) *Personal Influence: The Part Played by People in the Flow of Mass Communication*, Glencoe: Free Press.

Kavanagh, D (1995) *Election Campaigning: The New Marketing of Politics*, Oxford: Blackwell.

Kavanagh, D and Gosschalk, B (1995) 'Failing to Set the Agenda: The Role of the Election Press Conferences in 1992' in Crewe, I and Gosschalk, B eds, *Political Communications: The General Election Campaign of 1992*, Cambridge: Cambridge University Press.

Keane, J (1991) *The Media and Democracy*, Cambridge: Polity Press.

Kellner, D (1995) *Media Culture: Cultural Studies, Identity and Politics Between the Modern and the Postmodern*, London: Routledge.

——(2003) *Media Spectacle*, New York: Routledge.

Kerr, A and Sachdev, S (1992) 'Third Among Equals: An Analysis of the 1989 Ambulance Dispute' in *British Journal of Industrial Relations*, vol. 30, no. 1, pp. 127–43.

Key Note (2006) Public Relations Industry: Market Assessment 2006, Hampton: Key Note.

Keynes, J (1936) *The General Theory of Employment, Interest and Money*, London: Macmillan.

Kindleberger, C (2000) *Manias, Panics and Crashes*, 4th edn, New York: John Wiley.

King, A ed. (1998) *New Labour Triumphs: Britain at the Polls*, Chatham, NJ: Chatham House Publishers.

Kitzenger, J (1999) 'Some Key Issues in Audience Reception Research' in Philo, G ed., *Message Received*, Harlow: Longman.

Klandermans, B (1988) 'The Formation and Mobilization of Consensus' in Klandermans B, Kriesi H, Tarrow S and Greenwich, J eds, *International Social Movement Research*, London: JAI.

Klein, N (2000) *No Logo*, London: Flamingo.

Knightley, P (2003) *The First Casualty*, 2nd edn, London: André Deutsch.

Knudsen, J (1998) 'Rebellion in Chiapas: Insurrection by Internet and Public Relations' in *Media, Culture and Society*, vol. 20, no.3, pp. 507–18.

Kovach, B, Rosentiel, T and Mitchell, A (2004) *A Crisis of Confidence: A Commentary on the Findings*, Washington, DC: Pew Research Centre.

Kriesi, H (1991) 'The Political Opportunity Structure of New Social Movements' *Discussion Paper FS III*, Berlin: Wissenschaftszentrum.

Kurtz, H (1998) *Spin Cycle – Inside the Clinton Propaganda Machine*, New York: Pan Books.

Kynaston, D (1994, 1995, 1999, 2001) *The City of London*, vols 1–4, London: Chatto and Windus.

Lamont, N (1999) *In Office*, London: Little, Brown and Company.

Lang, GE and Lang, K (1983) *The Battle for Public Opinion: The President, The Press and the Polls During Watergate*, New York: Columbia University Press.

Langer, J (2003) 'Tabloid Television and News Culture: Access and Representation' in Cottle, S ed., *News, Public Relations and Power*, London: Sage.

Laraña, E (1994) 'Continuity and Unity in New Forms of Collective Action: A Comparative Analysis of Student Movements' in Laraña, E, Johnston, H and Gusfield, J, *New Social Movements*, Philadelphia, PA: Templeton Press.

Larraine, J (1983) *Marxism and Ideology*, London: Macmillan.

Lasswell, H (1927) *Propaganda Techniques in the First World War*, New York: Alfred Knopf.

Latour, B (1987) *Science in Action: How to Follow Scientists and Engineers Through Society*, Cambridge, MA: Harvard University Press.

Lazar, D (1990) *Markets and Ideology in the City of London*, Basingstoke: Macmillan.

Lazarsfeld, P, Berelson, B and Gaudet, H (1944) *The People's Choice*, New York: Duell, Sloan and Pearce.

Lees-Marshment, J (2001) *Political Marketing and British Political Parties: The Party's Just Begun*, Manchester: Manchester University Press.

——(2004) *The Political Marketing Revolution: Transforming the Government of the UK*, Manchester: Manchester University Press.

Lenin, VI (1970 [1902]) *What is to be Done?* London: Panther.

Lewis, J (1991) *The Ideological Octopus: Explorations of Television and its Audience*, London: Routledge.

——(2001) *Constructing Public Opinion*, New York: Columbia University Press.

Lewis, J, Inthorn, S and Wahl-Jorgenson, K (2005) *Citizens or Consumers? The Media and the Decline of Political Participation*, Milton Keynes: Open University Press.

Leys, C (2001) *Market Driven Politics*, London: Verso.

Lichtenberg, J (2000) 'In Defence of Objectivity' in Curran, J and Gurevitch, M eds, *Mass Media and Society*, 3rd edn, London: Arnold.

Lichter, S and Rothman, S (1988) 'Media and Business Elites' in Hiebert, R and Reuss, C eds, *Impacts of Mass Media*, New York: Longman.

Liebes, T and Katz, E (1990) *The Export of Meaning: Cross Cultural Readings of Dallas*, Cambridge: Polity Press.

Lievrouw, L (2004) 'What's Changed About New Media?' in *New Media and Society*, vol. 6, no. 1, pp. 9–15.

Lievrouw, L and Livingstone, S (2006) 'Introduction' in Lievrouw, L and Livingstone, S eds, *The Handbook of New Media*, 2nd edn, London: Sage.

Lindblom, C (1977) *Politics and Markets: The World's Political Economic Systems*, New York: Basic Books.

Lippman, W (1922) *Public Opinion*, New York: Harcourt Brace.

Littlechild, S (2000) *Privatisation, Competition and Regulation*, Occasional Paper 110. London: Institute of Economic Affairs.

Livingstone, S (1998) *Making Sense of Television: The Psychology of Audience Interpretation*, London: Routledge.

——(1999) 'Mediated Knowledge: Recognition of the Familiar, Discovery of the New' in Gripsrud, J ed., *Television and Common Knowledge*, London: Routledge.

——(2005) 'Critical Debates in Internet Studies: Reflections on an Emerging Field' in Curran, J and Gurevitch, M eds, *Mass Media and Society*, 4th edn, London: Hodder Arnold.

Lloyd-Davies, P and Canes, M (1978) 'Stock Prices and the Publication of Second-Hand information' in *Journal of Business*, vol. 51 pp. 43–56.

Lukes, S (1974 and 2005) *Power: A Radical View*, 1st and 2nd edns, London: (Palgrave) Macmillan.

Lull, J (2001) 'Superculture for the Communication Age' in Lull, J ed., *Culture in the Communication Age*, London: Routledge.

Lull, J and Hinerman, S (1997) *Media Scandals*, Cambridge: Polity Press.

Lusoli, W and Ward, S (2004) 'Digital Rank-and-File: Party Activists' Perceptions and Use of the Internet' *British Journal of Politics and International Relations*, vol. 6, no. 4, pp. 453–70.

——(2005) 'Logging On or Switching Off?' in Coleman, S and Ward, S eds, *Spinning the Web: Online Campaigning in the 2005 General Election*, London: Hansard Society.

Lusoli, W, Ward, S and Gibson, R (2006) '(Re)Connecting Politics? Parliament, the Public and the Internet' in *Parliamentary Affairs*, vol. 59, no. 1, pp. 24–42.

Lyotard, JF (1984) *The Postmodern Condition: A Report on Knowledge*, Manchester: Manchester University Press.

MAC Group (Messages, Actions and Communications) (03.03.05) Dgroup Email, Internal Documents/Emails.

——(11.03.05) Draft Ads PDF Document, Internal Documents/Emails.

——(13.06.05) Meeting Minutes, Internal Documents/Emails.

McCarthy, J (1997) 'The Globalization of Social Movement Theory' in Smith, J, Chatfield, C and Pagnucco, R eds, *Transnational Social Movements and Global Politics: Solidarity Beyond the State*, New York: Syracuse University Press.

McCarthy, J and Zald, M (1977) 'Resource Mobilization and Social Movements: A Partial Theory' in *American Journal of Sociology* vol. 82: pp. 1212–41.

McChesney, R (1997) *Corporate Media and the Threat to Democracy*, New York: Seven Stories Press.

——(2004) *The Problem of the Media: US Communication Politics in the Twenty-First Century*, New York: Monthly Review Press.

McChesney, R, Meiskins Wood, E and Foster, JB eds (1998) *Capitalism and the Information Age: the Political Economy of the Global Communications Revolution*, New York: Monthly Review Press.

McCloskey, D (1985) *The Rhetoric of Economics*, Brighton: Wheatsheaf.

McCombs, M and Shaw, D (1972) 'The Agenda-Setting Function of Mass Media' in *Public Opinion Quarterly*, vol. 36, pp. 176–85.

McKay, G ed., (1998) *DIY Culture: Party and Protest in 90s Britain*, London: Verso

MacKay, W, Hutton, M, Sandall, A, Robertson, M, Patrick, S and Wilson, R (2004) *Erskine May's Treatise of the Law, Privileges, Proceedings and Usage of Parliament*, 23rd edn, London: Lexus Nexus/Butterworths.

MacKenzie, D (2003) 'Long-Term Capital Management and the Sociology of Arbitrage' in *Economy and Society*, vol. 32, no. 3, pp. 349–80.

MacKenzie, D and Wajcman, J eds (1999) *The Social Shaping of Technology*, 2nd edn, Buckingham: Open University Press.

MacKuen, M (1984) 'Exposure to Information, Belief Integration, and Individual Responsiveness to Agenda Change' in *American Political Science Review*, vol. 78, pp. 372–91.

McLachlan, S and Golding, P (2000) 'Tabloidization in the British Press: A Quantitative Investigation into Changes in British Newspapers, 1952-1997' in Sparks, C and Tulloch, J eds, *Tabloid Tales: Global Debates Over Media Standards*, Lanham, MD: Rowman and Littlefield.

McLellan, D (1995) *Ideology*, 2nd edn, Buckingham: Open University Press.

McManus, J (1994) *Market Driven Journalism: Let the Citizen Beware*, Thousand Oaks, CA: Sage.

McNair, B (2000) *Journalism and Democracy: An Evaluation of the Public Sphere*, London: Routledge.

——(2003) *An Introduction to Political Communication*, 3rd edn, London: Routledge.

——(2006) *Cultural Chaos: Journalism, News and Power in a Globalised World*, London: Routledge.

McQuail, D (2000) *McQuail's Mass Communication Theory*, 4th edn, London: Sage.

McQuail, D and Suine, K (1998) *Media Policy*, London: Sage.

McSmith, A (1996) *Faces of Labour: the Inside Story*, London: Verso.

Major, J (1999) *John Major – The Autobiography*, London: Harper and Collins.

Malkiel, BG (1985) *A Random Walk Down Wall Street*, New York: Norton.

Manheim, J (1994) *Strategic Public Diplomacy and American Foreign Policy: The Evolution of Interest*, New York: Oxford University Press.

Mann, M (1986) *The Sources of Social Power, vol. 1: A History of Power from the Beginning to AD 1760*, New York: Cambridge University Press.

Manning, P (1998) *Spinning For Labour, Trade Unions and the New Media Environment*, Aldershot: Ashgate Press.

——(2000) *News and News Sources*, London: Sage.

Manning White, D (1950) 'The Gatekeeper' in *Journalism Quarterly*, vol. 27, pp. 383–90.

Mansbridge, J (1986) *Ideological Purity in the Women's Movement: Why We Lost the ERA*, Chicago, IL: University of Chicago Press.

Marchand, R (1998) *Creating the Corporate Soul*, Berkeley, CA: University of California Press.

Marsh, D ed. (1998) *Comparing Policy Networks*, Buckingham: Open University Press.

Marsh, D and Rhodes, R (1992) *Policy Networks in British Government*, Oxford: Clarendon.

Marston C (1996) *Investor Relations: Meeting the Analysts, The Institute of Chartered Accountants of Scotland*, Glasgow: Bell and Bain.

——(1999) *Investor Relations Meetings: Views of Companies, Institutional Investors and Analysts*, The Institute of Chartered Accountants of Scotland, Glasgow: Bell and Bain.

Martin, A, Culey, C and Evans, S (2006) *Make Poverty History 2005 Campaign Evaluation*, London: Firetail.

Martin-Barbero, J (1993) *Communication, Culture and Hegemony: From Media to Mediations*, London: Sage.

Marx, K and Engels, F (1938) *The German Ideology*, London: Lawrence and Wishart.

Media Information Centre (1971, 1982, 1992, 2002) *US Journalist Surveys*, Indiana University School of Journalism, IN: MIF.

Melucci, A (1989) *Nomads of the Present: Social Movements and Individual Needs in Contemporary Society*, Philadelphia, PA: Temple University Press.

Merrill Lynch (monthly poll, 2000–2006) *Global Fund Manager Survey*, London: Merrill Lynch.

Merrill Lynch/Gallup poll of UK Fund Managers 1999–2000 in *Gallup Political and Economic Index*, London: Gallup.

Meyer, T (2002) *Media Democracy: How the Media Colonize Politics*, Cambridge: Polity Press.

Meyrowitz, J (1985) *No Sense of Place: the Impact of Electronic Media on Social Behaviour*, New York: Oxford University Press.

Miliband, R (1969) *The State in Capitalist Society*, London: Weidenfeld and Nicolson.

Miller, D (1994) *Don't Mention the War: Northern Ireland, Propaganda and the Media*, London: Pluto Press.

——ed. (2004) *Tell Me Lies: Propaganda and Media Distortion in the Attack on Iraq*, London: Pluto.

Miller, D and Dinan, W (2000) 'The Rise of the PR Industry in Britain, 1979–98' in the *European Journal of Communication*, vol. 15, no. 1, pp. 5–35.

Miller, D, Kitzenger, J, Williams, K and Beharrell, P (1998) *The Circuits of Mass Communication*, London: Sage.

Miller, J and Krosnick, J (1997) 'Anatomy of News Media Priming' in Iyengar, S and Reeves, R eds, *Do the Media Govern? Politicians, Voters, and Reporters in America*, Thousand Oaks, CA: Sage.

Miller, P (1998) 'The Margins of Accounting' in Callon, M ed., *The Laws of the Markets*, Oxford: Blackwell.

Mills, C Wright (1956) *The Power Elite*, Oxford: Oxford University Press.

Mitchell, F, Sams, KI and White, PJ (1987) *Institutional Investors and Industrial Relations Data: An Empirical Study*, WP 88/23 Dept. of Business Studies: University of Edinburgh.

Mitchell, N (1997) *The Conspicuous Corporation – Business, Publicity, and Representative Democracy*, Ann Arbor, MI: University of Michigan Press.

Monbiot, G (2000) *Captive State: The Corporate Takeover of Britain*, Basingstoke: Pan.

——(2006) *Heat: How to Stop the Planet Heating Up*, London: Allen Lane/Penguin.

Moore, M (2001) *Stupid White Men*, New York: Harper Collins.

MORI (now Ipsos MORI) Polls (1974–2006) *Long Term Trends: The Most Important Issues Facing Britain*, London: MORI.

——(1983–2005) Poll Data in *British Public Opinion*, London: MORI.

——(1987, 1992, 1997, 1998) *Captains of Industry*, London: MORI.

——(December 1996) *Survey of Electoral Candidates*, London: MORI.

——(1997) *Survey of Members of Parliament*, London: MORI.

——(1998–2005) *Joining the Euro*, London: MORI.

——(summer 2000) *Attitudes of UK Institutional Investors and City Analysts*, London: MORI.

——(May 2001) *Business in the Environment*, London: MORI.

——(summer 2001, 2001/02) *Key Audience Research*, London: MORI.

——(summer 2002) *Corporate Social Responsibility*, London: MORI.

Morley, D (1980) *The Nationwide Audience*, London: British Film Institute.

——(1992) *Television, Audiences and Cultural Studies*, London: Routledge.

Morrison, D (1991) *Television and the Gulf War*, London: John Libby Press.

Mosco, V (1996) *The Political Economy of Communications*, London: Sage.

Moyser, G and Wagstaffe, M eds (1987) *Research Methods for Elite Studies*, London: Allen and Unwin.

Murdoch, R (1989) *Freedom in Broadcasting* (MacTaggart Lecture), London: News International.

Murdock, G (1982) 'Large Corporations and the Control of the Communications Industries' in Gurevitch, M, Bennett, T, Curran, J and Woollacott, J, *Culture, Society and the Media*, London: Methuen.

Murdock, G and Golding, P (1977) 'Capitalism and Class Relations' in Curran, J, Gurevitch, M and Woollacott, J eds, *Mass Communications and Society*, London: Edward Arnold.

Myners, P (2001) *Institutional Investment in the United Kingdom: A Review*, London: HMSO.

Nash, K (2000) *Contemporary Political Sociology: Globalization, Politics and Power*, Oxford: Blackwell.

Nava, M (1992) *Changing Cultures: Feminism, Youth and Consumerism*, London: Sage.

Negrine, R (1996) *The Communication of Politics*, London: Sage.

Negroponte, N (1995) *Being Digital*, London: Hodder and Staunton.

Negus, K. 1999 *Music Genres and Corporate Cultures*, London: Routledge.

Neil, A (1996) *Full Disclosure*, London: Macmillan.

Nelson, J (1989) *Sultans of Sleaze – Public Relations and the Media*, Toronto: Between the Lines.

Newman, K (1984) *Financial Marketing and Communications*, London: Holt, Rinehart and Winston.

Norris, P (1999) 'New Politicians? Change in Party Competition at Westminster' in Evans, G and Norris, P eds, *Critical Elections: British Parties and Voters in Long-Term Perspective*, London: Sage.

——(2000) *A Virtuous Circle: Political Communications in Postindustrial Societies*, Cambridge: Cambridge University Press.

——(2002) *Democratic Phoenix: Political Activism World Wide*, New York: Cambridge University Press.

Norris, P, Curtice, J, Sanders, D, Scammell, M and Semetko, H (1999) *On Message: Communicating the Campaign*, London: Sage.

NTO/Skillset (2002) *Journalists at Work: Survey by Journalism Training Forum*, London: NTO/Skillset.

NUJ (1994, 1996, 1998, 2006) *National Union of Journalists Surveys of Members*, London: National Union of Journalists.

——(March 2006) *Journalism Matters: NUJ Campaign Briefing*, London: National Union of Journalists.

Offe, C (1984) *Contradictions of the Welfare State*, Keane, J ed., Cambridge, MA: MIT Press.

Olson, M (1965) *The Logic of Collective Action*, Cambridge, MA: Harvard University Press.

Palmer, J (2000), *Spinning Into Control*, London: Continuum.

Panitch, L and Leys, C eds (1999) *Global Capitalism Versus Democracy*, Rendlesham: Merlin.

Parenti, M (1993) *Inventing Reality: The Politics of News Media*, 2nd edn, New York: St Martins Press.

Parsons, W (1989) *The Power of the Financial Press: Journalism and Economic Opinion in Britain and America*, London: Edward Elgar.

Patterson, T (2002) *The Vanishing Voter: Public Involvement in an Age of Uncertainty*, New York: Alfred Knopf.

Pavlik, J (1996) *New Media and the Information Superhighway*, Boston, MA: Allen and Bacon.

Peacock, A (1986) *Report of the Committee on Financing the BBC*, London: HMSO.

Pew Research Centre (1995, 1999, 2004) *The Pew Research Centre: For the People and the Press*, Washington, DC: Pew Research Centre.

Phillips and Drew (1999, 2000) *Investment Directions: Survey of Investment Management Arrangements*, London: Phillips and Drew.

Philo, G (1995) *Glasgow Media Group Reader, vol. 2: Industry, Economy, War and Politics*, London: Routledge.

Philo, G and Berry, M (2004) *Bad News from Israel*, London: Pluto Press.

PICT (Parliamentary ICT unit) (August 2006) unpublished internal House of Commons statistics on email traffic, produced by Parliamentary ICT unit, London: House of Commons.

PIPA (Programme on International Policy Attitudes), website: www.pipa.org.

Polat, R (2005) 'The Internet and Political Participation' in the *European Journal of Communication*, vol. 20, no. 4, pp. 435–59.

Poole, M, Mansfield, R, Blyton, P and Frost, P 1981 *Managers in Focus: The British Manager in the Early 1980s*, Aldershot: Gower.

Postman, N (1985) *Amusing Ourselves to Death*, London: Methuen.

Poulantzas, N (1975) *Classes in Contemporary Capitalism*, London: New Left Books.

Pratten, C (1993) *The Stock Market*, Occasional Paper 59, Cambridge: Cambridge University Press.

PRCA (1986) 'The Public Relations Yearbook', London: PRCA.

Price, L (2005) *The Spin Doctor's Diary: Inside Number 10 with New Labour*, London: Hodder and Stoughton.

Pritchard, D and Berkowitz, D (1993) 'The Limits of Agenda-Setting: The Press and Political Responses to Crime in the United States 1950–80' in the *International Journal of Public Opinion Research*, vol. 5, no. 1, pp. 86–91.

Protess, D, Cook, FL, Doppelt, JC, Ettema, JS, Gordon, MT, Leff, DR and Miller, P (1991) *The Journalism of Outrage: Investigative Reporting and Agenda Building in America*, New York: The Guilford Press.

Putnam, R (2000) *Bowling Alone: The Collapse and Revival of American Community*, New York: Simon and Schuster.

Quarmby, K (30.05.05) 'Why Oxfam is Failing Africa' in the *New Statesman*.

Radway, J (1987) *Reading the Romance*, Chapel Hill, NC: University of North Carolina Press.

Rawnsley, A (2001) *Servants of the People: The Inside Story of New Labour*, London: Penguin.

Rees-Mogg, W (1992) 'The Financial and Business Press' in Englefield, D ed., *Getting the Message Across – The Media, Business and Government*, London: Industry and Parliamentary Trust.

Reilly, F and Brown, K (2000) *Investment Analysis and Portfolio Management*, 6th edn, Fort Worth, TX: Dryden Press.

Richardson, J (1993) *Pressure Groups*, Oxford: Oxford University Press.

Rodriguez, C (2001) *Fissures in the Mediascape: An International Study of Citizens' Media*, Cresskill, NJ: Hampton Press.

Rose, N (1999) *Powers of Freedom: Reframing Political Thought*, Cambridge: Cambridge University Press.

Rosengren, K and Windahl, S (1972) 'Mass Media Consumption as a Functional Alternative' in McQuail, D ed., *Sociology of Mass Communications*, London: Penguin.

Ross, S (2004) *Toward New Understandings: Journalists and Humanitarian Relief Coverage*, New York: Fritz Institute/Reuters Foundation.

Routledge, P (1997) *Gordon Brown: The Biography*, London: Simon and Schuster.

Ruddock, A (2001) *Understanding Audiences: Theory and Method*, London: Sage.

Sanders, D and Edwards, G (1992) 'Consensus and Diversity in Elite Opinion: The Views of the British Foreign Policy Elite in the 1990s', Essex Papers in Politics and Government no. 92, Essex: University of Essex.

Sant, R and Zaman, MA (1996) 'Market Reaction to Business Week "Inside Wall Street" Column: A Self-fulfilling Prophecy' in *Journal of Banking and Finance* vol. 20, pp. 617–43.

Scammell, M (1995) *Designer Politics: How Elections are Won*, London: Macmillan.

——(2004) 'Crisis? What Crisis? Political Communication in the Blair Era' in *Political Communication*, vol. 2, no. 4, pp. 501–10.

Schattschneider, EE (1960) *The Semi-Sovereign People: A Realist's View of Democracy in America*, New York: Holt, Rhinehart and Winston.

Schiller, H (1989) *Culture Inc. – The Corporate Takeover of Public Expression*, Oxford: Oxford University Press.

——(1992) *Mass Communication and the American Empire*, 2nd edn, Boulder, CO: Westview Press.

——(1996) *Information Inequality: The Deepening Social Crisis in America*, New York: Routledge.

Schlesinger, P (1987) *Putting Reality Together*, 2nd edn, London: Methuen.

——(1990) 'Rethinking the Sociology of Journalism: Source Strategies and the Limits of Media-Centrism' in Ferguson, M ed., *Public Communication – The New Imperative*, London: Sage.

Schlesinger, P and Tumber, H (1994) *Reporting Crime: The Media Politics of Criminal Justice*, Oxford: Clarendon Press.

Schlesinger, P, Murdock, G and Elliott, P (1983) *Televising Terrorism*, London: Comedia.

Schlesinger, P, Miller, D and Dinan, W (2001) *Open Scotland? Journalists, Spin Doctors and Lobbyists*, Edinburgh: Edinburgh University Press.

Schlosser, E (2001) *Fast Food Nation: What the All-American Meal is Doing to the World*, London: Allen Lane.

Schorr, D (1997) 'Who Uses Whom?' in Iyengar, S and Reeves, R eds, *Do the Media Govern? Politicians, Voters, and Reporters in America*, Thousand Oaks, CA: Sage.

Schudson, M (1995) *The Power of News*, Cambridge, MA: Harvard University Press.

——(2001) 'The Objectivity Norm in American Journalism' in *Journalism: Theory, Criticism and Practice*, vol. 2, no. 2, pp. 149–70.

——(2003) *The Sociology of News*, New York: WW Norton.

Schumpeter, J (1952) *Capitalism, Socialism and Democracy*, London: Unwin University Books.

Scott, J (1991) *Who Rules Britain?* Cambridge: Polity Press.

——(1997) *Corporate Business and Capitalist Classes*, Oxford: Oxford University Press.

Sennett, R (2006) *The Culture of the New Capitalism*, New Haven, CT: Yale University Press.

Seymour-Ure, C (1996) *The British Press and Broadcasting Since 1945*, 2nd edn, Oxford: Blackwell.

Shaoul, J (2000) 'Privatisation: Claims, Outcomes and Explanations', in Philo, G and Miller, D, *Market Killing*, London: Longman.

Shiller, R (1989) *Market Volatility*, Cambridge, MA: MIT Press.

——(2000) *Irrational Exuberance*, Princeton, NJ: Princeton University Press.

Shleifer, A (2000) *Inefficient Markets: An Introduction to Behavioural Finance*, Oxford: Oxford University Press.

Siegal, J (1998) *Stocks in the Long Run*, 2nd edn, New York: McGraw Hill.

Sigal, LV (1973) *Reporters and Officials – The Organisation and Politics of Newsmaking*, Lexington, MA: Lexington Books.

Sigelman, L (1973) 'Reporting the News' in *American Journal of Sociology*, vol. 79, no. 1, pp. 132–51.

Silverstone, R (1994) *Television and Everyday Life*, London: Routledge.

Simonson, K (2005) *The Gleneagles Summit: NGO and Civil Society Perspectives on the G8*, Geneva: Centre for Applied Studies in International Negotiations.

Sklair, L (2001) *The Transnational Capitalist Class*, Oxford: Blackwell.

Smelser, N and Swedberg, R eds (2004) *The Handbook of Economic Sociology*, 2nd edn, Princeton, NJ, Princeton University Press.

Smith, M (1993) *Pressure, Power and Policy*, Hemel Hempstead: Harvester Wheatsheaf.

Smith, N (July 2006) *Discourses of Globalisation and European Integration in the UK and Ireland, 2004–05*, Colchester: UK Data Archive.

Smith, T (1996) *Accounting for Growth: Stripping the Camouflage from Company Accounts*, 2nd edn, London: Century Business.

Smith, W (1988) 'Business and the Media: Sometimes Partners, Sometimes Adversaries' in Hiebert, R and Reuss, C eds, *Impacts of Mass Media*, New York: Longman.

Smithers, A and Wright, A (2000) *Valuing Wall Street: Protecting Wealth in Turbulent Markets*, New York: McGraw Hill.

——(2004) *Stock Market Valuations*, London: Smithers & Co.

Snow, D and Benford, R (1992) 'Ideology, Frame Resonance, and Participant Mobilization' in *International Social Movement Research* vol. 1, pp. 197–217.

——(2000). 'Framing Processes and Social Movements: An Overview and Assessment' in *Annual Review of Sociology*, vol. 26, pp. 611–39.

Soroka, S (2002) 'Issue Attributes and Agenda Setting by Media, the Public and Policy-Makers in Canada' in *International Journal of Public Opinion Research*, vol. 14, no. 3, pp. 264–85.

——(2003) 'Media, Public Opinion, and Foreign Policy' in *Harvard International Journal of Press/Politics*, vol. 8, no. 1, pp. 27–48.

Soros, G (1994) *The Alchemy of Finance: Reading the Mind of the Market*, 2nd edn, London: John Wiley.

Sparks, C (2000) 'Media Theory After the Fall of European Communism' in Curran, J and Park, MJ eds, *De-Westernizing Media Studies*, London: Routledge.

——(2001) 'The Internet and the Global Public Sphere' in Bennett, WL and Entman, R eds, *Mediated Politics: Communication in the Future of Democracy*, Cambridge: Cambridge University Press.

Sparks, C and Tulloch, J (2000) *Tabloid Tales: Global Debates Over Media Standards*, Oxford: Rowman and Littlefield.

Spinwatch, website: www.spinwatch.org.

Sreberny Mohamadi, A and Mohamadi, A (1994) *Small Media, Big Revolution*, Minneapolis, MN: University of Minnesota Press.

Stauber, J and Rampton, S (1995) *Toxic Sludge is Good For You – Lies, Damn Lies and the Public Relations Industry*, New York: Common Courage Press.

——(2002) *Trust Us We're Experts: How Industry Manipulates Science and Gambles with Your Future*, New York: Tarcher/Penguin.

——(2003) *Weapons of Mass Deception: The Uses of Propaganda in Bush's War on Iraq*, New York: Tarcher/Penguin.

Stiglitz, J (2002) *Globalization and its Discontents*, London: Penguin.

Storey, J ed. (1998) *Cultural Theory and Popular Culture: A Reader*, 2nd edn, Harlow: Prentice-Hall.

Storey, J (1999) *Cultural Consumption and Everyday Life*, London: Arnold

Strange, S (1986) *Casino Capitalism*, Oxford: Blackwell.

——(1998) *Mad Money: When Markets Outgrow Governments*, Ann Arbor, MI: University of Michigan Press.

Strauss, A and Crobin, J (1998) *Basics of Qualitative Research: Grounded theory, procedures and techniques*, 2nd edn, London: Sage.

Street, J (1997) *Politics and Popular Culture*, Cambridge: Polity Press.

——(2001) *Mass Media, Politics and Democracy*, Basingstoke: Palgrave.

Sudarsanam, P 1995 *The Essence of Mergers and Acquisitions*, London: Prentice-Hall.

Swedberg, R (2003) *Principles of Economic Sociology*, Princeton, NJ.: Princeton University Press.

——(2005) 'Conflicts of Interest in the US Brokerage Industry' in Knorr Cetina, K and Preda, A eds, *The Sociology of Financial Markets*, Oxford: Oxford University Press.

Thompson, EP (1963) *The Making of the English Working Class*, London: Penguin.

Thompson, J (1990) *Ideology and Modern Culture*, Cambridge: Polity Press.
——(1995) *The Media and Modernity: A Social Theory of the Media*, Cambridge: Polity Press.
——(2000) *Political Scandal*, Cambridge: Polity Press.
Thornton, S (1995) *Clubcultures: Music, Media and Subcultural Capital*, Cambridge: Polity Press.
Thussu, D ed. (1998) *Electronic Empires*, London: Arnold.
Thussu, D (2000) *International Communication: Continuity and Change*, London: Arnold.
Thussu, D and Freedman, D eds (2003) *War and the Media Reporting Conflict 24/7*, London: Sage.
Tiffen, R (1989) *News and Power*, Sydney: Allen and Unwin.
——(1999) *Scandals: Media, Politics and Corruption in Contemporary Australia*, Sydney: UNSW Press.
Tilly, C (1991) *Coercion, Capital and European States, AD 990–1992*, Oxford: Blackwell.
Todd, M and Taylor, G eds (2004) *Democracy and Participation: Popular Protest and new Social Movements*, London: Merlin.
Tomlinson, J (1999) *Globalization and Culture*, Cambridge: Polity Press.
Treasury (March 1999, April 2003) *Budget Reports*, London: HMSO.
Truman, D (1951) *The Governmental Process*, New York: Alfred A Knopf.
Tuchman, G (1972) 'Objectivity as a Strategic Ritual: An Examination of Newsmen's Notion of Objectivity' in *American Journal of Sociology*, vol. 77, no. 4, pp. 660–79.
Tumber, H (1993) '"Selling Scandal": Business and the Media' in *Media, Culture and Society*, vol. 15, no. 3, pp. 345–61.
Tumber, H and Palmer, J (2004) *Media at War: The Iraq Crisis*, London: Sage.
Tunstall, J (1971) *Journalists at Work*, London: Sage.
——(1996) *Newspaper Power: The National Press in Britain*, Oxford: Oxford University Press.
Tunstall, J and Palmer, M (1991) *Media Moguls*, London: Routledge.
Turner, G (2003) *British Cultural Studies: An Introduction*, London: Routledge.
Tye, L (1998) *The Father of Spin: Edward L. Bernays and the Birth of Public Relations*, New York: Crown Publishers.
Underwood, D (2001) 'Reporting and the Push for Market-Oriented Journalism: Media Organisations as Businesses' in Bennett, WL and Entman, RM eds, *Mediated Politics: Communication in the Future of Democracy*, Cambridge: Cambridge University Press.
Useem, M (1984) *The Inner Circle: Large Corporations and the Rise of Business Political Activity in the US and the UK*, Oxford: Oxford University Press.
Van Ginneken, J (1998) *Understanding Global News*, London: Sage.
von Hayek, F (1945) 'The Uses of Knowledge in Society' in *American Economic Review*, vol. 35, no. 4, pp. 519–30.
Veljanovski, C ed. (1989) *Freedom in Broadcasting*, London: Institute of Economic Affairs.
Walgrave, S and van Aelst, P (September 2004) 'The Mass Media's Political Agenda-Setting Power: Towards an Integration of the Available Evidence', Paper for *APSA Conference*, Chicago.

Ward, S, Gibson, R and Lusoli, W (February 2005) *The Promise and Perils of 'Virtual Representation': The Public's View*, NOP Opinion Survey.

Waters, M (1995) *Globalisation*, London: Routledge.

Weber, M (1968 [1922]) *Economy and Society: an Outline of Interpretive Sociology*, New York: Bedminster Press.

Webster, F (2006) *Theories of the Information Society*, 3rd edn, London: Routledge.

Wetherilt, AV and Weeken, O (winter, 2002) 'Equity Valuation Measures: What Can They Tell Us?' in *Bank of England Quarterly Bulletin*, London: Bank of England.

White, J and Mazur, L (1995) *Strategic Communications Management: Making Public Relations Work*, Wokingham: Addison Welsey.

Wikland, H (2005) 'A Habermasian Analysis of the Deliberative Democratic Potential of ICT-Enabled Services in Swedish Municipalities' in *New Media and Society*, vol. 7, no. 5, pp. 701–23.

Williams, G (1996) *Britain's Media – How They Are Related*, London: Campaign for Press and Broadcasting Freedom.

Williams, R (1958) *Culture and Society 1780–1950*, London: Penguin.

——(1961) *The Long Revolution*, London: Chatto and Windus.

——(1977) *Marxism and Literature*, Oxford: Oxford University Press.

Winston, B (1998) *Media, Technology and Society: A History from Telegraph to the Internet*, London: Routledge.

Wolfsfeld, G (2001) 'Political Waves and Democratic Discourse: Terrorism waves During the Oslo Peace Process' in Lance Bennett, W and Entman, RM eds, *Mediated Politics: Communication in the Future of Democracy*, Cambridge: Cambridge University Press.

Woolley, P (May 2002) *The Passive Trap*, London: GMO Woolley.

——(December 2002) *Momentum: Private Gain, Public Cost*, London: GMO Woolley.

Wring, D (2005) *The Politics of Marketing the Labour Party*, London: Palgrave.

YouGov Opinion Polls (25.05.04) *YouGov/Daily Telegraph Survey on The European and Local Elections*, London.

——(06.12.04) *Assisted Dying for the Terminally Ill*, London.

——(June 2005) *YouGov/Sky News Survey on Britain, Europe and the G8*, London.

Zaller, J (1992) *The Nature and Origins of Mass Opinion*, Cambridge: Cambridge University Press.

——(1997) 'A model of Communication Effects at the Outbreak of the Gulf War' in Iyengar, S and Reeves, R eds, *Do the Media Govern? Politicians, Voters, and Reporters in America*, Thousand Oaks, CA: Sage.

Zellizer, B (1992) 'CNN, the Gulf War, and Journalistic Practice' in *Journal of Communication*, vol. 42, no. 1, pp. 66–81.

——(2004) *Taking Journalism Seriously: News and the Academy*, Thousand Oaks, CA: Sage.

# Index